Depth-Oriented
Brief Therapy

Depth-Oriented Brief Therapy

How to Be Brief When You Were Trained to Be Deep—and Vice Versa

Bruce Ecker and Laurel Hulley

Jossey-Bass Publishers • San Francisco

Substantial discounts on bulk quantities of Jossey-Bass books are available to corporations, professional associations, and other organizations. For details and discount information, contact the special sales department at Jossey-Bass Inc., Publishers. (415) 433-1740; Fax (800) 605-2665.

For sales outside the United States, please contact your local Simon & Schuster International Office.

Jossey-Bass Web address: http://www.josseybass.com

Manufactured in the United States of America on Lyons Falls Turin Book. This paper is acid-free and 100 percent totally chlorine-free.

Library of Congress Cataloging-in-Publication Data

Ecker, Bruce, date.
    Depth-oriented brief therapy : how to be brief when you were trained to be deep and vice versa / Bruce Ecker and Laurel Hulley.
        p.   cm.—(Jossey-Bass social and behavioral science series)
    Includes index.
    ISBN 0-7879-0152-0 (alk. paper)
    1. Brief psychotherapy. 2. Unconsciousness. I. Hulley, Laurel, date. II. Title.
III. Series.
RC480.55.E33 1996
616.89'14—dc20
                                    95-18735

HB Printing 10 9 8 7 6 5 4 3   FIRST EDITION

Contents

121603

To our parents,
Miriam and Sam Ecker
and
Ruth and Robert Shaffer
with gratitude

Preface

At a 1978 workshop, Italian family therapist and trainer Mario Andolphi was heard to say, "To make shorter the therapy, make longer the training." His words contain two important implications: making therapy shorter is desirable and making therapy shorter is a special skill.

Many therapists, however, regard brevity as highly *un*desirable because brief therapy is seen as sacrificing vital qualities of the work—the depth and durability of resolution reached; the thoroughness of change in the emotional and unconscious aspects maintaining the problem; the authentic, trust-based client-therapist relationship. Actually, with regard to many types of brief therapy, these skeptics are right. With regard to the therapy described in this book, the picture changes.

We have developed a brief therapy that preserves what we value most in the work: the complex depths of meaning and feeling in which human beings participate. Not only is it possible to retain this depth-dimension in brief practice, but it is also *by* working directly with the core elements of emotional and unconscious meaning that the therapy becomes so effective as to be brief.

When therapy no longer sacrifices its best qualities to be brief, then brevity becomes desirable.

Then there is the second point: that a particular kind of learning and skill are required for doing effective therapy briefly. Learning depth-oriented brief therapy involves a distilling and honing of the best skills and sensitivities of our profession. Anyone who loves the work of therapy will also love the challenge we offer in this book—the challenge of moving rapidly to the center of the client's world of meaning. Doing this will open up a new level of richness and satisfaction in time-effective work.

Our approach has a well-defined methodology, guided by a comprehensive conceptualization of problems and change. The presentation of our approach in this book is designed to be accessible and engaging to clinicians at all levels, from experienced professionals to graduate students.

Depth-oriented brief therapy is to our knowledge the first nonpathologizing brief therapy to fully address the emotional and unconscious aspects of the presenting problem on an equal footing with cognitive, behavioral, and systemic-interactional aspects. In our training activities we find that the integrative, constructivist character of depth-oriented brief therapy makes it appealing and highly useful to clinicians of all orientations. Its inclusion of emotions and the unconscious makes it relevant to psychodynamic therapists, and its use of empathic inquiry to find hidden emotional sense in the client's internal experience is familiar to self psychologists. Its strong emphasis on experiential and phenomenological methods is natural to humanistic and existential therapists. Its focus on current constructions and internal representations created in the course of development gives it much common ground with the object relations school and with cognitive therapies. Its systemic application with couples and families makes it pertinent to family systems therapists as well.

Both the methodology and the conceptualization of depth-oriented brief therapy contain significant innovation, such as an extension of the concept and technique of "second-order change" to third-order and fourth-order change, which we describe with detailed examples. The approach also expands the scope of postmodern constructivist thought and practice into including the full range of conscious and unconscious psychological activity. We have for many years felt that the therapeutic potential of constructivism is far greater than has yet been demonstrated, and our work for over a decade has focused on learning how to bring constructivism's nimbleness into the same depths of emotional and unconscious, autonomous process as is addressed by our psychoanalytic and psychodynamic colleagues—though we see those depths through a different conceptual lens. This is a domain of constructed reality that is largely disregarded by narrative constructivists and social constructionists, the influential domain of unconscious emotional meaning that is *not* always based in language.

What is new in depth-oriented brief therapy stands on a base synthesized from many influences across the spectrum of therapeutic schools. Our approach draws importantly from the work of Virginia Satir, R. D. Laing, and Carl Jung (for the coherence and positive function of the psyche in producing the symptom, the ontological unfoldment of self, and the conscious/unconscious dialectic); Gregory Bateson (for the hidden, epistemological aspect of human functioning and the logical types of constructs); Milton Erickson (for the nonpathologizing view of the client's unconscious process as readily accessible, responsive, and capable of cooperation with the therapist); Fritz Perls, James Simkin, and Carl Whitaker (for the therapist's use of self, the necessity of experiential engagement of the client, and the view of the client as the preeminent expert on her or his own experience); and Robert Shaw (for the accessibility of the hidden construction of the presenting problem and for the immediate availability of that epistemological and ontological structure for transformation).

In the many clinical examples that follow, the therapist is always one of the two authors. Session transcripts are in most cases transcriptions of tape recordings or videos, and in a minority of cases are a reconstruction of the session based on notes taken during or immediately after it. Identifying details have been altered to assure the confidentiality and anonymity of clients.

There are a number of acknowledgments we are pleased to make:

B.E.: My thanks and lasting gratitude go to psychotherapist Elizabeth Heaney for the steady enthusiasm, encouragement, and substantial efforts that brought about the presentation of depth-oriented brief therapy to the professional community. Also greatly appreciated is the energetic support and generous efforts of therapist trainer Vicky Stromee and family therapist Grace Manning-Orenstein in helping present our approach. My appreciation goes as well to psychologist Philip Manfield for viewing videos of the work and offering comments from an object relations viewpoint.

L.H.: I would like to express my appreciation to Professor John Watson of the infant developmental psychology department at the University of California at Berkeley, whose research and clarity of teaching regarding how human beings structure experience from the first hour of life became a lasting basis for my clinical perspective; to Professor James Coyne, under whom I worked at the Stress and Coping Project at UCB, for requiring me to become aware of the sociopolitical dimensions operating at all levels of psychotherapy and to seek an ever greater refinement of skills in each therapy hour; to Professor Kathleen Hulley of New York University for her always fresh views and knowledge of French deconstruction theory, a perspective I was later able to convert into a therapeutic tool; and to psychologist Felix Polk, for persistently prompting me further into my own difficult journey into unconscious emotional truth.

We jointly want to acknowledge and thank Dr. Robert Shaw, Director of the Family Institute of Berkeley, California, for his brilliant teaching and his contagious conviction that the therapist can and should find a way, moment-to-moment, to be effective in every session. Our gratitude also goes to Jossey-Bass editor and psychotherapist Hugh Grubb, who invited us to write this book and whose steady and sound advice we always followed; to our friend Gail Hann for her unstinting support in the care of our family while we wrote; and especially to our courageous and hard-working clients and therapist-trainees, every one of whom has been a world of learning for us.

Oakland, California   BRUCE ECKER
August 1995   LAUREL HULLEY

Depth-Oriented
Brief Therapy

Introduction: Joining "Deep" and "Brief" in Psychotherapy

Could it be possible for a therapy to move within the domains of the emotions and the unconscious, preserving the depth, authenticity and poignancy we value so highly in the work, and yet make an unmistakable difference in every session and therefore be brief?

Depth-oriented brief therapy developed out of our intention to find an affirmative answer to this question.

We were dissatisfied with the prevailing assumption in the traditional branches of the profession that it was inevitable for a significant number of sessions to be of unclear impact, leaving either the client or therapist privately not sure if the session had actually made a valuable and significant difference or if time and money had been well spent. Strategic and solution-oriented brief therapies emphasized making every session effective, but sacrificed depth and the quality of the therapist-client relationship in the process. Psychodynamic brief therapies, on the other hand, sought depth but insisted upon viewing clients through an exceedingly thick lens of pathologizing theoretical constructs, which too severely limited the therapist's view of the client's capacity for change, the allowed repertoire of therapeutic techniques, and the range of acceptable clients.

We examined thousands of our own therapy sessions with individuals, couples, and families for key moments in which deep, symptom-dispelling change took place. What distinguished these hours from others? What was it that we as therapists had to know and had to do or not do in order to generate that kind of effectiveness *all the time?*

We found consistently that the interactions that produced therapeutic breakthrough did not inherently require preparatory months or years of sessions. The crucial exchanges would in most cases have been equally effective if carried out in the very first sessions, if only the therapist had somehow known what they were. Depth-oriented brief therapy (DOBT) developed as we identified how to bring the client and therapist to those pivotal moments very rapidly, without reducing the therapist's role to one of technician or manipulator, as some other brief approaches seemed to do.

It emerged that the key condition for deep, brief work was the therapist's conviction that the unconscious constructs generating the client's problem are immediately accessible and changeable from the start of therapy. This book presents the comprehensive approach that developed as a result of reorganizing therapy around this central conviction. The fact of immediate accessibility means that profound therapeutic change can consistently be brought about far more rapidly than is allowed for in traditional in-depth approaches.

Our interest in effectiveness had led us to train in and affiliate initially with the systemic-strategic-cybernetic paradigm of psychotherapy, which in the 1960s and 1970s had opened up exciting new ways of conceptualizing problems and producing change, making new levels of clinical effectiveness possible. Increasingly we inhabited the constructivist ways of thinking and interacting that have characterized systemic family therapy from its inception.

In reaction to the psychodynamic orthodoxy that had preceded it, systemic and strategic therapy shunned the individual's intrapsychic process and eliminated emotions and the unconscious as legitimate areas of therapeutic focus. Family therapist and anthropologist Inga-Britt Krause, in summing up her review of the positions of the major forms of systemic family therapy with respect to emotion, writes, "For all of them motivation, articulated as feelings and emotions, was attributed to individuals and to address these was considered to be unimportant and perhaps even subversive to systemic theory and therapeutic practice. Representing what we may gloss as 'orthodox' family therapy, . . . the processes which take place inside individuals were considered to be outside the remit of observation and study."

Yet as we studied our own sessions we found that the ones in which key, in-depth breakthroughs occurred were precisely those in which we diverged from the systemic avoidance of emotional and unconscious material and worked directly with these dimensions of the client's problem no less than the cognitive, interactional, and systemic aspects. But we did so as constructivists, not as psychodynamic therapists, and found that we could evolve the assumptive base of constructivism in a way that enabled us to work with emotional and unconscious process with surprising effectiveness. (As theorist Michael J. Mahoney observes, "only recently has the term *unconscious* begun to be liberated from exclusively psychoanalytic connotations." This book participates in that important trend. We use the term *unconscious* broadly to encompass all cognitive, emotional, and somatic contents, states and processes that are outside of awareness. Specific degrees or types of unconsciousness will be indicated when necessary.)

We learned from our clients that what mattered most in triggering lasting change was for the client to find and experience the already-existing but hidden emotional meaning that the problem had for him or her. This was always the most strongly meaning-laden view of the problem and invariably opened avenues to rapid change. To arrive at this point required reaching into the client's constructions operating outside of awareness. When we began intentionally to seek the problem's *emotional truth*—an unconscious construction of passionately felt meaning—from the very start of therapy, our work began to reliably achieve the level of effectiveness we were seeking.

What distinguishes depth-oriented brief therapy from other brief therapies is this active engagement with the *full* phenomenology—emotional, cognitive, somatic (kinesthetic and somesthetic), and behavioral, conscious and unconscious—in the focused, efficient manner required for brief work and, at the same time, in the respectful and authentic manner required for a subjectively rich, meaningful, collaborative client-therapist relationship. Applied to this complete phenomenology, depth-oriented brief therapy's nonpathologizing, constructivist approach produces results that under orthodox assumptions are impossible—supporting the argument that the effectiveness of psychotherapy is limited more by the constructions put upon it by therapists than by the psychological makeup of our clients.

Depth-oriented brief therapy is able to integrate "deep" and "brief" by applying two convictions in tandem: (1) nothing underlies present problems but *present* cognitions, emotions, and kine/somesthetics, both conscious and unconscious; (2) unconscious, symptom-generating elements of the client's world of meaning are "in the room," always close at hand, immediately accessible, and therefore transformable.

In short, this approach holds that the elements necessary for in-depth resolution always are present and available for change. DOBT provides a practical methodology for rapidly and accurately locating and changing this key material. It is this *principle of immediate accessibility*—accessibility of unconscious, symptom-generating constructions—that dissolves the traditional opposition of "deep" and "brief."

As our many case examples will also show, the inherent effects of the methodology go beyond symptom relief and generate a new awareness of wellness and worth at the core of self.

It is no surprise that within the traditional frameworks of the psychoanalytic and psychodynamic schools, depth and brevity are seen as mutually exclusive qualities of clinical work. It is quite ironic, however, that even some of the postmodern, constructivist brief psychotherapies—strategic, solution-oriented, and narrative approaches—conform to the same root assumptions as mainstream orthodoxy in that they generally dispense with unconscious depth in order to achieve brevity, as noted earlier.

Our aim in this book is to point to the brief, fully in-depth psychotherapy that is made possible by a new assumptive base, constructivist in nature. Throughout the chapters of this book our clinical examples will show how depth-oriented brief therapy is carried out and how it differs from other approaches. DOBT has been successful with a wide range of clinical problems, including agoraphobia; anxiety and panic attacks; depression; addictive/compulsive behaviors such as compulsive eating, workaholism, and manic activity; sexual problems; symbiotic attachment and dependency; effects of trauma and abuse, such as dissociative states, shame, self-blame, and chronic low self-esteem; and couple, family, and interpersonal problems. We will also discuss the limits of the approach. Even highly effective therapy is not always brief, and we will explain why.

Overview of the Contents

Chapter One provides an introductory guided tour of the methodology and conceptual framework of DOBT, with several case examples. Chapter Two then demonstrates the approach in detail, applying it to clients whose presenting symptoms are driven by unresolved, lifelong emotional wounds. By the end of Chapter Two we will have seen DOBT deal with agoraphobia, low self-esteem, psychogenic pain, chronic depression, workaholism, and repetition compulsion. Chapter Three completes the conceptual picture sketched in Chapter One and points out important, supporting developments in cognitive neuroscience. Chapter Four describes the therapeutic stance for carrying out DOBT's methodology of discovery, *radical inquiry*, in preparation for Chapter Five's detailed survey of specific techniques of this methodology, including techniques for working with client resistance. Chapter Six likewise details techniques for DOBT's methodology of change, *experiential shift*. Chapters Five and Six continue the presentation of illustrative case material, including couple and family therapy.

The Constructivist Approach

A short statement of the constructivist basis of DOBT will be our point of departure. (For more extensive expositions of the range of constructivist perspectives in psychotherapy, we recommend the writings of Michael J. Mahoney, Robert A. Neimeyer, and William J. Lyddon, cited at the end of the chapter.)

In line with our insistence on experiential rather than analytical avenues to change, we begin by involving the reader in a *koan*-like problem: Consider a live goose inside a large, narrow-necked glass bottle. How to get the goose out of the bottle without hurting the goose or breaking the bottle? Ponder the problem as you read on, and we will return to it not far along.

Constructivism has two essential ideas at its base. The first is this: *Each person actively forms or assembles the experiential reality, the experiential world of meaning, that he or she inhabits and takes as independent, real, and self-evident.*

The constructivist view is that nearly all of this construing and assembling of reality is done *unconsciously*, both at the neurobiological level of synapses and neural networks and also at the social-psychological level of construing and assigning *meanings* to perceptions. We become completely absorbed in our own construction of reality precisely *because* we are unaware of our role as its construer-author. Even the stock versions of reality received from family and culture are not just passively experienced, but are actively if unconsciously invoked and applied by the individual (author*ized* if not authored).

In this view, whatever a psychotherapy client defines as the symptom or problem—compulsive eating, depression, a child's bed-wetting—is seen not as a sign of pathology but in less dire and rather more hopeful terms: The occurrence of the presenting symptom is dictated coherently by the individual's currently operating constructions of meaning. Therefore, the target of change, as described by therapist Laura Rice, is the client's specific "enduring constructions or schemes that are brought to bear on each new experience . . . [and] that are relevant to the recurrent situations in which the client reacts in unsatisfactory ways."

A *construct* is defined simply as any internal representation of any aspect of self or world. Every construct functions as an item of personal knowledge. However, use of the terms *construct, construction,* or *construing* in describing psychological processes does not in itself comprise the constructivist position. For example, object relations–oriented clinicians keenly appreciate that people construct their own representations and experiences of reality, yet these therapists are not necessarily constructivists. Constructivism involves this additional core idea: *There is no one objectively "correct" version of reality, no single "true" meaning of events, that distinguishes mental health or toward which a therapist should necessarily orient the therapy client.*

A constructivist therapist assumes there are any number of viable ways the client's view of reality could change that would dispel the presenting problem, and in a spirit of collaboration, the therapist and client consider and try out such possibilities. The differences among constructivist therapies are differences in how they select an alternate, symptom-free view of reality for the client to experimentally inhabit, and in how they invite and assist the client to do so. Their common ground is this: The therapist does not take the objectivist position of being a diagnostic authority on the "correct" view of reality, but rather offers expert skill in modifying realities so as to eliminate their unwanted consequences.

A constructivist therapist is rather like an anthropologist who accepts the validity of many different experiential realities and within broad limits does not presume to define how a person should think, feel, and live. This is a postmodern position in that it decenters any absolute, timeless truth about people's lives and instead recognizes a varying, local formulation of truth.

This epistemological position has sweeping implications for conducting psychotherapy. In contrast to (1) the traditional objectivist view of treatment as requiring discovery of factual, causal conditions in childhood and (2) the behaviorist-interactional view of the individual as controlled by the social environment, the constructivist view is that problems are generated entirely by the individual's cognitions and emotions comprising his or her present construction of reality. These present-time elements can, of course, include representations of past experiences, but these representations exist in the subjective present and should not be confused with an objective past. As theorist Gregory Bateson pointed out, if it really were past events in themselves that cause us to experience and act as we do, then "there could be no psychotherapy. The patient would be entitled and even compelled to argue, 'My mother slapped me down in such and such ways, and therefore I am now sick; and because these traumata occurred in the past they cannot be altered and I, therefore, cannot get well.'"

The therapeutic task is, therefore, to assist the client to further evolve his or her construction of reality, or matrix of meanings, in such a way that the presenting problem is alleviated. This is approached as an intrinsically progressive and creative process rather than a corrective or curative one. The therapist's view of the mind as an inherently active and potent meaning maker gives him or her a genuine conviction in the client's native capacities for meaningful change, a stance that is contagiously hopeful without necessarily being one-sidedly or glibly "positive." "There is nothing so obvious that its appearance is not altered when seen in a different light," wrote therapist George Kelly, a pioneer of clinical constructivism. "Whatever exists can be reconstrued."

However, the view of the client's problem as being entirely a consequence of how he or she currently construes reality has led many a constructivist into a naive analysis of the experience of trauma and hardship. Some have gone so far as to write, "as constructivists, we must insist that the 'trauma' of rape takes place in language, as part of a socially sanctioned narrative." The double error here is, firstly, a gross overestimation of the role of language and cognitive processes in generating experience and, secondly, the assumption that all suffering can be avoided by making the purely internal movement of adopting the right point of view. The latter position may be appropriate in the context of serious spiritual practice, but not in the context of psychotherapy. To suffer *is* an appropriate, meaningful response to experiencing such ordeals as grinding poverty, political oppression, or rape; the suffering, grief, and rage felt by people whose lives meet with such ordeals are not necessarily symptoms requiring a therapist's assistance. Rage over injustice and violation, for example, could be considered symptomatic only if it were expressed destructively, aimed at innocent targets, or not given any suitable expression over time.

In constructivist approaches, the therapeutic strategy is *not* to work directly on the symptoms in order to diminish them and produce more agreeable, less symptomatic conditions within the *same* view of reality—which would be *first-order* change. Rather, the approach is to usher the client into an alternate view of reality that does not include producing the symptom. This has been termed second-order change, a concept fundamental to constructivist brief therapies, and one which we further develop in this book.

For example, a very alienated and unhappy couple described their "communication problem": The wife complained that her husband viewed everything she said to him as criticism, and that he would therefore counterattack and behave in general as though they were adversaries. He agreed it always felt like they were adversaries but saw this as *her* fault; he felt she continually attacked him emotionally and verbally. The therapist witnessed a typical problematic interaction and saw that the husband did indeed respond to his wife's moderate comments as though he were under attack. The therapist then explained that he needed to do an experiment in order to find out how comfortable or uncomfortable the wife would feel if the husband *didn't* see her as attacking. He coached them through a replay of the earlier, combative interaction, a replay in which the husband, with the therapist's help, managed to respond to his wife's comments as "views shared between partners rather than as enemy fire."

After a few minutes of this atypical, amicable interacting, free of the construal of "attack," the therapist asked the spouses how they were feeling. The wife said, "Relieved." The husband said, "Defenseless." He was quiet for a few seconds and then added, "All I can tell you is, now I feel unjustified in sticking up for myself." A few more steps of inquiry drew out the unconscious emotional reality in which this man usually lived, a reality in which he is "bad and selfish" if he expresses his own views, wants, and needs, and in which it is legitimate for him to do so only if he is *under attack* (hence his great need to see his wife as attacking him, illustrating the constructivist view of perception as inseparable from presupposition).

His disentitlement to self-affirmation now became the focus. A change in that previously unconscious, disentitled position by the end of the next session allowed him to begin to feel justified in expressing himself autonomously even if *not* under attack. His now unneeded construal of his wife as attacking then fell away naturally over the next few sessions.

Here the "communication problem"—his great reactivity to her comments about him—was eliminated by second- and higher-order changes in how he construed interpersonal reality, with no change at all in her behavior. For the therapist to have focused on, say, improving "communication skills" within the original, unrecognized reality would have been a first-order change and would have encountered resistance or at best resulted in a fragile improvement lasting only until the next time his unchanged, unconscious presupposition of disentitlement came into play.

In the constructivist view, then, a client's presenting symptoms are the unacceptable costs or consequences of the client's current way of construing reality. Because it is the client who set up that construction of reality in the first place, it is the client who can change it, if skillfully guided to do so, in order to eliminate those unwanted consequences. Competently executed, this approach tends to result in particularly durable therapeutic change and can occur rapidly.

The hallmark of constructivism is the creation of new meaning and the plasticity of experiential reality. However, the position of constructivists is *not* that "anything goes" or that people are free to make up any reality they wish. People have neither the current ability nor the ethical license to arbitrarily or immediately create *any* wished-for reality, such as "I am a cardiologist." Rather, the constructivist point is that people have much more ability *than they realize* to modify the reality they currently inhabit. Constructivism does not maintain that all alternative realities are equally acceptable; that is, it does not reject values, but neither does it prescribe them.

Within its metastrategy for problem resolution in psychotherapy, constructivism coordinates and integrates the use of "a variety of therapeutic techniques originating from many different therapeutic traditions without . . . encountering the dangers of an arbitrary eclecticism." Clinical examples throughout this book will indeed demonstrate a wide range of techniques used to carry out our particular constructivist approach to problem resolution. The reader will undoubtedly recognize some of these techniques (cognitive, Gestalt, Ericksonian, and so forth) and should remember that *it is the therapeutic design being served by the technique, not the technique itself, that constitutes the DOBT/constructivist dimension of the work.*

At this point we pause to ask the reader how he or she is doing with getting that goose out of the bottle without hurting the goose or breaking the bottle. There *is* a way, very simple, already at hand. Ready? There! Poof! It's out!

The problem existed only as a construction in the reader's imagination. It never consisted of a physical goose in a physical bottle and was not governed by the same properties as physical objects. If the reader construed the imaginary goose and bottle as having to have the properties that a physical goose and bottle would have, the reader unconsciously invented a world and then took it to be real—and gets, in retrospect, a glimpse of our constant but unconscious use of the mind's ability to construct and inhabit realities. An imaginary goose is easily removed from an imaginary bottle in which it suffers unnatural confinement, without hurting the goose or breaking the bottle. Likewise, the very real suffering of therapy clients is due to conditions and constraints that clients themselves have unwittingly put into effect in response to external events, and which clients therefore have the capacity to dissolve. Even in the midst of objective hardship, the difference between a triumph and a collapse of the spirit is the difference in how the ordeal is construed—the construction of meaning by which the individual relates to circumstances.

Notes

P. 2, *characterized systemic family therapy from its inception:* See, for example, J. Bogdan (1988), "What's All the Fuss?" *Family Therapy Networker, 12*(5), 51; J. S. Efran, R. J. Lukens, and M. D. Lukens (1988), "Constructivism: What's in It for You?" *Family Therapy Networker, 12*(5), 26–35.

P. 2, *eliminated emotions and the unconscious as legitimate areas of therapeutic focus:* See, for example, P. Watzlawick, J. Beavin, and D. Jackson (1967), *Pragmatics of Human Communication,* New York: W. W. Norton; J. Haley (1978), "Ideas Which Handicap Therapists," in M. M. Berger (Ed.), *Beyond the Double Bind,* New York: Brunner/Mazel; E. Lipchik (1992), "A 'Reflecting Interview' with Eve Lipchik," *Journal of Strategic and Systemic Therapies, 11,* 59–74; I.-B. Krause (1993), "Family Therapy and Anthropology: A Case for Emotions," *Journal of Family Therapy, 15,* 35–56.

P. 2, *"For all of them . . . the processes which take place inside individuals were considered to be outside the remit of observation and study:"* I.-B. Krause, *op. cit.* (p. 43).

P. 3, *"only recently has the term* unconscious *begun to be liberated from exclusively psychoanalytic connotations":* M. J. Mahoney (1991), *Human Change Processes: The Scientific Foundations of Psychotherapy* (p. 107), New York: Basic Books.

P. 5, *Michael J. Mahoney:* M. J. Mahoney (1991), *Human Change Processes: The Scientific Foundations of Psychotherapy,* New York: Basic Books; M. J. Mahoney (1988), "Constructivist Metatheory: I. Basic Features and Historical Foundations," *International Journal of Personal Construct Psychology, 1,* 1–35; M. J. Mahoney (1988), "Constructivist Metatheory: II. Implications for Psychotherapy," *International Journal of Personal Construct Psychology, 1,* 299–315.

P. 5, *Robert A. Neimeyer:* R. A. Neimeyer (1993), "An Appraisal of Constructivist Psychotherapies," *Journal of Consulting and Clinical Psychology, 61*(2), 221–234.

P. 5, *William J. Lyddon:* W. Lyddon and J. McLaughlin (1992), "Constructivist Psychology: A Heuristic Framework," *Journal of Mind and Behavior, 13,* 89–107.

PP. 5–6, *level of synapses and neural networks:* H. von Foerster (1981), *Observing Systems,* Salinas, CA: Intersystems; H. von Foerster (1984), "On Constructing a Reality," in P. Watzlawick (Ed.), *The Invented Reality* (pp. 41–62), New York: W. W. Norton.

P. 6, *level of construing and assigning* meanings *to perceptions:* P. Berger and T. Luckman (1966), *The Social Construction of Reality,* New York: Doubleday; C. Geertz (1973), *The Interpretation of Cultures,* New York: Basic Books; W. B. Pearce and V. E. Cronin (1980), *Communication, Action, and Meaning: The Creation of Social Realities,* New York: Praeger.

P. 6, *"enduring constructions . . . in unsatisfactory ways":* L. N. Rice (1974), "The Evocative Function of the Therapist," in L. N. Rice and D. A. Wexler (Eds.), *Innovations in Client-Centered Therapy* (p. 293), New York: Wiley.

P. 6, *additional core idea:* See, for example, B. Held (1990), "What's in a Name? Some Confusions and Concerns About Constructivism," *Journal of Marital and Family Therapy, 16,* 179–186.

P. 7, *As theorist Gregory Bateson pointed out:* G. Bateson (1972), *Steps to an Ecology of Mind* (p. 272), New York: Ballantine.

P. 7, *wrote therapist George Kelly:* G. Kelly (1969), *Clinical Psychology and Personality: The Selected Papers of George Kelly,* B. Maher (Ed.), New York: Wiley.

P. 8, *"the 'trauma' of rape takes place in language":* J. S. Efran, R. J. Lukens, and M. D. Lukens (1988), "Constructivism: What's in It for You?", *Family Therapy Networker, 12*(5), 29.

P. 8, *second-order change:* See, for example, P. Watzlawick, J. Weakland, and R. Fisch (1974), *Change: Principles of Problem Formation and Problem Resolution,* New York: W. W. Norton; W. Lyddon (1990), "First- and Second-Order Change: Implications for Rationalist and Constructivist Cognitive Therapies," *Journal of Counseling and Development, 69*(6), 122–127; R. A. Neimeyer (1993), "An Appraisal of Constructivist Psychotherapies," *Journal of Consulting and Clinical Psychology, 61*(2), 221–234.

P. 9, *constructivist view of perception as inseparable from presupposition:* See, for example, C. Sluzki (1990), "Negative Explanation, Drawing Distinctions, Raising Dilemmas, Collapsing Time, Externalization of Problems: A Note on Some Powerful Conceptual Tools," *Residential Treatment for Children and Youth, 7*(3), 33–37.

P. 10, *"a variety . . . dangers of an arbitrary eclecticism":* G. Feixas (1990), "Approaching the Individual, Approaching the System: A Constructivist Model for Integrative Psychotherapy," *Journal of Family Psychology, 4*(1), 27.

CHAPTER 1

What Is an Effective Therapy Session?

Sometimes we have to be reminded that we have capacities we forgot we have.
VIRGINIA SATIR

Wanting to describe the nature of her therapy experience, one of our clients shared the fable of the musk deer—the deer who endlessly searches the forest for the wonderful source of an exquisite perfume she always smells, and in the end finally discovers that the wonderful source is herself. It is characteristic of depth-oriented brief therapy for the client to experience just such a complete reversal of meaning and to discover, "It is I who create the very experience I thought was happening *to* me, and I who can transform it."

This remarkable discovery happens in a most natural way. The therapist's intentionality is focused fully on finding, and drawing the client into experiencing, what we term *the emotional truth of the symptom*—a kind of lost continent of meaning in the client's evolving world. It is this discovery that has the liberating effect.

The emotional truth of the symptom can be understood as one of the more influential formations within the person's world of meaning. In depth-oriented brief therapy, such formations of meaning are conceptualized principally in terms of what we call *positions*.

Positions

A *position* is essentially a constructed version of reality plus a strategy for responding to that reality. A position consists of a linked set of conscious or unconscious feelings, beliefs, images, memories, values, presuppositions of meaning, and bodily tensions or sensations, which activate together in response to situations that appear pertinent to them, triggering a strong predisposition to respond in a particular, preset way.

Recall the man, described in the Introduction, who felt "attacked" by virtually any substantive comment his wife would make to him. As already described, the therapist brought to light this man's unconscious presupposition that within close family relationships, he was not entitled to be assertive and autonomous unless under attack. This in turn made it very important to construe his wife as attacking him, so that he could legitimately be self-assertive. This whole, unconscious, cognitive-affective construal of reality, including the self-protective behavior of finding every opportunity to see his wife as attacking him, constituted a *position* he held in relation to her. Cast into words, this position could be phrased, "I have no right to differ with you or assert my own wants and needs unless you are attacking me, and since I have no intention of being powerless with you, I will see you as attacking whenever I possibly can." *That* was the emotional truth of the symptom. However, he had been aware of neither holding this position nor of powerfully asserting it, because he was unconsciously presupposing its truth. Consciously he felt quite the opposite, felt himself to be a victim of her "attacks" and unable to get her to stop attacking him. He had no inkling that it was his own position creating this bubble of experiential "reality" ("illusion" would be more accurate) that seemed so real.

More exactly, we define a position as a linked set of conscious and/or unconscious emotions, cognitions, and somatics that (1) constitute the person's construal of meaning for a certain kind of situation, creating an experiential reality; (2) are activated when current perceptions seem in some way to match the stored representation ("memory") of that kind of situation; and (3) distinctly predispose the person to respond to the situation with specific *protective actions* designed to secure safety or well-being or avoid harm or suffering. This ready, pre-set response, which is behavioral and/or internal (as in dissociating, obsessing, psychogenic pain, and so on), is itself an integral element of the position.

As useful as the concept of position proves to be in understanding symptoms and change, the notion of position by and large does not arise in the spectrum of psychotherapies. In the few places where it has been systematically used—in the brief strategic therapy model of the Mental Research Institute and in some conceptual analyses of narrative therapy—the concept of position denotes already or incipiently conscious views and attitudes of the client. In depth-oriented brief therapy, the full inclusion of truly *unconscious* positions in the methodology and conceptual picture results in fundamental and sweeping differences from other brief approaches and forms a comprehensive psychotherapy with altogether new capabilities.

Positions organize reality. Oddly, a human being can harbor simultaneous, divergent positions that establish quite different realities in relation to the same item of experience, and therein lies the genesis of nearly all problems that bring people to therapy. This heterogeneous construction of reality is a central feature in DOBT's view of people, problems, and change. Specifically, a therapy client has two divergent positions that are of utmost relevance to the therapist's task.

The Anti-Symptom Position

Nearly always, therapy begins as follows: The client comes in and describes a problem or symptom (by *symptom,* we mean the specific, identifiable features of the presenting problem[s], such as spousal arguments, anxiety attacks, compulsive eating, child cutting school, and so on). In the client's description she directly or indirectly expresses the following views and attitudes:

- She sees the problem or symptom as senseless or irrational.
- She sees the problem or symptom as completely valueless and undesirable and therefore wants it to stop.
- She sees herself as its victim—that is, she views the problem as an involuntary experience and views herself as powerless or having no control over the external situation and/or herself.
- She takes the problem to *mean* certain negative things about herself or others (for example, she is [or they are] bad, shameful, defective, crazy, stupid, inadequate, uncaring, and so on).

The client has, as all people do, a fundamental need to make sense of all experience and so resorts to these consciously available ways of construing the problem. In DOBT this set of views and attitudes—the client's initial, conscious constructions in relation to the presenting problem—is termed the client's *conscious anti-symptom position.*

The Pro-Symptom Position

Experience shows that the conscious, anti-symptom position gives an incomplete account of the client's emotional relationship to the problem.

As we will demonstrate many times over in this book, the client inevitably also has an unconscious, *pro*-symptom position toward the problem, an unconscious construction of meaning that proves to be the key to rapid, in-depth resolution and is the central focus of DOBT both methodologically and conceptually. This pro-symptom position contains the truest emotional significance of the symptom and the full phenomenology of how the client generates it. In contrast to the makeup of the conscious, anti-symptom position described above, reality in the unconscious, pro-symptom position consists of the following knowings and attitudes:

- The symptom or problem has deep sense and compelling personal meaning.
- The symptom or problem is at certain times vitally necessary and is of crucial, positive value, so it must *not* simply stop or be disallowed.
- The symptom is created and authored by me myself and is implemented by me as needed.

A pro-symptom position is an unconscious model of reality in which the symptom seems necessary to have, and it is from this position that the client produces or implements the symptom. The man who felt attacked by his wife had an unconscious, pro-symptom position in which the view of reality—"I am unentitled to autonomy unless attacked"—made it emotionally very important to construe "attack," despite the fact that in his conscious position he strongly disliked this experience. This pro-symptom position involved an *emotional wound* related to autonomy, a *presupposition* of when autonomy is legitimate for him, and a consequent *protective action* of construing attack in order to avoid being deprived of autonomy.

As a rule, these three elements—*emotional wounds, presuppositions, and consequent protective actions*—are the primary components of pro-symptom positions.

Very often the client's presenting symptom *is* a protective action, though it may be unrecognized as such. Protective actions avoid the occurrence of any unwanted experience or event. Protective actions take an extremely wide range of forms, including dissociation, obsessing, depression, anger, blaming, shame, low self-esteem, and such addictive-compulsive (mood-altering) behaviors as binge eating, workaholism, manic activity, and many others. A protective action associated with an emotional wound serves to protect against directly experiencing the emotional pain of an unhealed emotional wound and/or against ever again receiving any similar violations, blows, or losses.

In the course of the next two chapters we will more closely define presuppositions, emotional wounds, and protective actions and see how they are organized within a position. Here our focus is on the fundamental fact that within the view of reality created by emotional wounds and presuppositions in the pro-symptom position, the presenting symptom is compellingly important to have. As the example in the next paragraph shows, the client is at first thoroughly unaware of how needed and meaningful the symptom is to her or him, since the pro-symptom position is unconscious. A central feature of DOBT is the therapist's direct work, from the first session, with these unconscious constructs that are creating and maintaining the problem.

Consider the client whose symptom of "procrastination" was destroying his graduate school career, which had only recently begun. He felt himself to be "a failure," wanted therapy to get him to carry out his schoolwork, and saw the problem self-blamingly in terms of "weakness of character," "laziness," and "self-sabotage"—all elements of his conscious, anti-symptom position. He was amazed to discover his pro-symptom position, fully unconscious at the start of therapy, which consisted largely of the conviction that it was urgently important not to submit to a life program that he himself didn't actually want, this graduate program having been decided upon by his parents. When therapy ended four sessions later, he had direct, feeling-centered awareness of this as his own emotional truth; knew his non-pursuit of this graduate program to be not a weakness or failure but an actual success at keeping his life his own; and had decided to drop out of the program because it was not what he wanted for himself.

In this case, the symptom of procrastination was a protective action that the client affirmed and retained once he experienced his actual purpose for implementing it. This is an extremely simple, almost transparent example, yet the therapeutic process it illustrates—arranging for resolution on the basis of discovering an unconscious emotional truth or pro-symptom position—is extremely broad in application.

This example also shows that the client's best interests are *not* necessarily served by defining success in brief therapy as achieving an outcome agreed to by client and therapist at the *start* of therapy, as it is in other brief approaches. In depth-oriented brief therapy, the in-depth work involves discovery of the unconscious construction of the presenting symptom, which as a rule results in the client experiencing a thorough transformation of the conscious meaning of the problem. Consequently, the outcome desired by the client often changes greatly or even reverses, as it did in this example. Here the client's initial desired outcome definition was "I would be doing everything necessary to complete my course work and program requirements without significant delays." This *sounds* like a positive and verifiable behavioral goal—very much the kind of goal established in solution-oriented, strategic, and behavioral therapies. Suppose the therapist had designed the therapy to bring about this conscious agenda of completing his graduate program and had creatively generated enough motivation for him to do that—and to continue to unwittingly override his still-unconscious reasons for wanting not to. The therapy would count as a "success" in a study of short-term outcomes. However, this man's fundamental alienation from his field and his about-to-erupt autonomy issues would have remained hidden, and his emotional involvement in his line of work would have been built on quicksand. We would predict that the same collapse of motivation that first brought him into therapy would recur farther along his path, perhaps with an even greater sense of personal failure.

In our view, the client is served much better, and more ethically as well, by gaining full, felt awareness of his emotional truth, his pro-symptom position, and then reassessing what the outcome of therapy should be. We take the client's initial definition of the outcome seriously, but what we are committing and agreeing to wholeheartedly at the start of therapy is not tie client's initial concept of resolution, but the client's arriving at a genuine, lasting resolution, knowing that this will not necessarily be what the client originally pictured.

If we as therapists are aware that the client's initial concept of a desirable outcome is a product of the same limiting view of self and world that is generating the problem itself, then we are ethically obligated to invite a reassessment by the client of the desired outcome in light of some fuller view of the client's own purposes. Therapies that neglect the unconscious are, of course, free of this inconvenience.

The client's anti-symptom position insists upon change ("stop the symptom"), while his or her pro-symptom position insists upon stability ("keep the symptom"). Thus DOBT's handling of the dialectical tension between these two positions is a way of working simultaneously with the client's two-sided commitment to both change and stability.

At the start of therapy, the client's pro-symptom position, despite being unconscious, is the emotionally governing one, in this sense: The client keeps manifesting the symptom despite consciously and even desperately wanting not to do so. While the pain or trouble of the presenting symptom motivates the client to get rid of it, the very fact that the client keeps producing (or, in a couple or family, co-producing) the symptom means that, given everything—in particular, given the imperative emotional themes in the client's pro-symptom position—*having* the symptom is actually a higher priority than *not* having the pain and trouble it brings. The therapist's work in DOBT is at all times guided by the active conviction that *the symptom is the way it is because some position of the client wants or needs it to be exactly that way.* Every aspect of every symptom is a coherent manifestation purposefully and precisely implemented or expressed by a coherent position of the client. The symptom is never the client being out of control or defective, though that is how the client's conscious, anti-symptom position construes it.

The Therapist's Two Top Priorities

In DOBT the therapist empathizes with the client's suffering and accepts the client's wish to be rid of the symptom.

Then the therapist's first main task is to achieve clarity into those imperative but hidden emotional themes that constitute the client's pro-symptom position and that make the symptom actually more important to have than not to have. The specific methodology of DOBT for rapidly achieving this decisive clarity is called *radical inquiry*. It is "radical" because of its swiftness and accuracy in discovering the problem's hidden root (*radical* deriving from the Latin *radix*, meaning *root*) and because of its assumptive framework, an application of constructivist epistemology that departs radically (root level) from traditional conceptions of the unconscious.

Having discovered the client's pro-symptom position (or a significant part of it) through radical inquiry, the therapist's second task is to carry out DOBT's methodology of change, which overall we call *experiential shift,* to emphasize the necessity of experiential rather than analytical or interpretive approaches to change. The therapist is now seeking for the client to have an actual experience of change in the constructs comprising his or her pro-symptom position.

The phrase *experiential shift* refers to either the *process* of change or to the change itself, in the same way that the word *change* may refer to the process or to the final result of change; the appropriate meaning is always clear from the context. In depth-oriented brief therapy, both the process and the final result of change are always experiential.

As both radical inquiry and experiential shift require the client to face and feel emotionally unresolved or dystonic material, they require of the therapist empathy, sensitivity, skill with emotional and cognitive process, and a strong ability to establish warmth and safety in the client-therapist relationship.

Radical inquiry is the therapist's highly focused process of bringing to light the client's pro-symptom position(s) involved in the problem. Experiential shift is the equally focused process of involving the client in directly altering pivotal pro-symptom constructs. Since an effective session in DOBT is one in which radical inquiry or experiential shift is carried out, these two activities are the therapist's two top priorities in every session.

With sufficient commitment to the notion that the important symptom-generating positions and processes can be immediately contacted, the therapist will shape interventions that experientially bring this about. The therapist's genuine readiness to meet the client's emotional truth, right now, communicates itself and lets the client know on conscious and unconscious levels that here, now, it is safe and appropriate to let this happen. Engaging clients experientially in their own pro-symptom material makes everyone present know that something of moment is occurring in each therapy hour. In contrast, talking *about* the problem or its resolution, accurate or insightful as such talk might be, rarely produces in-depth, lasting resolution.

In depth-oriented brief therapy the rule is: *radical inquiry and/or experiential shift in every session, from the first session.* The therapist stays on purpose and does not let the session drift away from these two pursuits, both of which focus on the client's *pro*-symptom position. This is the basis for consistently doing deep, brief, unmistakably effective work with lasting results with individuals, couples, and families.

We find in training clinicians in DOBT that many therapists habitually focus on the client's *anti*-symptom position in an effort to build up that position to the point of defeating the symptom. In this they conform to the expectations of clients, who naturally believe that the path to being free of the symptom is through attending to their anti-symptom position—working *against* the symptom and trying to get *away* from it. Many therapists conceive of therapy in the same way and devote sessions to empathizing with the client's *anti*-symptom views and feelings and supportively encouraging the client's attempts to not have the symptom happen.

This is, however, a prescription for ineffective work, because it puts the therapist in the same ineffective position the client has been in, unknowingly trying to override a hidden, emotionally powerful pro-symptom position, a situation almost guaranteed to produce resistance, relapse, symptom substitution, prolonged therapy, or a sense that the therapy is superficial and cannot deal with "the real problem."

In DOBT the therapist focuses the work on the client's *pro-symptom* position as soon as possible in the first session and then keeps it there, making momentary exceptions for the purpose of maintaining emotional rapport and empathy when the client relates from his anti-symptom position, and then drawing the focus back to working with the client's pro-symptom position through radical inquiry or experiential shift.

Radical Inquiry

Radical inquiry has several aspects that operate together. We will briefly introduce some of these aspects here and illustrate them with case material; Chapters Four and Five provide a more thorough discussion.

Radical inquiry is the therapist's methodology for finding the symptom's emotional truth, which makes it lucidly clear how, and why, the presenting symptom is actually more important to have than not to have. This is a phenomenological-experiential process of discovery, carried out entirely within the terms of the client's subjective world of meaning. As such it involves no attempt to get the client to accept theoretical analyses or interpretations, does not use psychiatric diagnostic categories, and is completely non-pathologizing. Finding the emotional truth of the symptom also involves no inventing or grafting of a "better narrative," however collaboratively constructed. The symptom's emotional truth is completely the client's own already-existing but unrecognized construction of meaning, and it is through the recognition and further evolution of *that* construction that change occurs in depth-oriented brief therapy.

Radical inquiry, like the constructivist perspective it serves, is not defined by any specific psychotherapeutic techniques or interventions; a great many techniques may be applied, adapted, or devised. The defining feature is this: Whatever techniques are utilized, any step of radical inquiry is crafted by the therapist in such a way that responding to it inescapably brings the client into an *experience* of the hidden, pro-symptom position, the hidden emotional truth of the problem.

Let's take an example from couples therapy. A couple in their late twenties described their problem as "emotionally ugly verbal battles that keep happening and keep us from feeling close. We both jump right in." They said they were able to stay harmonious for at most three or four days, at which point one of these bitter fights would inevitably erupt. Hearing this information, the therapist in DOBT feels interest in finding out what makes it overridingly important for these two individuals to have fights that end the closeness. The therapist does not impose ready-made views of why couples fight, why intimacy is frightening, why a couple system would homeostatically reestablish distance after closeness, and so on. In this case the therapist began radical inquiry by asking, "If you were to stay close for long periods, weeks and weeks, as you want, there are ways in which that would be so good, so enjoyable. But I want to know in what way would it be in some way a difficult problem in itself to remain close and happy, on and on?"

The therapist then held the focus upon this question and had each of them construct and actually sample in imagination the experience of day after day, week after week of harmony. This is an example of how, in order to respond to a radical inquiry intervention, the client must experientially access and report on some part of the emotional truth of the problem. Within a few minutes each experienced something completely new, but in fact very old: for each of them, the very fact of being in happy harmony unconsciously had the distinct if indiscriminate meaning, "I've lost myself in this relationship; I'm being passive and controlled." Each held a strong, unconscious conviction that harmony equals submission equals loss of self, and each kept a stance of sharp vigilance against being dominated in a relationship. Three or four days of closeness were enough harmony to trigger an unconscious alarm, and they would "both jump right in" and have a fight that restored to each a most reassuring sense of assertive independence. This explanation was not what systems theorist Barbara Held terms a "predetermined explanatory content" imposed by the therapist, but a *direct, vivid, experiential realization* and acknowledgment by each of the partners. The unusual degree of sameness in their unconscious positions made it especially easy in this case for a new kind of mutual empathy to develop regarding these feelings and concerns. In their next session two weeks later they reported that incipient fights were now quickly fizzling out because "we're now so aware of what we're really up to, and we just kind of look at each other." Now that they were out of their unconscious reactive pattern of distancing, they were able to face and work fruitfully with their fears of being controlled by allowing closeness.

From the initial, conscious position of both of them, the presenting symptom of fighting appeared to be a completely undesirable problem. From the unconscious, pro-symptom position, the symptom was actually the very needed *solution* to a problem, an initially unacknowledged problem, but a problem so important that its solution—the symptom—was actually more important to have than not to have, despite all the suffering it brought. As occurs in many cases, the therapist here found the problem to which the symptom was the clients' solution.

Experiential Shift

Experiential shift, the methodology of change in depth-oriented brief therapy, has two stages. The first stage is to usher the client into consciously inhabiting and integrating the discovered pro-symptom position. This phase of the work we refer to simply as *position work*. Here there is no attempt whatsoever to change the pro-symptom position; position work is purely a matter of having the client incorporate this previously unconscious position into how he or she consciously experiences the problem.

In many cases position work resolves the problem. When it does not, an additional phase of experiential shift is required, the *transformation of constructs*, which involves revising or dissolving the emotional reality in the pro-symptom position so that there is no longer any version of reality in which the symptom seems needed.

The client's pro-symptom position, being unconscious, may be "comprised of a set of meanings that are felt to be incompatible with, unacceptable to, and threatening to the system of meanings constituted in consciousness," as psychoanalyst Thomas Ogden describes. The client's conscious, anti-symptom position acts as an obstacle or barrier to discovering and owning the unconscious, symptom-generating position. This process may require sensitive therapeutic facilitation (as shown by two cases detailed in Chapter Two).

When the pro-symptom emotional reality has been deeply unconscious, the client's initial experiencing of it is a very state-specific knowing, a quite altered state that may be lucid at the time but is likely not to be retained in awareness when the client returns to the very different reality in his or her habitual, conscious position. This is to be expected, and so a focused process of integration is needed in order for the client to maintain access to the pro-symptom view of reality and consistently relate to the problem from it, rather than from the anti-symptom position. Position work carries out this vital step of integration. It will be illustrated in many examples throughout these chapters and systematically reviewed in Chapter Six.

With the couple described just above, position work brought the partners to a stable awareness of actually implementing the symptom of fighting as a solution to the problem of having a faltering sense of autonomy, even though each hated the fighting. This was a conscious integration of the *pro*-symptom emphasis on the *value* of having the symptom with the *anti*-symptom emphasis on the *pain* of having it: the partners directly apprehended that having the symptom of fighting was, for them, *worth* the considerable pain and trouble that accompanied it. The client in position work both experientially discovers and explicitly acknowledges how the emotional worth or meaningfulness of having the symptom in fact outweighs its costs. This is a crucial point in the work, a point we term the *pro/anti synthesis.* Achieving this synthesis is a profound change in the construction of the problem, and in many cases resolution is an immediate result.

The acknowledgment that having the symptom has been worth the costs of having it does not mean the client's suffering is any less real or deserving of empathy. It means only that the therapist must not confuse suffering with real readiness to live without the symptom: the client wishes genuinely to be free of the symptom or problem but simultaneously has even higher priorities that require keeping it. The existence and potent influence of these initially unconscious higher priorities is not theoretical but empirical, a matter of unmistakable experiential fact for the client. In depth-oriented brief therapy the therapist empathizes with both the client's suffering *and* the subjective priorities found to be necessitating and maintaining the symptom. The therapist never naively takes the client's anti-symptom position as the full story and there-fore never attempts merely to eliminate the symptom or to have the client eliminate it without full clarification of the importance of the symptom in the client's world.

Problem Resolution: Congruence of Positions

Finding and then integrating the pro-symptom emotional truth of the symptom is the prelude to two possible types of resolution: either (1) the client's *pro*-symptom position will be changed so that the symptom no longer appears necessary to have and therefore disappears, or (2) the client's *anti*-symptom position will be changed by the revelation of the pro-symptom reality so that having the symptom no longer appears to be a problem and the symptom continues as a now valued or at least acceptable item in the client's experiential world.

In either case, the result will be that one of the positions has come around to the other's view of the symptom as desirable or undesirable to have. When this agreement or congruence of positions is reached, there is no longer any basis for the symptom to exist or to be regarded by the client as a problem.

As the client's initial, fragmentary view of his own relationship to the symptom becomes more complete in the course of the work—as the client contacts the emotional truth of the symptom and the meaning of the symptom undergoes a transformation—he may reassess and come to regard the symptom as something he wants to retain. We refer to this as *reverse resolution,* since it entails a reversal in the status of the symptom from unacceptable to acceptable.

If the symptom remains unacceptable even in light of its emotional truth, and the client's original desire for the symptom to stop continues to define the outcome of successful therapy, we refer to this as *direct resolution.*

A simple example of reverse resolution is the work described earlier with the graduate student "procrastinator." Consciously, he was attributing to his symptom negative meanings of personal defectiveness that are culturally prevalent but had nothing to do with the unconscious emotional truth of his procrastination (his pro-symptom position). Upon contacting and recognizing this emotional truth—that what he had been calling procrastination was actually an unconscious refusal to follow an unwanted path in life—he took his stand on it and carried it out fully. What had seemed an undesirable symptom underwent a transformation of meaning and became a desirable strength of self-determination that he wanted to retain. His *anti*-symptom position ("stop this procrastination") was transformed and brought into agreement with his pro-symptom position ("keep this self-determination") as a result of coming into conscious contact with it.

In direct resolution, the symptom continues to be unacceptable even in full view of its emotional truth. A woman seeks therapy because she wants to lose weight but has been unable to do so. In her first session of therapy she experiences her pro-symptom position, in which being overweight is very important as her foremost form of preserving autonomy against a mother she has experienced all her life as extremely controlling. Being overweight now makes deep new sense and is no longer the "weakness of willpower" she had thought it to be—yet she still wants to lose weight. Therapy then focuses on arranging for this, either through disengaging weight as the arena of the power struggle, or better still, through transforming how she construes her relationship with her mother so that the power struggle ends, making weight loss acceptable. This change would constitute a new construction of reality in which being overweight is now unnecessary, allowing direct resolution to occur. The client's pro-symptom position would be transformed into a new position that does not require the symptom, and that agrees with the anti-symptom position that the symptom is unnecessary.

In general, then, since every client has the two divergent views of the problem—anti and pro—problem resolution in DOBT consists of transforming either the anti-symptom or pro-symptom position, bringing the one construction of reality into alignment or agreement with the other regarding the symptom's unacceptability (direct resolution) or acceptability (reverse resolution). One of these two positions is going to prove to be a goose in a bottle and lose its reality. *Which* one will dissolve always becomes self-evident, either from the nature of the symptom at the start of therapy or through the identification of the client's pro-symptom position.

The following case vignette provides a more complete example of direct resolution and illustrates radical inquiry and experiential shift more fully, showing how an effective therapy session is one in which these two priorities are carried out. The inherent capacity of DOBT's methodology to produce in-depth benefits beyond symptom relief will also be apparent.

Case Example: "Agoraphobia" with "Delusion"

A middle-aged woman came in and explained that for many years she had been experiencing difficult levels of anxiety over leaving her house, even for such ordinary tasks as going to the grocery store. The intensity of the anxiety had been increasing over time and had become so strong that she now avoided going out on such trips. She wanted relief, and she also expressed her very troubling concern that this irrational fear meant she was going insane; she urgently wanted to arrest what she saw as growing madness.

As many clients do, she was assuming a therapist would need a great deal of personal history in order to get to the source of the problem and help her, so she started telling her life story. But in order to work deeply and briefly—and, in particular, in order to carry out radical inquiry—the therapist has to maintain focus on obtaining a certain kind of information, namely that which answers the question, What construction exists that makes having the symptom more important than not having it? So the therapist instead asked her what she actually experiences while walking down the street that triggers fear for her. This was a first step of radical inquiry, a first step of looking for the client's purposeful unconscious activity, the value of which is worth the fear it brings.

She had not previously looked closely at exactly what she experiences that triggers fear, so to answer this question she had to go to a new level of awareness of how her fears develop and, to some extent, reexperience that process right there in the room—another example of how a radical inquiry intervention always brings the client into an *experience* of the hidden positions and processes driving the symptom.

She quickly identified specifically what triggers her fear: Whenever she is out walking down a street, just going about her business, she becomes concerned that a former therapist of hers, a woman who moved out of state, is somewhere nearby on this street and is watching her. She becomes involved in the idea and the feeling that her former therapist is there, has noticed her, and is looking at her.

She first feels self-conscious, burdened, and annoyed over being watched by this woman and no longer having privacy, but then, because she is aware she is imagining all this and yet regarding it as real, she starts to think she's truly going crazy. And then, in turn, the idea that this is a psychotic experience triggers intense anxiety.

When struggling there on the street against feeling her therapist's presence, it was clear to her that this delusion meant insanity, but this was too frightening to remember in detail at other times. All she knew as she prepared to leave her house was that "out there" she would start to lose her mind. This is the "fear of fear" commonly labeled agoraphobia. Within the first fifteen minutes of the first session on this problem, this much was now clear.

In standard diagnostic terms this woman would be labeled not only agoraphobic but also obsessional and delusional, with symbiotic separation anxiety and paranoia. However, a diagnostic label does not denote a phenomenological entity; it reveals nothing of the hidden processes of thought, feeling, and behavior that generate the symptoms, and that are within immediate reach. It is these very specific positions and processes that the therapist aims to discover through radical inquiry. In the next twenty minutes or so, all that was needed of the hidden process and the unconscious, pro-symptom position generating this woman's symptoms was discovered.

The therapeutic strategy at this point—the strategy of radical inquiry—was to identify exactly how her symptom of imagining her former therapist was valuable for her. To this end, the therapist asked her to close her eyes and, very simply, to imagine walking down the street and to see what would happen if she *didn't* start to think or feel that this woman was present.

This is a technique we term *viewing from a symptom-free position.* Having the client experience what happens if the symptom doesn't occur is a frequently useful technique for radical inquiry. The point of experiencing what happens if the symptom doesn't is *not* to get the client to desist forevermore from producing the symptom, but only temporarily—just long enough to find out what valuable effects of *having* the symptom are lost, and are revealed through their loss, when the client is without the symptom in circumstances where usually it would be occurring. Often it is expedient to have the client carry out viewing from a symptom-free position in imagination rather than *in vivo,* making direct use of the client's ability to construct an experiential reality and sample it.

Coached by the therapist, this client went through the experience in imagination of finding out what would happen if she did not start thinking her former therapist was nearby as she walked all the way to the store, did her shopping, and then walked back home.

She readily experienced what would happen: she described feeling a deep, old loneliness, a very painful feeling of being left all alone. The therapist now understood her pro-symptom position, and therefore began to do position work in order to bring the *client* into awareness of that position. The therapist's first step of position work was simply to say in response, "So if you don't imagine she's there, then you feel this painful feeling of being left all alone." This adds no new information; it simply focuses the client's attention on what she loses by being without the symptom, and as a result, she said, "Oh,—and I *don't* feel all alone if she's there, too—if I think she's there with me."

Therapist and client had identified the problem for which the symptom was the solution. From this little exercise it became clear to the client that she imagined her therapist was there, watching her, to avoid this old emotional wound of feeling alone and abandoned. She *experienced* that that was her *own* emotional truth, and it was deliberate on the part of the therapist for her to have just such a direct encounter with what her symptom was doing for her.

It was now a small step to reach the client's pro/anti synthesis. The therapist said, "Yes. And you kept imagining her for this important purpose, *even though* you think that's insanity and *even though* that scares you so much. What do you make of that?" She thought momentarily and answered, "I guess it's more important to me to not feel that feeling of being so alone." This was an explicit acknowledgment of her pro/anti synthesis, the recognition by the client that the symptom has had a value that has in fact been worth its costs. Position work was now well established.

Consider the experiential shift already produced for the client: In realizing that she visualizes her therapist in order not to feel alone, her worry about insanity and pathology was already nearly obsolete, as was her view of the symptom as involuntary. A powerful reframe consisting of second- and higher-order changes has occurred, a change of categories defining the very meaning of the symptoms, even with no explicit comment on these points from the therapist. This reframe was not an externally applied invention of new meaning, but an internal discovery of unconscious meaning. We call this *reframing to the emotional truth of the symptom,* and it is brought about through position work. The client apprehends and feels the governing, personal significance of the symptom and makes new sense of the symptom in relation to compelling emotional themes that had been unconscious. Quite often this is an extraordinary experience for the client, a profoundly meaningful and memorable moment of self-understanding. (The concept of the emotional truth of the symptom is more fully and technically defined in Chapter Three.)

The experiential nature of this work is crucial. The client is not taking the therapist's word for it. The therapist is not theorizing, diagnosing, or interpreting but is bringing the client into a direct encounter with her own psychological material, her own emotional truth.

Until now, though, the woman's conscious mind wasn't in on this arrangement for avoiding feeling alone and abandoned. The only way her conscious mind had been able to carry out its need to make sense of the symptom was by construing that to imagine her therapist was present meant she was going crazy. As described earlier, a therapy client's conscious view of the symptom is often no more than a grab at whatever ideas place the symptom in some familiar category of sense, such as "insanity," even if this category is itself very disturbing.

There then was one further step of radical inquiry: The therapist, continuing to evoke the moments and the experience of being on the street, said "As you continue to be there, let yourself have this feeling, this deep, old feeling of being alone in this way. And as you feel this alone feeling, there on the street, you can just notice what, if anything, it *means* to you, or means *about* you, that you feel alone. And what is it that you notice?" Here the therapist is asking her to identify and reveal any presuppositions involved in this state of feeling alone. She reflected with eyes closed for just a few seconds and said, "It means I'm unlovable." This in itself was a powerful part of the structure of the symptom—an ontological presupposition, a construction of meaning that strongly influences the kind of being she "knows" herself to be. From her facial expression and tone it was clearly new for her to be aware of making the all-alone feeling mean "I'm unlovable." (Presuppositions, a key component of pro-symptom positions and an essential area of discovery in radical inquiry, are discussed in Chapter Three.)

The session still had another ten minutes, but even if it had ended right here, it would have been an effective one, because (1) through radical inquiry the therapist gained major clarity into the client's pro-symptom position, that is, why the symptom is more important to have than not to have, and (2) the process of radical inquiry has produced three significant experiential shifts for the client, each a bringing-to-awareness of an aspect of the unconscious, symptom-generating process: going into fear by imagining her therapist, carrying out the *protective action* of imagining her therapist in order not to feel painfully and frighteningly alone (her activated *emotional wound*), and assigning the meaning "I'm unlovable" to the state of feeling all alone (her powerful presupposition), all were brought experientially into the client's awareness. All three of the components that make up pro-symptom positions—protective action, emotional wound, and presupposition—are apparent.

In this case, it was clear that direct resolution would be required—that is, alleviation of the symptom through a transformation of her pro-symptom position. In general, with sufficient clarity and empathic reach into the hidden sense and construction of the symptom, entirely new possibilities emerge for how the client might be able to transform her experience of the problem. The therapist sees that if a certain presupposition or emotional wound in the pro-symptom construction were dissolved, the position as a whole would dissolve or lose its power to create an experiential reality. Each component of the client's pro-symptom position is a potential avenue of resolution that is invisible until the position becomes clear. The therapist then carries out methods of experiential shift (using well-known techniques or inventing new ones) that seem most promising for altering these particular elements and rendering the presenting problem obsolete. For this purpose, learnable steps are spelled out later in this book. In practice and with experience, however, radical inquiry brings the therapist to such a degree of clarity that avenues to *denouement* spontaneously become apparent. In fact, it is when this begins to occur that the therapist knows radical inquiry may be complete.

That is what now occurred in the session. The therapist saw that the client's delusion-solution worked only if she was *unaware* of her purpose for implementing it. If it was arranged for the client to become aware of her purpose at the crucial moment, while walking along the street, the delusion could no longer be automatic and autonomous.

The therapist therefore now said, "What's wrong with thinking about your therapist, to *remind yourself that you have an important connection with her.* But whenever *you really do want to be free of the feeling that she's present,* all you have to do is *ask yourself, really ask yourself,* 'Am I willing to feel alone right now?'"

The question prescribed at the end of this communication has the client consider the emotional truth of the symptom consciously at exactly those moments when previously she would resort to the symptom unconsciously. This question is simply a way to have the client, right there on the street, self-administer the reframe to emotional truth that position work had produced: conjuring up her therapist no longer means she is insane. It now means she feels painfully alone and wants relief from this feeling—and this registers very strongly as true for her. So the main trigger of her anxiety, the idea that this is psychotic, is gone.

Note that the new construction of meaning was not an invention and was not co-constructed, as in other constructivist brief therapies, but was a utilization of the client's own unconscious material, which makes it virtually irresistible, a perfect psychological fit. The reorientation brought about by contacting her unconscious position was relatively straightforward for this client.

There are many ways to carry out reframing to emotional truth, and the type of question prescribed in the intervention detailed above is only one of them. Other techniques could no doubt also have been used just as effectively. The assigned question, "Am I willing to feel alone right now?" keeps the reframe in place between sessions, that is, it keeps the client *aware* of the symptom's emotional truth, which can easily slip back into the dark unless anchored into awareness in some way; and in addition, it is a double bind that puts her in the position of being at choice on whether or not to resort to imagining her therapist. DOBT provides a particularly effective form of double bind because, as already indicated, the bind's reframe is constructed using the emotional truth of the symptom, and so it is subjectively compelling.

Note especially that the prescribed question, like all interventions made in DOBT, is *not* a message to the client to stop producing the symptom. It is a way to position her consciously in the emotional truth of the symptom, which is a position of having choice over whether or not to resort to the symptom. Implicit and explicit messages to the client to stop producing the symptom are therapeutically ineffectual in general, a point already well known to brief therapists since the 1960s.

As mentioned earlier, radical inquiry and experiential shift are not defined by the specific techniques used to carry them out. Chapters Five and Six survey a wide range of specific techniques we find useful. In the therapist's key communication, for instance, he used evocative modulations of voice tone both to focus attention and to invite the client to feel and experience rather than only think. He said, "What's wrong with thinking about your therapist, to [pause; tone drops, softens, and slows] *remind yourself that you have an important connection with her?*" This message acknowledges the deep sense of the symptom—the deep validity of the need that the symptom was meeting, the need for a sense of connection to caring figures—and gives her permission to continue to meet that need, but to meet it overtly, rather than covertly through a symptom.

One might think that for this woman to face rather than suppress her feeling of aloneness would only exacerbate her anxiety, but it did not. (Most therapy clients, we find, are not nearly as fragile as is assumed in psychodynamic approaches.) One week later, in the next session, she said that from using the prescribed question she immediately did get control over imagining the presence of her therapist, and the anxiety about going out had diminished greatly. In order for in-depth therapy to be highly effective and therefore brief, it is essential that it not be the *therapist's* limiting assumptions that are cutting off the therapeutic possibilities in each session. The *client's* limiting assumptions are more than enough to deal with.

In this second session she also said that using the question made her experience a new awareness of going through life in the role of being an abandoned child. She said that even though she was forty-six, she didn't feel herself to be a grown-up, and that, although it took some courage, choosing to feel alone on the street began to open up a sense of being an adult who is no longer hoping for some parent to enfold her. So this work also forwarded the separation-individuation issues in this woman's life.

During this second session, in order to continue to solidify the client's awareness of the emotional truth of the symptom, the therapist, in a natural way, referred several times to how much sense it had turned out to make that she would think of her former therapist when feeling too alone. The therapist also warmly chided her about thinking she was crazy, and told her that if ever again she thinks she's crazy, it is a definite sign that she is actually on the verge of discovering another important, hidden meaning in her life.

In the third session she reported that the anxiety, a problem that had troubled her for years, was completely gone; she said she was no longer imagining her old therapist at all. Ten months later she came in to deal with some other issue (involving her adult daughter, who was moving back into the state and wished to live with her), and when asked if the previous work had held, she said it had held very well.

Although this was a problem with rather complex roots, the actual breakthrough took about thirty minutes. The breakthrough had great simplicity, yet the rapidity and depth of the change did not involve any "tricks," strategic or otherwise. The work with this client did not extend explicitly into her emotional wound of abandonment in her family of origin for two reasons: first, it proved unnecessary to do so for resolving the presenting problem; second, the client was not requesting such a focus and in fact wanted not to address it. Nonetheless, the work was perceived by both client and therapist as experientially deep. The moment in which position work brought the emotional truth of the symptom into awareness was a moment in which the client experienced a sudden depth of self-connection and cogency of self: an expansion of self-understanding and a surprising sense of functioning with more coherent meaning than she had realized (more on this point at the end of this section). Also, the client's choice to inhabit an adult identity at times of aloneness was a fundamental change in her way of being in the world.

With some clients the work does go directly into major, unresolved emotional wounds carried since childhood, as Chapter Two will show in detail. For depth-oriented brief therapy we go as deeply into unconscious constructs as is necessary for resolving the presenting problem, and no further, *unless* the client has motivation to do so and defines the further depth as a new focus for therapy.

Let's review the process of change that occurred in terms of the client's positions, bearing in mind what is axiomatic in DOBT: *Change is blocked when a person tries to move from a position that he or she does not actually have as a governing emotional truth. Therefore, for a client to achieve rapid change, first have the client take the pro-symptom position he or she actually has.*

The client's conscious, anti-symptom position was, in effect, "Feeling that my therapist is there when I'm walking down a street is unwelcome and very frightening, because it's psychotic. I want it to stop." This conscious position turned out to be an emotionally incomplete account of the situation, as we have seen.

Her unconscious, pro-symptom position was, in effect, "Walking down a street all alone means I am abandoned, all alone in the world, and unlovable. All this is too painful to let myself feel, so it's necessary to avoid this hurt by dreaming that my old therapist is nearby and aware of me." This was found to be the emotionally governing position, where "governing" means simply that this position was prevailing in her experience and behavior, regardless of opposition from her conscious position. The unconscious, pro-symptom position is by definition emotionally governing, since the symptom would not occur if it weren't.

In other words, before this woman came in for therapy, when her pro-symptom position was still fully unconscious and unknown to her, she nevertheless asserted it through the symptom of imagining realistically that her therapist was present there on the street, even though consciously she knew better and consciously wanted not to do so. This shows the autonomy of unconscious positions, and of course it is because of that autonomy that symptoms are so mysterious and upsetting to the conscious attitudes.

Constructs comprising unconscious positions are kept separate from incompatible conscious constructs. Bringing her pro-symptom position into full, felt awareness had the effect of bringing its constructs into contact with conscious constructs she harbors. *Contact of incompatible constructs and the resulting dissolution of one by the other occurs only when both are in awareness and experientially vivified simultaneously.* For, example, when the unconscious, nonverbal, pro-symptom construct "the hallucination of the therapist is necessary in order to avoid feeling abandoned" was brought into contact with the conscious construct "this hallucination is psychotic," the latter was dissolved. Likewise, when that same pro-symptom construct also came into contact with the other conscious construct of knowing that she *could* tolerate feeling alone on the street, the latter in turn dissolved the pro-symptom need to dream up her therapist.

Intervening at the level of the emotional truth of the symptom produces resolution and healing of a deeper kind than is the current norm or aim in the brief therapy field. In discovering the presenting symptom's emotional truth, the client discovers the great sense hidden in what she thought was her worst nonsense. The woman in the vignette didn't just get rid of her presenting symptom of fear of going out onto the street. What she thought was insanity—a profound defectiveness in her being—turned out to be full of emotional sense and personal meaning. Turning "craziness" into deep emotional sense illuminating important life themes did more healing of her core self-worth than did merely getting rid of a painful symptom.

Once symptoms fall away, people generally do not think of them any longer and even forget they ever had them. But what clients gain through the realization of their pro-symptom position, their emotional truth, is an awareness of having an inner self that operates throughout its depths with remarkable coherence, active intelligence, and complete emotional sense. That makes a deep and lasting impression. That is an *ontological* healing, a transformation in the kind of being the client knows him- or herself to be. The phenomenological-constructivist spirit of depth-oriented brief therapy, which clients experience as profoundly respectful of their subjective world, is well suited to reveal this innate coherence and gives the approach a natural capacity to time-effectively produce changes well beyond symptom relief. We will more fully describe the part played by an individual's ontology in the structure of his or her positions in the course of the next two chapters.

Summary

Depth-oriented brief therapy is based on the clinical experience that a therapy client's conscious, *anti*-symptom position in relation to the presenting problem is always accompanied by an unconscious but emotionally governing *pro*-symptom position. For the client to inhabit and experience that pro-symptom position is to experience the emotional truth of the symptom—the construction of reality in which the symptom is necessary to have. In working with the pro-symptom position, client and therapist are working directly with the emotional and unconscious meanings that structure the very existence of the problem.

The essential methodology of depth-oriented brief therapy is simple: empathize accurately and sensitively with the client's anti-symptom position, knowing that a pro-symptom position awaits discovery; one-pointedly find that pro-symptom position; usher the client into experiencing the emotional truth of that position; and then, as necessary, assist the client experientially to transform that position. The effectiveness of depth-oriented brief therapy results from adhering closely and fully to this methodology.

Several case examples have demonstrated how an effective depth-oriented brief therapy session is one in which the therapist (1) carries out radical inquiry for achieving clarity into the unknown, pro-symptom constructs and/or (2) facilitates an experiential shift, producing actual change in how those constructs are held by the client. These are the categorical objectives in *every* session.

Radical inquiry by definition is experiential and not analytical or interpretive. When radical inquiry is complete—when the emotional sense and necessity of the symptom in the client's world are lucidly clear—the therapist engages the client in experiential shifts that integrate the pro-symptom emotional reality—the process of position work—and that transform or dissolve constructs in the positions involved in the problem. These changes occur either in the pro-symptom position, so that the symptom is no longer necessary and therefore ceases to occur (direct resolution), or in the anti-symptom position, so that the client's objections to having the symptom dissolve and the symptom is retained (reverse resolution).

From this overview of depth-oriented brief therapy, we turn next to a closer look at the moment-by-moment process of the client-therapist interaction in the course of rapidly resolving long-standing emotional wounds.

Notes

P. 13, *"Sometimes . . . forgot we have":* V. Satir (1983, November), spoken comment at clinical workshop, San Francisco.

P. 15, *in the brief strategic therapy model of the Mental Research Institute:* R. Fisch, J. Weakland, and L. Segal (1983), *The Tactics of Change: Doing Therapy Briefly,* San Francisco: Jossey-Bass.

P. 15, *in some conceptual analyses of narrative therapy:* See, for example, H.J.M. Hermans, H.J.G. Kempen, and R.J.P. van Loon (1992), "The Dialogical Self," *American Psychologist, 47*(1), 23–33.

P. 18, *as it is in other brief approaches:* See, for example, P. Watzlawick, J. Weakland, and R. Fisch (1974), *Change: Principles of Problem Formation and Problem Resolution,* New York: Norton; S. de Shazer (1985), *Keys to Solutions in Brief Therapy,* New York: W. W. Norton; M. S. Wylie (1990), "Brief Therapy on the Couch," *Family Therapy Networker, 14*(2), 26–35, 66.

P. 19, *the client's two-sided commitment to both change and stability:* See, for example, P. Papp (1983), *The Process of Change,* New York: Guilford.

P. 23, *"predetermined explanatory content":* B. Held (1990), "What's in a Name? Some Confusions and Concerns About Constructivism, *Journal of Marital and Family Therapy, 16,* 179–186.

P. 24, *"comprised of a set of meanings . . . in consciousness, ":* T. H. Ogden (1994), *Subjects of Analysis* (p. 16), Northvale, NJ: Aronson.

P. 34, *a point already well known to brief therapists since the 1960s:* See, for example, Watzlawick, Weakland, and Fisch, *Change.*

P. 34, *Most therapy clients, we find, are not nearly as fragile as is assumed in psychodynamic approaches:* See, for example, A. J. Horner (1994), *Treating the Neurotic Patient* in *Brief Psychotherapy,* Northvale, NJ: Aronson (original work published 1985).

CHAPTER 2

Resolving Emotional Wounds

Our remedies oft in ourselves do lie.
WILLIAM SHAKESPEARE, *All's Well That Ends Well*

One of the more daunting challenges facing a therapist is the situation in which a new client walks in with a deep, unresolved emotional wound carried since childhood and generating symptoms —and the client wishes or needs to resolve the problem briefly.

Unlike physical injuries, emotional injuries do not automatically heal with time. They are peculiarly timeless. This, however, has its advantages, in that the *healing* of emotional wounds also does not necessarily take place in or require time.

It is here that the effectiveness of depth-oriented brief therapy is most apparent. In this chapter we usher the reader step-by-step through the therapy sessions of two clients—sessions in which the discovery and resolution of major emotional wounds is central to the work. The immersion in actual therapy sessions in this chapter is intended to give the reader a direct view of DOBT in action and to show how the conceptual picture chalked out in Chapter One is put to clinical use.

These examples will also begin to show how clients' constructs that define reality are organized within a position, an important conceptual feature of DOBT. In the clinical commentaries below we will extend the well-known concept of second-order change by defining third and fourth orders of change. This four-level scheme of the structure of positions will prove to be a useful map of how human beings construct and organize their experiential reality and of how therapeutic change takes place. (Chapter Three provides a unified, comprehensive review and synthesis of this conceptual framework.)

Emotional wounds are among the main components of an unconscious, pro-symptom position, the others being presuppositions and protective actions, as noted in Chapter One. A therapy client's presenting symptom is likely to be the client's experience of either the emotional wound itself or the protective action associated with it. Protective actions perceived as symptoms include obsessing, dissociation, raging, intellectualizing, blaming, addictive and compulsive behaviors, screen emotions (such as guilt, depression, shame, anger), and screen cognitions (such as self-blame: "I was abused because I deserved it."). Symptoms that are an aspect of the emotional-cognitive-somesthetic construction of the wound itself include perceptual and somatic memory flashbacks and feelings of helplessness, anguish, violation, dread, panic, loss, or depression incongruent with present circumstances.

In both of the following cases we will see how radical inquiry quickly reveals the emotional truth of the symptom, the view of reality in the client's unconscious, pro-symptom position that makes the symptom more important to have than not to have. Both cases also require direct resolution, that is, transformation of the client's unconscious, pro-symptom position, because even in light of the revealed emotional truth of the symptom, the client still wants the symptom to stop happening.

Cut to the Core: Thirty Years of Tormented Self-Regard

The client here is a married woman, age forty-five, and the setting is a biweekly group that had recently formed and met several times. What follows is the complete transcript (with minor changes for clarity) of this woman's first personal, therapeutic work in the group, a thirty-minute interaction with the male therapist that decisively dispelled a deep, painful, lifelong emotional wound of low self-esteem.

This single-session example is not meant to suggest that DOBT is an easy miracle cure. However, it is important to show

how extraordinarily effective DOBT can be. The point is not that requiring only one session is to be routinely expected. What is routine in DOBT is the therapist's high level of intentionality toward finding and meeting the emotional truth of the symptom, right now, in this very session, from the first session. As a result of that stance, resolution is reached in the shortest possible time. The example is intended to show how very real is the possibility of rapid resolution even of lifelong emotional wounds.

The client is herself a psychotherapist, which should not lead the reader to assume that the work was therefore necessarily easier in any sense.

> *Client:* I'm not sure if this problem is even workable, so let me just say what it is and see if it makes sense. I got in touch with a real old piece of really negative self-esteem that's very hard for me to—makes me real anxious to even dance around it a little bit. It's like a shard of glass inside me, and every so often I get cut. But in some senses I'm pretty conscious of this so I can sort of not get cut on it, mostly. You know, I can sort of, "Oh, that's that old piece there. I'm not going to pay attention to it right now." I can function *around* it.
>
> *Therapist:* But it stays there.
>
> *Client:* But it's there, and I don't know how to release it. I've never been able to. I guess I'm sort of—I would love to release it but I don't have faith that it *can* be released, so if there's a possibility of releasing it—
>
> *Therapist:* [Smiling] There *is*.
>
> *Client:* —I'd like to risk doing it. [Laughs]
>
> *Therapist:* There's a possibility, for sure.
>
> *Client:* All right. All right. As long as you're sure that it's a possibility.
>
> *Therapist:* Yep, I am.
>
> *Client:* So, so I'll be more specific. [Laughs]
>
> *Therapist:* Yes.

[In response to the client's overt need for assurance, the therapist's first three responses have communicated his relaxed conviction that profound change can certainly happen here in this deep, old emotional wound. This conviction is a fundamental element of the therapist's stance in DOBT, and communicating it to the client, whether explicitly or implicitly, significantly fosters the client's capacity to work deeply and generate change.]

> *Client:* All right. So, the way I got to it is realizing that I've developed a pretty, um, coherent persona of being competent and poised and intelligent and knowing what I'm about and not being able to be rattled very much. It works pretty well for me. And what I got in touch with is, how come I needed to put this persona in place? And what's underneath it is—that I was—we had moved when I was ten and then we moved again when I was twelve. And from the time I was five to ten I was sort of a real competent leader with younger kids. I was the oldest one, and I was a leader of both boys and kind of was a leader with girls in sewing. I sort of did the gamut, and—and it was fun! I mean, I felt very self-assured and had a lot of fun being the one who was in charge of all these younger kids. And then the two years after that not much happened, but then came age twelve, and I remember this, this moment when I went on the new school yard, and I still believed that I could pull my weight with the boys, and I could sort of be their equal or even be a little more than their equal. And they like, "Go away!" You know, "Get out of our territory!" Just absolutely a *total* brush-off. It was like a real shock that I couldn't do this number anymore. And then, somewhere around there, puberty happened, and my sense of me now as a woman was that I was really ugly and didn't know how to do anything to hide that. And, um, even ugly enough to be repulsive. I mean, you know, the word that came up when I got in touch with it, that fit this, is that physically I'm a very repulsive person. And, um—[Silence] Um—
>
> *Therapist:* Is that the shard?
>
> *Client:* That's the shard. What just went blank is the thing that locked it in—the shard. [Pause]

[The therapist is going along with the client's historical account because he feels the content is giving him an understanding of the current emotional truth of the symptom of an emotional and psychogenic pain, a cutting shard of low self-esteem.]

Client: There was one afternoon I was walking to a drug store, and I remember that I was a little pudgy, and I had shorts on, and I never shaved my legs, and my hair was sort of a mess, and I had pimples on my face and no makeup, and I walked down to the drug store—and I was about twelve or thirteen or so—and this teenage boy, who I never saw before or after, said, "Yuk!" Something like that, some word like that. And it's like it just—Uhhh! It went right in there. And it's like, I mean that's really where in some way, as a feminine presence, I've never in some way got past that. I mean, I'm here, I've got success, but I know I get caught there. And then what I did was put all this accomplishment over it. I mean, that's what I did when I felt, "Ohh-*kay,* I can't run boys anymore" and "Ohh-*kay,* I can't make it as a girl at all, not after *that.*" So what I would do is make it as an intellectual. Professional. Accomplished. So that's what I did. I mean, that's what I plugged in. And so whenever I expect to be really challenged intellectually—if I feel I can't use all this defensive stuff I put in place—then I feel I'm going to be totally disarmed, I get very anxious, and really I'm getting cut on the shard, actually. Oh! And it's not only the—and the belief about being so ugly and so repulsive then puts me into a place where I get totally tongue-tied and awfully self-conscious.

Therapist: Yes.

Client: So if I'm not in a professional mode, then I don't have a way to relate to people, because I'm so self-conscious. So that, *that* is the shard. I think that's most of it.

[Her sharply negative self-esteem and her lack of "a personal way to relate to people" seem at this point deep-set and unlikely to resolve quickly, despite her psychological sophistication. Since age twelve and possibly earlier, her self-concept, her social identity and interaction, and her personality had formed around (1) the belief that as a female she is utterly unacceptable to others and (2) the strategy of using her competence and intelligence as a distracting display in order to avoid humiliating exposure.]

Therapist: Yeah. Yeah. You know, listening to that story—I mean it's a very—it's a powerful story.

Client: It is for me, still. I couldn't *believe* they were saying it, those boys: "I don't *want* you."

Therapist: Yes, those adolescent and preadolescent feelings of self-consciousness and torment over how accepted or unaccepted we are, are *so* intense. I mean, God they're passionate. And what strikes me in your description of it all is that—how we *do* go through a really awkward stage in development. I mean, I looked so awful during that corresponding stage, it's just ridiculous how gawky and ugly—I mean, pimply, and you don't know how to do your appearance, and you *can* be ugly for a while. But *you* seem to have gotten the idea that that's the bottom truth about you.

Client: Yes, exactly.

Therapist: And it stuck.

Client: That's right.

Therapist: And it never became apparent to you that it's a phase you pass—I mean, down in your feelings, where it counts—that that's a stage, a developmental stage you passed through.

Client: Right.

Therapist: And came out of.

[The therapist has begun by empathizing with the intensity of the client's experience of the problem, especially her feeling "I'm forever ugly." The therapist simultaneously noticed that his own, genuine view of the larger, developmental context could serve as a reframe that might weaken her construction of herself as forever ugly, so he shared this idea in a natural way, combined with some self-disclosure. This developmental perspective challenged the meaning of her adolescent ugliness, shifting it from an eternal, mythic truth that excludes her from humanity to an ordinary, temporary stage that actually includes her in the human family. The therapist saw this as only a first step in dispelling the apparent reality of her "I'm ugly" position. Several weeks later she commented on how effective this shifted perspective was in immediately starting to loosen the hold of the old reality.]

Client: Right. It's somehow that everything above it is defensive so that I won't pay attention to that's the reality.

Therapist: Let me see if I understand what that means: At the point where you felt you were ugly—and might have been, at that point, the way we get as teenagers—you completely pitched your attention into creating a persona that was going to impress people, and you got totally invested and involved in *that,* and it's like you never again reopened or reassessed the question of how you actually look.

Client: Yes. When I look in the mirror it's *yuk!* You know, the old thing never—it never went away.

Therapist: What would be the bad thing, the dangerous thing, the scary thing, the difficulty you'd have to face if you—let go of that old view of yourself as ugly? If you—let it in, that you moved through a developmental phase and—now you're a lovely, grown woman.

[The therapist was struck by the client's words "it never went away." These words express a victim position of powerlessness (the symptom has a life of its own and happens *to* her), but if symptoms are always coherently and purposefully generated, then the fact that her view of herself as ugly "never went away" points to some important if unconscious purpose for actively holding on to this view. So the therapist next invites her to contact the value this "I'm ugly" construction has for her by evoking, through voice tone, a contrasting experience of being without this construction—that is, an experience of being an agreeable-looking woman. This is a step of radical inquiry, an experiential discovery of what makes the symptom important to have.]

Client: Well, the thing that just came up without my having any control over it [Laughs]—

Therapist: Good.

Client: —was sexuality.

Therapist: Yes.

Client: So, since that's not allowed, and since that's—I'm finally feeling control of it, I can choose what I'm going to do with my sexuality after all these years. Um—But, certainly, if I'm ugly, and if I'm convinced that any man will be totally repulsed by me—aside from the fact that I'm married and really love my husband—but if I didn't, and if that weren't the case, what I really want—this is *very* hard to say—but what I would really like to do is be tremendously seductive. And I never, *ever*—except with my husband—allow myself to do that.

Therapist: Allow, and *allowed.*

Client: Allowed, allowed—because of this belief that I was out of that league.

Therapist: The belief that you don't qualify.

Client: Yes, I totally don't. It would be repulsive.

Therapist: You would shame yourself further.

Client: Yes, I would be very humiliated, because obviously no one would be turned on by a woman who looked like me. So—so that works, because sexuality was scary for me. It wasn't permitted.

Therapist: Was it scary in itself? Even aside from the question of "I'm ugly, so I shouldn't be sexual because then I'll be even more humiliated"?

Client: Well, I have to say one more point that's even *more* difficult to say. There's some way that got locked in at about the same time I was experiencing this sense of being very ugly. I was also very religious. That's when I believed in this very present God, and I had a lot of conversations with Him, and at the same time I had this *tremendous* drive to masturbate, which I could not stop. So my belief system was that the reason I was so ugly was that it was *evil* to masturbate, and I was being punished by being made ugly. That was my punishment. So, that also got locked in.

Therapist: So that's a big part of it. OK. I want to see if I understood that last part. It seems that believing you're ugly—still ugly, truly ugly, always—is a key part of how you keep your sexuality in check, which is spiritually necessary, within your spirituality.

Client: Archaic spirituality. I don't believe that any more.

Therapist: Well, up here, "don't believe," but below the neck it might still be around. I don't know.

Client: Right, right.

Therapist: So to cut loose sexually means you're a sinner, and you're gonna be condemned or whatever.

Client: Right. And I think probably—I mean, again not so much now, but there was certainly a period in my life where it would have been totally OK up here to be really seductive and to play out—and I would have wanted to, but what I told myself was no one who looked like me had the right to do that.

[Radical inquiry has revealed two important parts of the emotional truth of the symptom of staying in "I'm ugly" and viewing herself as certain to be rejected: (1) it keeps her from risking any more devastating humiliations as a female, and (2) it avoids spiritual disaster by keeping a lid on what otherwise felt like uncontrollable sexuality. It has become explicitly clear that the symptom, her "I'm ugly" construction, is a protective action operating in the contexts of sexuality and spirituality. Bringing the client into direct awareness of how the symptom is strategically serving her will diminish the plausibility of the symptom's content. In other words, this reframing to emotional truth puts the client meta to the content level of the symptom, weakening the apparent reality of the content, "I'm ugly." In this case, focusing on the past was a useful way to find the present, hidden, prosymptom constructions maintaining the "I'm ugly." Having accomplished that, the therapist now wants to shift the focus from the past to the present and discover the degree to which the symptom is currently needed to protect against being sexual. This is crucial information to obtain before attempting any experiential shifts to fully dispel the symptom, since the client will not be willing to live without "I'm ugly" if that belief still seems vital for suppressing her sexuality.]

Therapist: I find myself wondering if you're in the classic position of, you didn't sow your wild oats, you didn't experiment with sexual energy and sexual experience the way you wanted to and the way it's in you to do, and "I'm ugly" is a major if not *the* major way you keep the lid on that. And to—I wonder if there's a part of you that's frustrated or very much wanting to have that missing experience of being overtly sexual in the world, and having, you know, sowing your wild oats.

Client: Well—

Therapist: To stop thinking or feeling you're ugly would be to take the lid off of that, and you'd have to deal with those desires—open Pandora's box, in a way. And you're married, and you've got everything nice and stable and put together. It would make a mess. It just sounds like staying with "I'm ugly" is doing some very important things for you.

Client: Well, you know, in a way, that's—there's some level where that really isn't true anymore, because—

Therapist: Yes, I believe that. But I'm interested in seeing if there's a level where it *is* true.

Client: [Pause] At the level where it *is* true today, I think, I think I could probably toy around at being more sexual because I'm not really afraid any more of losing control and being unfaithful. I really choose not to be unfaithful in my marriage.

Therapist: Good. So would you be willing to do—

Client: But I could be a little more sexual, when I chose to, if I didn't feel it would be ridiculous. I think that's it. And that would not be—that would be clean. That's why I said at this point it's different. There *were* times when I didn't feel I had as much choice about my sexual energy. If I let it out, boy, it was not controllable.

Therapist: I see.

Client: And that was injurious for a lot of years. It really was. It *did* almost destroy my marriage, actually.

Therapist: So it *was* important, then, to feel you're ugly as a way of keeping all that in check.

Client: That's really, I mean, how that ties together is, I was married, and at the end of the first year I had an affair with my boss, who was the boyfriend of my best friend. The stupidest, most common, garden-variety kind of affair. And when I was in the midst of it and trying to decide what to do, my mother and I went for a walk to talk about it, and we were walking by and we went into a clothes shop or something, and she said to me, "You know, I wouldn't let your husband go by, because with your kind of looks you're not going to have a lot of chances." That was twenty-five years ago. So what it meant—the message that I've been telling you happened at twelve—well, there's a whole *earlier* piece around that, that I got somewhere, because that—I mean, that was a very strange thing for her to say. That wasn't the issue. I was trying to decide what to do with my *life* at that point.

[As often happens once the client connects with parts of the emotional truth of the symptom, other linked areas of emotional truth begin to emerge.]

Therapist: So there's this whole other area there, where if you get it that you're not ugly, there's some old business with mom that's pretty intense.

Client: I don't know. [Laughs]

Therapist: Sounds like it.

Client: Oh, yes. Because actually the first place that came from was, she told me a man wasn't going to like me because I didn't have enough to grab onto up here. I mean I do have a lot of messages from her that I wasn't—

Therapist: Well, sounds like she needed you to be below her on the ladder. Is that right?

Client: Well, I don't know. What I'm thinking about—I mean, that's the amazing thing. The way I explain it to myself is, she was very overweight for a big chunk of her adolescence and young adulthood and had very low self-esteem, and so in some ways she's very identified with me, and it was so important for me to have the perfect looks that she didn't have, that instead of telling me, as I do with my daughter, how wonderful I am, she was always telling me how I fell short. But maybe it was just my rationalization that she was doing it [Laughs] for my own good, because [Laughs]—so that I would— actually, I think I have to reassess.

Therapist: Yes. Because that's part of what's keeping this stuck, it seems. It seems that it is. Because look, to get it that you're not ugly refutes all those messages from her.

Client: Yes, right. But see, I can't really—even as you say that to me, I can't really—I can't—you know, as you say that, inside what I'm feeling is, mm-mm, that's not true.

Therapist: About what?

Client: That I'm not ugly. See, I can't really—I can't take that in.

[This is an important moment. "I can't take that in" is a message of a certain kind, an opportunity the therapist must recognize. The client is not merely saying, "I don't believe it that I'm not ugly." As a result of the previous work, the client is speaking from a position meta to the content "I'm ugly." She is saying, "I can tell there is something not allowing me to harbor the view of myself as not ugly." In other words, she is commenting on an experience of feeling a mysterious, invisible barrier. This resistive barrier is the active unwillingness of her unconscious, pro-symptom position to allow the construction "I'm not ugly" to exist. She has no words for this nameless experience of resistance other than "I can't take that in." Although earlier she began to glimpse the emotional themes in her pro-symptom position, she is not yet positioned in it, and it is still unconscious. At this point, however, she is right up against that pro-symptom position, and if the therapist recognizes this, it is a simple matter to have the client, like Alice, step across into a different reality and actually inhabit her pro-symptom position. Bringing this about through suitable experiential intervention is what we term *position work*. In depth-oriented brief therapy, the resistance of the client's pro-symptom position always serves as a valuable point of access to that position. To this end, the therapist is going to invite her to voice a "trial sentence" that overtly expresses what her pro-symptom position is doing right now.]

Therapist: Would you right now try out saying, "It's very important to me to believe I'm ugly."

Client: [Big, fast, loud sigh]

Therapist: Just try it out.

Client: OK. So—

Therapist: See how it feels. Without thinking about it. Just say it
and see how it feels.

Client: I'm trying—it's very hard. Those words have—It's very
important to me—[Long pause; visible squirming in
chair; eyes down]—to believe I'm ugly.

Therapist: How does that feel?

Client: I don't know. I didn't—I can't make it real.

Therapist: Would, would you look right at me—

Client: [Bursts into shrill laugh] No!

Therapist: —and, yeah, just look at me and—You know the thing
that just happened? What you just felt? That big "No"?
Try looking right at me and saying it more fully in
words: "Bruce, I *refuse* to let it in, that I'm not ugly."

Client: [Under her breath] OK. All right.

Therapist: Look right at me—

Client: [Exhales a spasm of laughter]

Therapist: —and say, "Bruce, I refuse to let it in that I'm not
ugly."

[The therapist is using the concreteness of the person-to-person
interaction in the room to produce actual integration of the
unconscious position. If the client said the sentence in an autistic
reverie while gazing at the floor, the material would remain split
off, but to express it to another person, a male person, face to face
necessitates that her usual conscious position participate in the
"knowing" of this emotional truth.]

Client: [Long pause; laughs; pause] It's too direct. If I say it
direct with you, I have to let it in a little bit.

Therapist: Say it because it's your true position. This thing that
happened, these are the words for that. And that's
simply the truth of what you're expressing, and I want
you to do it overtly in words. [Pause] Not trying to
change anything.

Client: Well, I know that. It's just that—it's almost physically

impossible! Even though I know that, to make myself
say it overtly—[Pause] It's just too direct, too direct.

Therapist: I understand that you—

Client: And it's like I hide that from the world. There's no
one—I've never told *anyone* that that's the truth,
because I don't play that in the world. I pretend like
I'm fine about my looks. I don't ever ask anyone what
I should wear, and I seem very *confident* about my
looks.

[The therapist experiences her now as diverting from the unbearable exercise, and so brings her back to it.]

Therapist: Even though the directness feels off the charts—

Client: Yes.

Therapist: —you can now extend your range of directness to
include *this* degree of directness.

Client: [Laughs] Right. Right, because then I have to put
aside—[Laughs loudly]

[As she says "put aside," she begins using her hands to move an
invisible something that is right in front of her, off to one side. Evidently her construction of the problem has a strong kinesthetic-
spatial component that has now also come into awareness, and she
is now spontaneously working with that.]

Client: I have to then put aside the piece that—actually, Bruce,
what I want to have you believe is that I'm actually *confident* about the way I look in the world and the communication I make, and it doesn't even concern me; I
don't have a lot of psychic energy on it; I don't pay a lot
of attention to it, because I feel fine and confident
about it. So I have to take away that [Shoves it aside],
which is what I nonverbally tell people in the world all
the time, because it's so painful for me to say anything
else and say, "OK, I'll be divulged."

Therapist: Mm-hm, there it is.

Client: Which makes me feel very cold. OK? I mean I'm feeling really cold now.

Therapist: Yes.

Client: Yes. Because that's my protection. [Laughs]

Therapist: I see that. And you've just bravely put your protection aside.

Client: Yes, and it's really scary. That's why it's so hard to say those words you asked me to say.

Therapist: Got it. I understand. You want a blanket before you say it? I can get a blanket for you.

[The therapist keeps the focus on the task of saying those words. From the client's voice, facial expression, and overall manner, it is clear that she has now willingly waded in and immersed herself in the emotional waters that she earlier was describing from the shore.]

Client: Yes. No. We don't have time. OK. Um. So, I can barely remember it, but I think what it is I'm supposed to say is, Bruce, it's really hard for me—

Therapist: "I'm unwilling—"

Client: Oh. I'm unwilling not to believe that I'm ugly.

Therapist: Good. OK, that's *very* close to what I said. I want to say it again to you—

Client: Yeah.

Therapist: —so you can try it out. "Bruce, I'm unwilling to let it in that I'm not ugly."

Client: [Pause; slowly] Bruce, I'm unwilling to let it in that I'm not ugly. [Silence]

Therapist: How is it to acknowledge that to me?

Client: Well, it's like I'm fighting. It's, it's, it's, it, it, it's actually—I have to [Laughs]—I'm fighting to keep that other part [the "confident" persona that she pushed aside] from coming back in front of my face. Because the *other* part is—OK, the first part is, you know, this front that I'm really OK. Then the other thing that's in there, that really we're like not even addressing, is that I feel ugly. Not only do I feel ugly, but I feel repulsive, repulsively ugly. So then—we're going to move *that* one a little bit *that* way, because if that's out there—See, I didn't move that one out of the way. That's why I was still fighting it. OK?

Therapist: Mm-hm.

[In response to the therapist's persistent request that she overtly take her pro-symptom position in the form of saying a certain sentence, the client became aware of the subjective obstacles to her doing so, two obstacles that are distinct cognitive-emotional-kinesthetic formations: the "I'm fine" construction of her persona, and her strategic construal "I'm ugly." To inhabit the position of the sentence "I refuse to let it in that I'm not ugly" would be to take a position meta to both of these constructions, separating her from them—which is exactly why the therapist worded the sentence this way and why these two obstacles take externalized form as she tries to say it. She is now in the process of finding her own way of literally moving these obstacles aside.]

Client: So, right. So there are two there. So if I move *this* one out of the way, then there's some way that I have to take this one—this really stupid but very strong one that I am repulsively ugly—and get *that* one out of the way. And then I might be able to even say—as my head shakes, which means I'm unprotected. It's the first time I ever held it open. God, this physical stuff is so true!

Therapist: Yes. Yeah. Let yourself really register how this feels.

Client: I mean, because before I was closed to it and—so you thought I—If I put one over here and one over here—and I'm open.

Therapist: Right.

Client: Man!

Therapist: Yeah. Stay with it.

Client: [Long silence; quietly] This feels very strange.

Therapist: Unfamiliar?

Client: Yeah, it's very strange. [Pause] So, now we're at a place where I can say it.

Therapist: OK.

Client: Bruce, I'm unwilling to let in the possibility that I might not be ugly. [Pause] I am! That's true! That's true!

Therapist: You are unwilling.

Client: That's pretty stupid, isn't it!

Therapist: Well, I think we've already seen what it's about,

haven't we. And it's not about being stupid, is it. Seeing yourself as ugly has been doing some *very* important things for you, and to live without that would be a
big change, a big change in a number of important
ways. Change that seems scary.

Client: Now it seems really sad.

Therapist: Sad.

Client: In terms of not—if that really wasn't true, suppose.

Therapist: Yes, yes.

Client: Then it would be really sad to realize that I felt so
awful all my life for nothing.

Therapist: Yes, I see. [Pause]

[The arising of this poignant feeling of sadness is a key indicator
that the client has owned and is integrating her pro-symptom position, largely de-potentizing it and clearing the way for a sudden,
fuller view of her life experience—a shift from the emotional reality of "I'm ugly" to the emotional reality of "How sad to have
thought of myself as ugly all my life, when I wasn't." Right now, for
the first time in over thirty years, the client is in a new position free
of the reality produced by the old pro-symptom construction. Recognizing the significance of this moment, the therapist's next
words are intended to further vivify and establish this new view of
herself and her life.]

Therapist: Just think how sad it would be to *keep* feeling you're
ugly from now until the day you *die,* if it's not true.

Client: [Silence] Well, you know what it does.

Therapist: What's "it"?

Client: Keeping in place the belief that I'm repulsively ugly
and that if anybody got through my persona they
would know that, and it would be humiliating. [Pause]
To have someone go, "Yuk!" again would be unbearable. So, in order to never—OK, that's it, that's it
exactly. If I hold onto that I never have the chance of
somebody ever saying, "Yuk!" to me again, because *no*
one is ever going to get close enough.

Therapist: Yes. So that's—so you made a decision never to be vulnerable to somebody going, "Yuk" again.

Client: Mm-hm.

[In saying, "You made a decision," the therapist is now deliberately using language that emphasizes the client's role as the active author of the symptom rather than its victim. He does this now because the client's immediately preceding statement showed the therapist that she is now in a position to experientially recognize her own potent role as the creator and purposeful implementor of the reality "I'm ugly." Therefore, the therapist knows that naming her authorship of the symptom will now be empowering for her, rather than implying blame or pathology.]

Therapist: And part of that decision was to never again trust that you're not ugly, because trusting that you're not ugly would mean you'd let somebody really see you.

Client: That's right.

Therapist: And then they might go, "Yuk!"

Client: They *would.* [Laughs]

Therapist: And that was *so* painful—a big shard of glass in you. So the pain of thinking you're ugly is *worth* the safety it gives you from any more shards.

Client: [With decisiveness] That's right.

[The client has reached a point of being experientially so aware of her pro-symptom position—her purposeful authorship of the symptom—that once again, the therapist could say his last sentence and know she would recognize it as her own emotional truth, rather than as an interpretation being imposed by him. That particular sentence is the apex of the position work, because it captures the essence of her pro-symptom position and of her new awareness of that position. To establish a new reality based on that exact awareness would certainly render the problem obsolete, so the therapist reiterates it.]

Therapist: It's very painful to think you're ugly. Common sense says you'd be happy to discover you're not ugly, but actually it's protecting you so massively, you feel, to feel you're ugly. Everything hinges on that protection. [Pause] Maybe even your relationship with your mother is protected by thinking you're ugly.

Client: My mother is probably a year from dying right now, and sort of vulnerable.

Therapist: It would not be comfortable to go into rage at her at this point, for example.

Client: It wouldn't make any sense to do it.

Therapist: No, I don't mean actual confrontation.

Client: Well, it *might* make some sense.

Therapist: [Laughs] So, we're out of time. Are you OK with stopping there?

Client: Yes.

At the next group meeting, two weeks later, she made these comments: "That was the most powerful piece of therapeutic work I've ever experienced. The shard isn't there any more. I feel different. I'm really amazed. Our work allowed me to reach a sense of profound clarity and to make a palpable, internal shift."

Then no other comments were exchanged about this work until ten weeks after the session, when the therapist asked how the results of that session were holding. Her response: "It's holding remarkably well, and I'm really pleased about that. I really do have a different inner position about the issue of how I look. Sometimes I have to work at it to think it through again, but I think I'm really able to let go of the idea that I am both ugly and repulsive and have always been that way. I really have been able to mostly keep some perspective on that.

"One of the things I did was go back through photo albums for years and years and years, just to take another look from a different perspective. That was helpful.

"The other, the major change is that I'm not—I don't have so much negative chatter going on when I'm passing myself in the mirror. There's quite a bit less negative chatter, and that's really nice. And I have been able, I think, to really drop a good chunk of defensiveness that I have had between me and people, so that I have less anxiety being around people, and I don't have as much of a wall up. That's a lot to say, but I—that's the way I experience it. It's just easier to be with people, because I'm not guarding against that unconscious belief that people are going somehow to see, if I'm not very guarded. So, it's *wonderful,* it's really good! And, I still am feeling very grateful and quite amazed."

In another follow-up four months after the session, she reported with great amusement that at an occasion with some friends who were talking about self-image, she had spontaneously thought of herself as "cute" and had actually said so. Explaining, she said, "'Cute' meant both physically and personality. I couldn't *believe* I was saying this to these people!"

Commentary

This work illustrates the direct accessibility, through radical inquiry, of the client's unconscious, pro-symptom construction, leading to rapid resolution of a raw, lifelong emotional wound in self-regard.

Since the presenting symptom was low self-esteem that physically felt like a cutting shard of glass in her abdomen, it was clear from the start that the problem involved an unresolved emotional wound and therefore that direct resolution would be necessary. That is, the symptom would indeed have to be eliminated (rather than reconstrued and reclaimed as a strength), requiring a transformation of the pro-symptom position in which the emotional wound was a central element.

The therapist did nothing but carry out the two top priorities of depth-oriented brief therapy, namely, (1) radical inquiry in search of the emotional truth of the symptom (the subjective reality within the client's pro-symptom position), followed by (2) experiential shift, here in the form of position work, which means having the client experientially inhabit and consciously integrate her previously unconscious, pro-symptom position.

The transference aspect of this session warrants comment. Transference-minded readers may be biased toward interpreting the session as a "transference cure" rather than as showing the effectiveness of the methodology of DOBT. The argument presumably would be that hearing the male therapist support a view of her as lovely dispelled the client's view of herself as ugly. However, the client herself showed that this was not occurring when, following the therapist's final comment on her being lovely or not ugly, she had an experience that she described by saying, "See, I can't really—I can't take that in." Whatever positive transference may have been occurring clearly did not sweep away her still unconscious attachment to her view of herself as ugly. It was the subsequent position work that enabled her to release this view. A positive transference would, of course, have inclined her to cooperate with this work, but it was not central to how resolution was achieved. A lifelong, negative self-concept is virtually always accompanied by a tenacious, core belief that receiving any positive regard only means the other person has been successfully fooled.

Through radical inquiry and position work, therapist and client discovered, and the client experienced, the emotional truth of the symptom, namely that "I'm ugly" was all along serving to protect her in various important ways. In the arena of gender attractiveness she had received a cutting blow so deep and painful that she would rather resign forever as a player than risk being slashed like that again. She resigned by creating a construal of herself as a lost cause, rationalizing her withdrawal from the field. Forming this construal was a strategic protective action shielding the vulnerability of the emotional wound. In addition, "I'm ugly" protected her from spiritual and marital ruin due to uncontrollable sexuality and from refuting her undermining mother's view of her and possibly rupturing their relationship.

A governing or superordinate element of her pro-symptom position was her purpose of maintaining safety from these dangers through the strategic, protective construal, "I'm ugly." Inviting her to own and assert this purpose (in the form of a refusal to be without her strategic, protective device) was the pivotal position work of the session. Asserting this superordinate purpose allowed her to extract her identity from all of the other, subordinate elements of her pro-symptom construction including the belief "I'm ugly." She experienced that it was the *protective* value of this belief, not the *truth* value, to which she was clinging. Exposing what the symptom is covertly achieving is the deconstruction of the symptom—not merely a conceptual deconstruction, as in literary criticism and political and clinical analysis, but an experiential deconstruction, the client's living encounter with her symptom's unseen but crucial value to herself.

Already wounded in her view of herself by her mother's messages of inadequacy, it was with stunning finality that she heard the teenage boy's "Yuk!" as confirming the objective visibility of her shameful insufficiency. She experienced his view of her as sharply cutting. The important point, however, is this: In all subsequent moments it was her own view of herself as ugly that kept cutting. It was she herself who continued unconsciously to insist on applying the cutting shard of "I'm ugly" for its protective value. In other words, her own solution to the problem of vulnerability was to hold tight to the very construction that was a shard in her body. Through the position work of overtly owning her covert use of "I'm ugly" for self-protection, she rendered it useless for that purpose and so became willing to relinquish it. In removing "I'm ugly" from her view of reality, she also removed its kinesthetic aspect, the shard, from her body.

The therapist did not conceptualize her view of herself as ugly as a cognitive error requiring "correction." There is no such conceptualization in depth-oriented brief therapy. Rather, the therapist "knew" from the start that her view of herself as ugly existed as part of a coherent, if hidden, unconscious construction of meaning: her pro-symptom position. In the client's world, whatever is, is because some position of the client needs it to be that way.

The session is also useful to consider in terms of the orders of change occurring. The therapist knew very well that his first-order demur that she was not in fact ugly had very little therapeutic power (even though he genuinely meant it), because her "I'm ugly" position had second-, third-, and fourth-order components that this first-order refutation would not budge. A *second-order construction* is the meaning attributed to particular perceptions and experiences. As a second-order process, the therapist offered a developmental perspective designed to change the very meaning of the client's adolescent experience of being ugly. The meaning of her appearance at twelve shifted from "assessment of permanent, essential self" to "snapshot of transient, developing self."

Most of the session, however, was an execution of third-order change. The *third order of structure* within a position is comprised, by definition, of the constructs that determine which among all possible second-order constructions of meaning will be applied to particular perceptions or experiences. Specifically, the third order is the domain of *purposes served* in selecting constructions of meaning. It emerged that this woman had three different unconscious, protective purposes for harboring the strategic, second-order construction "I'm ugly": prevent further trauma of slashing rejection, prevent sexual sinning, prevent alienation from mother. When she realized these purposes and relinquished them (a third-order change), then the "I'm ugly" construction of meaning itself became free to change as well (a subordinate, second-order change flowing from third-order change). Having relinquished her protective purposes, she now can let it in that she's not ugly. In general, an unconscious, third-order purpose served cannot survive becoming fully conscious and integrated in position work, and when that third-order purpose dissolves, the second-order strategic construction it had been supporting is no longer viable.

Third-order constructs of purpose derive in turn from *fourth-order constructs* of the fundamental nature of the self, others, and the world, that is, constructs in the domain of ontology. Based on my fourth-order constructs of the kind of being I presuppose myself to be, and the kind of world I take myself to be in, I form third-order purposes or priorities that govern how I will attribute meaning in concrete situations (my second-order constructs). To give a simple example, if I construe my being to be whole, lovable, and well connected into the fabric of existence, I form purposes of creative expression of wellness, interconnectedness, and trust, and I then construe concrete situations as presenting specific opportunities to enact such purposes. If unconsciously I construe my being as wounded, deficient, unlovable, and disconnected from the fabric of existence, I form unconscious purposes of self-protection, competition, and survival, and I then construe concrete situations as venues where by necessity I must carry out those purposes. The woman in the foregoing example had a fourth-order construction of herself as fundamentally deficient in her essential qualities of gender and as being slashed to the core by others' harsh rejection of this deficiency. This fourth-order construct generated the survival-oriented third-order purpose of preventing any repeat of such cutting rejection, which she carried out by maintaining the strategic construction "I'm ugly."

Unhappy No Matter What

The title we've given this vignette captures the essence of the problem presented by a thirty-seven-year-old, chronically depressed, compulsively workaholic woman. Her melancholic depression had dominated her emotional life since high school if not earlier, and would soon darken any enthusiasm felt over new developments in her work or personal life. She remained functional but would frequently lose momentum, begin "procrastinating," and see herself as incapable of succeeding at things she valued, such as her urban planning projects at work or her relationships with men. She had been married for three years in her twenties and had just one month earlier left a two-year relationship because of feeling hurt and angry over the man's too-ambivalent feelings. However, she and he were now tentatively resuming their involvement.

Despite previous episodes of psychotherapy in her life, she was at a loss as to what was keeping her in a mood of unhappiness that prevailed over all circumstances. These previous therapies were open-ended and unfocused, and now she wanted brief, focused work. Her ten sessions of depth-oriented brief therapy involve addressing symptoms and pro-symptom positions of greater complexity than we have previously considered.

Session One

Given that the client was unaware of what in her view of reality warranted being depressed, the therapist in the first session made a wide range of inquiries aimed at identifying a symptom-positive context, a specific area of life experience in which her depression was necessary and meaningful. Asked when she gets depressed, she thought and said, "When I get excited and things are going well and I feel successful and happy, a moment comes when I notice that, and then immediately I get depressed." To a therapist who thinks in terms of DOBT, this last remark has a particularly strong stamp of a hidden, pro-symptom position that is incompatible with feeling successful and happy. In an attempt to invite more of that pro-symptom emotional truth into awareness, the therapist gave her as a between session task an index card on which she had written the sentence fragment, "If I let myself stay successful and happy—" The client was to look at the card daily and notice what occurred to her.

Sentence completion tasks are often useful for radical inquiry because an unconscious position generally cannot resist the opportunity to complete a sentence that is highly relevant to the position's central theme. The person experiences the completing words autonomously suggesting themselves, revealing the views, needs, or agenda of the hidden position, showing specifically why the symptom is important to have. In this case the sentence fragment was worded to set up an experience of viewing from a symptom-free position. That is, the sentence was worded to evoke the unwelcome consequences of being without the symptom of rapidly going into depression when happiness arises.

Other noteworthy material to emerge was the following: The clients' parents always "drank a lot" socially. Father's anger was "severe and unpredictable," and he was unexpressive of affection, never once saying the words, "I love you" to her (he'd say, "Likewise," if she said she loved him). Father was now seventy-nine, and she was aware of still feeling much anger at him for his blasts of emotional harshness at family members. Father wanted her to be either a business executive or a lawyer, so she worked for four years in a management position but finally realized this did not suit her and changed careers. Even though she would exhaust herself with overachievement and overwork, "It's been very, very hard for me to feel I can do something well or carry through. . . . I have a sneaky way of always managing to see myself as bad. I'm constantly on my own case for not living up to my potential."

The next session was scheduled for the following week. Based on what she learned in session one, the therapist could at this point make sense of the client's depression most easily as an unconscious state of hopelessness or despair over feeling unloved by her father as well as over seeing herself, by his standards, as fundamentally a failure—more than enough to keep her endlessly depressed. Although she was a fairly psychologically minded person, her factual or intellectual awareness of the unloving manner of her father did not appear to be accompanied by a corresponding emotional awareness of being depressed over this. The therapist therefore approached session two intending to carry out radical inquiry that would experientially test these themes for emotional truth.

Session Two

At the start of the session the client reported that the only thing that occurred to her in carrying out her task (completing the sentence fragment, "If I let myself stay successful and happy . . .") was that "I turn into a monster and become insatiable if I don't get enough emotional understanding from the man I'm with." To the therapist, this response, a seeming non sequitur, indicated that her unresolved wound of emotional neglect by her father had an urgency that overrode even a contemplation of being happy.

It also indicated that she might be trying to set right the painful story of her relationship to father by connecting with similarly emotionally insensitive men and pursuing the meaningful struggle to get them to become emotionally sensitive and loving. In this common pattern, rather than face, grieve, and accept the fact of never having been given direct emotional love by her father, she denies and avoids feeling this sizable loss by unconsciously struggling to undo it: she will get an unloving male to become loving. This never succeeds, and the struggle continues ad infinitum. What Freud termed *repetition compulsion* is understood in DOBT to be the strategic protective action of unconsciously construing an irreversible loss to be reversible and struggling to bring about that (impossible) reversal.

To check on whether these constructions were actually present, the therapist carried out radical inquiry using a form of viewing from a symptom-free position, which took about three minutes. The therapist asked her to imagine being in a relationship with a man who from the very start readily and appropriately supplies the emotional attention and sensitivity she so much wants. The therapist had her visualize this, evoking a few different scenes of daily life with such a man, and then asked her how it feels. The client said, "It might be boring . . . . Somehow there's never been an attraction for me with someone like that."

This response confirmed to the therapist that despite having a conscious position of wanting to be with an emotionally sensitive, unambivalent man, unconsciously her top emotional priority was not to be with such a man, but to be with an emotional replica of her father and win a change of heart in him. This was the compelling, meaningful struggle for rapprochement that she unconsciously expected would finally bring a very unhappy story to a happy ending and, perhaps most importantly, reverse her view of herself from an unlovable, insufficient person to a lovable, sufficient one. (Of course, this is a doomed strategy for resolution, since the chances of any partner significantly changing his or her basic emotional style to suit the other's needs are remote. The result is a rewounding rather than a resolution.) A man who is emotionally sensitive and loving from the start is simply the wrong man, totally irrelevant to her unconscious plan and therefore not an emotionally interesting figure. This was the reality within her unconscious, pro-symptom position on relationships with men.

Recall that one of her presenting symptoms was a strong pattern of "always managing to see myself as bad." It was clear at this point that a classic construction of low self-esteem was operating. Her unconscious commitment to maintaining her fragile emotional bond with a rejecting father required construing herself as bad, insufficient, unlovable. The only way she had for sharing an emotional reality with him was to agree with him about herself— that is, to regard as objectively true all the feelings of inherent unlovableness she had when with him. To let go of this negative construction of herself would also be to let go of her familiar sense of connection to him. In her pro-symptom position it was important to preserve her negative self-sense in order to (1) stay in the same experiential reality as her father and (2) keep pursuing her plan to have him reverse her negative view of herself with his love. If she were to unilaterally shift into regarding herself as worthy and lovable, she would be letting go of her need for father without having the happy ending she seeks. In short, the classic construction of low self-worth is maintained for the purpose of protecting against irreplaceable loss of the emotional bond in the primary relationship in which the negative view of self was learned. The symptom of low self-worth, which to the client's conscious mind is a problem, is actually her *solution* to still-higher-priority problems, such as how to preserve emotional connection to a rejecting parent. Changing the client's solution (symptom) is of course much easier when the therapist knows what problem it is solving. (We provide a review of the higher-priority problems "solved" by staying in low self-esteem in Chapter Six. Readers versed in object relations theory will recognize a similarity, though not an equivalence, of these ideas with, for example, those of Fairbairn.)

Since being lovable is of the most fundamental importance to each person, to construe oneself as inherently unlovable generates a pervasive depression (whether consciously recognized or not) as well as chronic fears of intimacy and rejection. These are the costs of maintaining low self-worth in order to protect a primary emotional bond. The fact that the client's mind clings tenaciously to this protective construction shows that the high price is worth paying. When the unconscious, pro-symptom position is "Dad feels I'm unlovable, and agreeing with him is the only way to preserve my emotional connection with him," then the depression generated by agreeing that "I'm unlovable" is merely a side effect to be endured. This illustrates an important general principle: *The unconscious mind pursues its present solutions to perceived, high-priority problems with indifference to the pain these solutions (symptoms) cause the conscious personality.* The presence of this pain or limitation does not in itself motivate the unconscious, pro-symptom position to change.

With this understanding of her pro-symptom position, the therapist set out to do the position work of having her consciously realize and own the purpose of her negative self-construal: protecting her connection with dad. This type of position work is an experiential shift that we often use in DOBT to unlock a low self-esteem position. (It is third-order position work, because it consists of having the client own a superordinate purpose served by how she is construing the situation. The therapist, however, is not analytically thinking "third order" but is aware of encountering the presence of a governing purpose and is seeing the possibility of having the client own it.)

As a first step, the therapist set up a simple experiential task that would Socratically bring her attention to her own position. She asked her to visualize her father and also, standing behind him, all the past boyfriends and lovers who turned out to be ambivalent or emotionally unexpressive. This image formed easily and vividly. The therapist then asked her to speak to them by completing this sentence, without pre-thinking the ending: "If I know that I'm OK . . ." After a few rounds of this, each with a new, spontaneous ending, one arose that she knew was *it:* "If I know that I'm OK, I won't need to try to get it from *you* anymore." This immediately brought tears along with the realization that "being pleasing," especially to men, was organizing the whole emotional tone of her daily life. This simple, Socratic position work of sentence completion had produced a significant breakthrough. She had reached an initial awareness that she herself was actively maintaining the

"I'm *not* OK" position for the purpose of preserving connection and carrying out a plan of rapprochement. After the wave of feeling passed she explained that with those words, she felt for the first time in her adult life that, "I don't have to do it this way. I don't have to try to please them."

As a further step of owning her purpose for staying in low self-worth, the therapist invited her to go further into viewing her father from a symptom-free position. While she was still looking at him in her mind's eye, the therapist asked her, evocatively, to "just try on for a minute or two, purely through imagination, as an experiment, the identity of knowing—you are fully OK, fully a good, lovable, worthy person. As you look at your father, you can see what it's like to look at him, from this imagined position of knowing that—you are really OK, and sufficient, and lovable. Just for a minute, as an experiment, allowing this positive sense of yourself. And as you look at him from this position of well-being, just notice if anything changes in how he seems to you, or in how it feels between you. [Pause] What is it that you notice?"

She said, "He becomes smaller and less significant," and explained that she meant visually smaller and emotionally less significant. This "incredible shrinking parent" effect, a useful diagnostic indicator, experientially confirmed the therapist's understanding of her pro-symptom position. Her familiar construction of connection with her father—as represented in her visual image of him—was incompatible with a positive view of herself, so his image diminishes when she inhabits a positive construction of herself. She had just experienced this for herself, which is crucial for the work to be nonspeculative and brief.

While she was still seeing this diminished image of her father, and in order to go beyond radical inquiry into position work—that is, to have her consciously integrate the emotional meaning of what she had just perceived—the therapist then said, "Just notice whether or not it feels OK to you to have a position of knowing that you're actually OK, fully OK, if the *cost* of being in this new position of OK-ness is that your father becomes smaller and less significant. [Pause] And what do you notice?"

She said, "It feels a little sad—but OK, actually. [Pause] You know, what I'm noticing also is that *not* being OK is how I get my friends to give me special attention. I didn't realize that." This, too, was accompanied by a series of recognitions of how she "used" boyfriends and friends "to make me feel OK," after which she said with tears, "I'm so glad to be getting to this."

Having her view her father from a symptom-free position was not intended to shift her into that position permanently, but only for a few minutes, in order to have her become aware of what changes when she is operating without the symptom. In this experiential way it becomes clear what the symptom is doing for her that makes the symptom important to have. If, as in this case, the client in addition begins to integrate and transform her (third-order) purpose for maintaining the symptom and her (fourth-order) construal of essential self from which that purpose springs, then an even bigger step has been taken.

As a between-session task of position work, the therapist gave the client for daily reading another index card on which she had written, "Am I willing to know I'm actually OK, if the costs of knowing I'm OK are that Dad becomes smaller and less significant in my life and that I'll lose a familiar way of inviting caring concern from my friends?"

Sessions Three, Four, and Five

One week later, at the start of the third session, she reported that she had looked at the card every day, and though she had no specific new thoughts or feelings about what it said, to her surprise it was now feeling significantly easier to choose to stay happy. She said, "It's not as hard as I thought it would be." This again illustrates the capacity of position work alone to produce deep change rapidly, here in only two sessions. That is, simply by consciously taking what in fact was a governing emotional position—"I see myself as not OK in order to keep dad's importance from diminishing"—she spontaneously became free to move off of it.

She also reported having the realization that in her relationship of the past two years she had been using her boyfriend as a "sewer" into which to "pour out all my bad feelings so that I'd feel better—but I didn't, really. I suddenly saw that I didn't have to do that—that what I wanted was to be happy—happy to *begin* with." To the therapist this new, unilateral intention to be happy indicated a significant shift out of her unconscious plan to get an emotionally closed man to open up and heal her unhappiness with his love.

Asked by the therapist what she felt the most valuable focus for the session would be, she addressed her problem with work and career. She said she was still finding that while carrying out her work—short-term consultation jobs—feelings of enthusiasm, purpose, or motivation would soon dissipate and be replaced by a sense of mechanical effort and pointlessness. To the therapist this sounded like yet another aspect of her depression, and it reminded her of the client's previous description of shifting abruptly into depression upon noticing that she feels "excited and things are going well and I feel successful and happy." Evidently there was an unconscious, pro-symptom position incompatible with having energy and forward movement in her work life, so to identify this position the therapist formulated a more pointed form of an earlier task of radical inquiry for her to carry out between sessions. She was to find and feel whatever would be distinctly unwelcome, difficult, or scary about living in her energetic state of enthusiasm and success.

In session four she reported that as a result of the task, she now felt "very troubled and conflicted" in a new way. She was experiencing a new level of excitement at work and had thoughts of getting her Ph.D., but she couldn't see how to follow these interests *and* have children. At thirty-seven, she felt time was short. A key construction then emerged: She construed "career" to be a "hermetically sealed big thing that crowds everything else out," including family, friends, traveling, sitting and reading, and so on. In the past she had indeed carried out all her academic and professional endeavors this way. To allow excitement, purpose, and motivation at work to persist and develop into a "career" was to agree to have no other life, which had become unacceptable to her. She had done the between-session task quite well, actually experiencing how it was "unwelcome, difficult, or scary" to sustain enthusiasm at work: to get at all serious about work was to lose control and binge on it, becoming, as she said, "ridiculously workaholic." This now began to make sense of her quick suppression of these positive, energetic feelings.

It seemed to the therapist at this point that her pattern of total immersion in career, to the exclusion of all else, was probably an important protective action against feeling her chronic depression. If so, the way to dispel the workaholism and make "career" safe and tolerable was to dispel the depression that made it necessary to be totally immersed in work. A true resolution of that depression should show up as a falling away of the workaholism.

The therapist's interest was drawn toward her father's own compulsive behavior, his alcoholism. The therapist asked specifically how it was for her, in her childhood, that her father drank. The client said the problem wasn't the drinking in itself, but her father's sudden explosions of anger when all seemed well and daddy was happy (after drinking). After an intense flare of scorching anger at one or more of the children, he would be fine again within minutes, couldn't understand why the children weren't, and would get angry at them for *that*. She was always afraid of him, she said, because of the unpredictability of his explosions.

Therapist: So how did you cope with always being afraid, that danger of him exploding?

Client: I just became silent. If my parents were together and either of them asked me anything about myself, I just wouldn't answer. I never felt dad listened to me anyway, so I just didn't offer anything. . . . We just stopped talking to each other at all. Later his hearing deteriorated, and dad just receded, for me.

Therapist: Would you be willing to picture him, the way he looked when you were younger, and say some things to him?

Client: OK. [Closes eyes]

Therapist: Let me know when he's there. [Pause]

Client: Ready.

Therapist: As you look at him, try saying, "I'm really unhappy I have a daddy I'm afraid of."

Client: I'm really unhappy I have a daddy I'm afraid of. [Gets teary and sniffly] It's also true that—I'm really unhappy I have a father that doesn't understand me. And actually [Now nearly crying] what I'm really saying when I say that is, a father that doesn't *care* about me, because I always felt that if

he really cared about me or loved me, he would try
to understand me.

Therapist: So, the truth of the feeling you've been carrying in
your life is, "My father doesn't really care about me."

Client: He doesn't love me.

Therapist: "He doesn't love me." You feel unloved by him.

Client: Yeah, uh-huh. Yes.

Therapist: And part of you is always in great downheartedness, or
depression, about that.

Client: I guess.

Therapist: So, that part *isn't* so clear. So let's just stay with the
truth that you actually feel—that you feel unloved.

Client: Yes.

Therapist: And what I'm understanding from what you've said is
that, feeling uncared-about and unloved is the worst,
troubling part—worse than the fear of his anger.

Client: Yeah, mm-hm. To this day, the only way I can talk to
him is to talk about things that *he* cares about. I can't
talk to him about things that matter to *me.*

Therapist: So it's always all about him. And even though, as
you've told me before, he's a very dedicated family
man and does lots of things for people, what you're so
unhappy about, and what's hurt you, is that he doesn't
show real interest in *your* world, a personal interest in
getting to know you in your own right, the self that *you*
are.

Client: Right. That's it exactly. If the focus is on his agenda,
then we had something to talk about and could get
along. And that's why I was in business.

Therapist: Now, feeling unloved by a dad is a big thing, a big
unhappiness. Maybe this is what makes sense of this
mystery that you've described to me of how your own
enthusiasm and happiness in life don't hold up, don't
sustain—you get them going but then they just collapse, quickly. Seems like those current happinesses
are standing on a foundation that's so unhappy. I wonder if you're carrying around a really big unhappiness
that in some parts of yourself seems a lot bigger than
these current happy developments.

Client: [Cries softly]

Therapist: You look like you have a feeling when I say that. What is it you're feeling?

Client: [Speaking through tears] Well, I'm feeling the unhappiness.

Therapist: Yeah, it's a big unhappiness.

Client: I suppose it's something to become aware of it, but—I mean it's not the kind of thing that goes away. [Cries] I mean it's me, it's part of me.

Therapist: Well, I believe that your life is a broad enough river, that there's room for a current of sorrow over on one side. A good life can include some sorrow, too. But to reach that balance you have to first know the emotional truth of how it is, and has been, for you.

Client: I suppose if I face it, then there are ways I can work with it.

Therapist: Yes. So, how about if I give you a card to help keep this emotional truth in plain view?

Client: OK.

[The therapist writes out and hands her a card that says, "The truth is, up to now my unhappiness over feeling unloved by my dad is bigger than any happiness I've been able to have."]

Client: [Reads card; begins to cry, her face appearing to the therapist deeply anguished] It's true.

Therapist: Yes. [Pause] It's true, and it's so painful that I don't know if you'll be willing to live with the truth of that, this week. Do you think you could read it twice a day, morning and night?

Client: OK. I will.

Here in the fourth session, the therapist engaged her in the position work of facing, feeling, and accepting this central emotional truth of her depression, immediately upon discovering it. It was now clear that for her to begin to feel distinctly happy over anything in her current life only served to remind her, unconsciously, of a much bigger unhappiness, collapsing her happy mood, as she had described in the first session. The card was a simple device to foster the position work of inhabiting the emotional truth of that bigger unhappiness without attempting to change it or get her out of it in any way.

In session five, one week later, the client said that the words on the card were profoundly true and had led her into reflections on the lifelong sweep of this big unhappiness. She described feeling abandoned by both mother and father at age six, when her brother was born and her father began traveling often on business. She still had her older sister, but at eleven her sister reached puberty and sister's interests went elsewhere, a final abandonment that "made me hatefully angry at her, and that was a rift that lasted until only a few years ago."

The therapist asked her to visualize father, mother, and sister and to try out saying to them, "I'm so angry at you for abandoning me." She tried the sentence two or three times. To the therapist's surprise, she said that she wasn't connecting with it, but that another sentence was insistently coming to mind. The therapist encouraged her to try that one, and to her three family members she said, "I'm right about the problems in our family." This instantly came to life with emotion and tears, an upwelling of a complex mixture of feelings. She repeatedly commented on how satisfying it felt to her to say those words, so the therapist suggested saying them a few more times, which she did. She explained that she had always made sense of her unhappiness as caused by her own "weakness of character" and emotional defectiveness, so to take the position "I'm right about the problems in our family" was simultaneously a major (fourth-order) change in her view of herself as well as a liberating step of separation from her parents' view of the family. The therapist gave her those words written on a card, plus another phrase that the client welcomed in order to enable her to hold this position even when she imagined her parents arguing against it: "and I'm right even if you deny it."

Sessions Six and Seven

Asked how it went for her with the words on the card, she said, "It was actually pretty great. That card was a lot more than a card. I had a real image. I didn't have to keep remembering the words; I could remember the image and the feeling that went along with it, and it was very powerful, and I guess pretty profound, because it was something I had been coming to for a while—I mean, for twenty years or thirty years or so—and it's something that I've been wanting to say—you know, that I was right, I could see that things were wrong. And it's been having a very real effect, because knowing I'm right about how things were is actually giving me the confidence to make decisions and do things that I might not have the confidence to do. Yeah. Other therapy I've had didn't make the same kind of progress."

Since the improvement was so marked in both her mood and her confidence in making the decisions facing her, she brought up the possibility of ending therapy within a few more sessions and suggested meeting less often than weekly, to which the therapist readily agreed.

The ultimate stage of separating from one's family's view of reality is to hold a different reality while in their presence. To this end the therapist invited her to do a simple rehearsal of being with her family while in the symptom-free position of knowing she's right. This exercise would foster any further experiential shift that might be necessary for sustaining this degree of autonomy.

Therapist: Can you imagine what it would feel like, to actually be in the room with your family members, with you privately knowing that you're right about the problems in the family?

Client: Well, as you were just saying that, I had an image of just laughing with them. I think what it does is, it allows me to see where they're healthy, too. Because there's also a lot of support and strength in my family. [Cries softly]

Therapist: [Silence] What are these tears about?

Client: It's a relief. I think it's that, when you're in a state of confusion and you don't trust what you're right about, and you don't trust what you see as the problem, it's really hard to let yourself see what's really good. But then, the fact that there's a lot of good there makes it hard to know if you're right about the bad. And it gets all tangled up, so it's a big relief to know that you can acknowledge that it is healthy in some ways. In the past I didn't have room for that.

Therapist: I see, yes. After many years in that confusion, this is
    quite a relief.

[The client has just described the transformative effect of simply
taking her emotionally true position in relation to her family members. By doing so she spontaneously moved into an unexpected
new position of perceiving and appreciating what is positive in her
family relationships, a significant step of individuation. She had
been trying to see her family in a genuinely positive light for
decades and could not, because she had been striving to do this
from a position that was incongruent with her own emotional
truth.]

She then said she was in fact about to visit her family (on the
opposite coast). The therapist asked if, in light of the work she'd
done in these sessions, there was a specific goal she wanted to have
for this family visit. She said that "the hardest and most damaging
thing" about visiting her family was the depression she inevitably
goes into as a result of comparing her own life and the choices
she's made with the affluence, career stability, and advanced levels
of achievement of her family and friends, and especially the fact
that her friends have children. She starts to feel "left out, and I
hate feeling left out and left behind. I start to feel that I'm not OK
and don't belong." The therapist asked if her choices in life, being
right for her (a deliberate invocation of her new clarity of knowing she's right in her assessments), have entailed both certain
losses and certain differences from her family and friends, which
she vividly sees during a visit. She agreed with this description.

The therapist then gave her a task of position work. She suggested she deliberately get depressed about these losses and differences ahead of time, before the visit. She explained that since
her choices, though right, have entailed some actual loss and separation, sad feelings over the loss and separation are entirely fitting, but she could face and feel these feelings knowingly, before
arriving, rather than unknowingly have her mood deteriorate due
to half-conscious comparisons triggered during a visit.

The task of deliberately getting depressed before the visit may
appear to be a paradoxical intervention because it prescribes the
symptom, but it was not a strategic, "trick" type of paradox. Position

work in DOBT is exactly the process of having the client own her symptom-affirming position. The therapist was inviting this woman to preestablish herself in sharp awareness of the emotional truth of her situation, which is that she is a choice-making person who accepts, with some sadness, the costs of her choices and is not a victim of those costs. She said, "That sounds good—I mean, I'm already feeling it that way—I think it comes from my dad and my sister had a real tight relationship, and I was kind of left out. There's a long history of that feeling . . . . Can I have a blank card, to write that down?" She said she would write, "My choices are right for me, even if I'm sad about some of the consequences."

She also wanted the therapist to know that she had just successfully finished a major project at work, but that "it was almost too easy. I didn't have a lot of struggle and agony over it, which I'm so used to thinking is a part of the formula for something to be worthwhile, that it's got to be agonizing." More on her workaholism now emerged. For all of her adult life she felt that "if work isn't an all-consuming, colossal effort, it can't be very meaningful." She has always worked long hours, often until 10 P.M. She said, "There's a real high that you get" from that kind of strenuous, total immersion in the effort. This portrait of a chronically depressed person whose workaholism gives not just thorough distraction from her personal life but an intense "high" corroborated the therapist's sense that this habit was her main protective action against feeling that depression.

In session seven, three weeks later, she reported on her family visit. She said, "At times it was pretty intense. . . . A couple of situations happened that were identical to the 'I'm right about the problems in the family even if you deny it.' It was really uncanny, actually."

She described an incident in which she was with her parents. All were in a fine mood (dad had already had his afternoon martinis), and since her parents began discussing some of the emotional tensions between dad and her sister, she offered her view of the problem, which included how dad, and not just sister, was contributing to the tension. This seemed to be going well, but at some point dad told her she was crazy, and when in response she told him not to do that, his mood abruptly changed and he was suddenly right in her face, yelling at her and waving his finger. After he stopped she was visibly shaken by his emotional assault, but for the first time in her life, "I didn't feel diminished by this, which is the way I'd always felt. I didn't feel small, physically small, or confused; I didn't feel at all confused." Dad, now very defensive, said, "Basically what you're saying is that you hate me." She told him that actually she loved him very much, and then said, "You know what, dad? Something that I've wanted to say for a long time is that *you* have never said that you loved me. And that's felt like a real gap in my life." Dad responded, "Well you know, that's true. You're probably right. I'm fairly certain that I haven't. I thought that was just something you said to your wife, and didn't need to say to your kids." She said, "Well, it really does make a difference." The subject then changed and normal activities resumed. Several minutes later, as they were about to go their separate ways, her father said, "Just a minute," walked over to her, hugged her, and said, "I love you." She said this was "a surprise, and really nice. I didn't think there would be any impact, or that he would've remembered."

By transforming her unconscious position from "he's unloving to me; I'm unlovable" to a conscious position of "he's unloving to me; that's very wrong," she could then relate to her father in a new way that required him to answer to her legitimate grievance. This in itself was the transformative and healing shift, quite aside from any favorable response from her father. In fact, we pointedly tell clients in such circumstances not to expect a favorable response, and that the purpose of taking a self-validating, self-affirming position in relation to an abusive parent is to establish oneself as self-affirming, regardless of response. It was a bonus that this woman's father responded, momentarily, with the loving behavior a dad ought to express. No other such displays of feeling occurred.

The therapist asked if anything during the visit connected with the central emotional truth that had emerged in a previous session in the words, "My unhappiness over feeling unloved by my dad is bigger than any happiness I've been able to have."

She said, "Most of the time I felt a lot lighter than I've felt in years, which comes from the awareness of that. I think that was a real key thing for me to acknowledge. I was really aware of how much more buoyant I felt, just in general—how much easier it was for me to be silly and to have fun and just to be positive. . . . Being so much more able to have fun is to me a strong sign that despite the baggage I've been carrying around about my dad, I'm able to get free of that now."

While that central emotional truth was unconscious as a position of hopelessness, she was depressed. Having consciously embraced, validated, and begun to grieve it, she had moved out of it and now described herself as buoyant, positive, readily silly and having fun—strong indications of depression dispelled and the position of hopelessness dismantled. Current happinesses now stood on their own ground. Her newfound appreciation of and capacity for fun was a manifestation of her new position of knowing she's right and following her own (instead of dad's) interests, dissolving her old position of staying connected with dad by subordinating her reality to his.

Sessions Eight and Nine

In session eight, two weeks later, she said she wanted to focus next on her uncertainty over how to develop her career. The session was spent entirely on considering what for her actually is fun and enjoyable in work and what isn't, including the "shoulds" that she told herself seemed meaningful but actually were not enriching. She came to a definite knowledge that what she most wanted in the immediate future, regardless of the details of what she chose to do, was to "relax and have fun" in the course of choosing it and doing it—a significant desire for a veteran workaholic.

In session nine, five weeks later, she shared a new development, explaining, "I've met this guy, and in the course of conversations with him, I began to realize that he really listened and he was interested and enthusiastic about me, and was really supportive of me. He came to visit last week, and we had a wonderful time together. For several days before he came, I would wake up in the middle of the night and think about him and have this excitement. I'd be lying there wondering, 'What's going on? Am I just fantasizing something I want that's not really there? Or is this person really wonderful?' Ultimately I realized that this wasn't so much about him, but that I was having this feeling, a feeling of elation, or of expanding and just sort of rising and getting bigger. And then I remembered your asking, 'What would it feel like if there was a man in your life who was sensitive and supportive from the beginning?' And I thought, 'This is what it would feel like!' And I realized that that was another thing that has come out of the sessions: getting to where I expect to be taken seriously, and feel happy about it happening instead of unhappy over *not* being important. And there's also the event that happened when I was visiting my parents, and we had done visualizations and it had *happened,* and it struck me how powerful this work is, because it gets to the heart of what's important to me."

To the therapist it was significant that she felt excitement over a man who from the start was emotionally open and mutual. Since the client once stated, "There's never been an attraction for me with someone like that" (session two), this excitement indicated a fundamental transformation of her unconscious, pro-symptom position from commitment to getting a man like dad to bestow love and make her lovable, to knowing she is inherently lovable and being with a man who already appreciates that.

Her focus now returned to the previous session's themes of work and career. She reported that despite remembering what she wanted to do—relax and enjoy her work, whatever it would be— she had immediately consumed herself in planning an ambitious project, knowing all along that "this had nothing to do with relaxing at all." However, after weeks of planning, she abruptly dropped the project. Concerned about this bout of workaholism, with which she coped by again abandoning serious work, she explained that she wanted "to develop a pattern that allows me to accomplish things in a scaled-back way, so that I don't have to have this big push and long hours of work."

She went on to say, "There's another thing that's going on," and introduced something she suspected might be making her reluctant or even fearful of getting fully reinvolved in work. It had to do with a job she'd had for almost five years, ending two years ago. "I think I have to face that my experience in Jack Smith's office [fictitious name] was really painful, and the idea of going back into full-time work is very frightening to me, actually. I'm afraid to go back to work for somebody because I'm afraid that I'll be a bad employee, basically—because things were so awful at Jack's, and it was never clear to me what I was doing wrong. [Pause] I think I need to go over that [Beginning to cry] because it's still really painful."

The therapist asked what had actually happened. "Jack was in a terrible mood for months on end, and he never would say what was bothering him, so we were always trying to figure it out. Either there wasn't enough money because clients hadn't paid or there weren't enough new projects. And he would start being critical of everyone's work, often mine. Or he'd be in a really *good* mood, even though the projects were spinning out of control. I was called the project manager, but I didn't have any experience managing big projects, and I didn't actually have any control. I would do all the work, and he would take all the credit; we'd go to the meetings and he'd make all the presentations. I'd sit there and get these *awful* backaches, and finally I couldn't bear sitting in those meetings anymore, because I felt invisible. Then there were a couple of times at big meetings when, without warning me at all, he'd tell *me* to do the presentation, without having given me any chance to prepare. To this day I don't know if he was being purposely cruel or just totally thoughtless to spring that on me. Everything with him was so chaotic, but I just assumed that that was the way work went, and it was up to me to make the best of it."

Asked if this resembled her experience with her father, she said, "Oh, definitely. The good-mood/bad-mood thing, and never knowing what was wrong. And being barked at without explanation." Clearly this boss and father figure further traumatized her and taught her to expect emotional abuse and high anxiety in the work setting, so that she now dreaded the prospect of full-time, long-term employment and was avoiding it.

The therapist asked her what she would need in order to feel ready to again take a full-time position. She thought and then said, "To know that I wouldn't take on all the guilt, that I wouldn't feel responsible, because I think what was more damaging than anything else is that I felt responsible for the problems." This now emerged for her as yet another facet of how she had construed reality on that job in the same way that as a child she had construed her father's emotional abuse and neglect: as meaning she was in the *wrong,* was *wrong* about her perceptions, and dad was *right.* A revision of her history with Jack Smith clearly was needed, and the therapist saw this as an opportunity for her to bring to bear her new ways of making sense of such experiences.

The therapist made this suggestion: "How about picturing him, and letting yourself say everything you need to say to him, everything that wants to come out?"

Speaking through tears to her image of her former boss, she said, "The fact is, Jack, it was mostly *your* fault for being such an awful manager. [Pause] I tried really hard to make you a better manager and to make it easier on both of us. I sat down with you and told you what the project needed, and how I needed your help, and you'd sit and listen and agree, and then nothing ever changed after that—it just went right back to the way it always was. Finally I just gave up. But I was wrong to feel guilty for everything getting out of control, because it was your responsibility. [Cries harder; sobs] And you know, I'm really sorry we couldn't end our relationship better, with more respect and appreciation, and I tried hard to do that, too, but I could see that you just wanted to build up a sense of resentment and victimization, because in your eyes somehow I let you down. But I just couldn't provide what you needed, and I didn't deliberately let you down. [Cries]" To the therapist she then said, "You know, I depended on Jack a lot for an image of *myself,* and in the end, when he accused me of being a bad team member, I really questioned what I was doing and what was really going on."

That she had replayed with this boss the emotional patterns experienced with her father was now even more strikingly clear to her. She said she felt better from saying these things and that she needed them to be a mantra that she keeps repeating. Asked what the specific words of the mantra should be, she said, "It's not my responsibility that the projects were over budget and out of control." It was clear that these words were a reassertion of her earlier breakthrough, "I'm right about the problems in the family." The therapist wrote the "mantra" on an index card and handed it to her. Reading the card, she said, "It makes me feel really good just to look at that."

Session Ten

The next session occurred three weeks later. The client reported, "I've actually been feeling a lot more relaxed about what's going on for me right now . . . I've been spending time figuring out what I want to do with my time and what feels right for me, over the next several months. I've come around to thinking it's OK for me to just take it easy a little bit more, and just take a couple of classes I've been wanting to take, and kind of scrape off a lot of the obligations I've created for myself, and try to simplify my life more, and get more sleep." That she had actually been tolerating and enjoying feeling relaxed and was intentional about reorganizing life to sustain that, indicated that her intense, workaholic "high" was no longer a needed alternative to depression. She was beginning to replace the high with sober self-care.

She said she didn't have a sense of there being anything to work on in the session and was feeling that maybe it was time for her to assimilate the effects of the sessions rather than work on anything new. The therapist supportively agreed, making a point of showing respect for her own knowledge of what's right for herself. If more therapeutic assistance were needed, she would be more inclined to get it if the therapist now demonstrated respect for her judgment.

She decided to use the rest of the session for a discussion of the difficulty of choosing a direction for her work. After a while she explained that one of the chief difficulties is "a nasty voice inside" that accuses her of being "just a dilettante" who never sticks with anything long enough or deeply enough and never chooses a direction on a sound basis. It emerged that according to this voice, it didn't count for much that she had spent four years in business, two years in graduate school, and then nearly five years in Jack's office. From the position of that voice, to change is to be a dilettante, period. In the ten remaining minutes of the session, the therapist focused the following process of radical inquiry and experiential shift on the position this voice was expressing.

Therapist: Sounds like that part of you doesn't give any value to following your *interest*. Almost as though that part of you says, "You should stay with what you're doing, whether you feel interested in it or not. That's real character. That's a serious worker."

Client: Yeah, yeah. It's true.

Therapist: Stay in one place and build that career. That's the only measure of your character.

Client: Yeah. Completing the thing.

Therapist: What's "completing" mean in a career?

Client: I guess, getting to a point of feeling confident and recognized for being able to do the job.

Therapist: OK, so this part of you has these values, that much more important than interest in the work is staying in it long enough to achieve a certain level of confidence and recognition.

Client: Actually—staying *longer* than that point is what's been damaging.

Therapist: When you say that, it sounds like a different voice than the one that says, "Stay no matter what, or you're a dilettante." What you just said recognizes that you shouldn't stay longer than is healthy for you.

Client: Yeah, that's true. [Pause] I feel like just in this last week, that "Stay no matter what" has shifted. I mean, I'm not totally confident about it, but now it's feeling that what I'm doing—making a change again—is OK. And it helps to talk about it this way. . . . I don't like that voice that tells me that I have to keep doing what I've been doing.

Therapist: That voice—I wonder what the emotional truth of that voice is. "Stay no matter what." Any sense of what that's really about?

Client: I think it's responding to my *father.* I really think it's his approval that's involved.

Therapist: In other words, do only what will make him want to connect with you?

Client: Something he can respond to, yeah.

Therapist: So that voice is actually saying, "Stay with what dad can relate to, or he won't respond to you."

Client: And as a kid I used to do things like trying to create fossils and playing with worms, and he'd never connect with me in that. The support I got from him was for being a lawyer or going into business. It never *occurred* to me that I would do anything else.

Therapist: So, your lifelong experience is that following your own real interest takes you further and further away from anything dad might know how to connect with.

Client: Yeah, yeah, definitely.

Therapist: So that might be the emotional truth of that voice. So when that voice gets going, it would be so interesting, I think, if you were to turn to it and respond by saying, "I know how scared you are that dad won't be able to follow us, where we're headed."

Client: Yeah.

Therapist: You look as though something stirred in you just then.

Client: Yeah. That makes me feel very emotional.

Therapist: And what's the specific feeling?

Client: *Relief.* [Cries]

Therapist: Relief over what?

Client: [Spoken through tears] Well, it's the idea of taking the child who would've liked to have heard that a long time ago and giving her ways to have a lot of joy just doing things that are fun and exciting.

Therapist: Yes.

Client: As long as I can remember, there wasn't a single person who could do those kinds of things with me. I did them alone.

Therapist: I'm not sure if this is connected, but I get even more of a sense now of how special it is—almost like, "Could this be real?"—that you're almost beginning to have that kind of experience with this new man in your life. "Could it really happen that someone recognizes and respects and supports what really interests *me?*"

Client: Right. It seems very eerie.

Therapist: Eerie—stepping into a different reality.

Client: Yeah.

Time was now up. She said it still felt right not to schedule another session, and that she would call if and when needed.

Commentary

The therapist was often at sea in the midst of the unfolding complexity of this client's pro-symptom positions but had a compass, a direction: radical inquiry into the emotional truth of the specific symptom currently in consideration. Persistence in radical inquiry revealed the various facets of her pro-symptom emotional truth until the full picture was in clear view.

At times, symptoms continued despite significant steps of radical inquiry and experiential shift. The therapist took this as indicating that there were additional pro-symptom positions to find and shift, so she reinitiated radical inquiry. By cycling back and forth between processes of radical inquiry and experiential shift as needed throughout these ten sessions spanning eighteen weeks, all significant pro-symptom positions were identified and changed sufficiently to relieve the symptoms, in depth, to the client's satisfaction: happy and enthusiastic feelings were now readily accessible and persisted without sudden, mysterious reversion to depression; she was now self-affirming rather than self-invalidating as a basic interpersonal stance (and actually held her self-validating position in the presence of her father, eliciting from him the never-before-heard words "I love you"); she was elated at her involvement with the emotionally generous kind of man for whom she had previously felt no attraction; she felt a new freedom and willingness to follow her own actual interests in her work life, regardless of her father's directives; she felt highly intentional about working in a nondriven way, and was now in a position to make this change because she no longer needed a workaholic "high" to keep her out of depression; and she was now extracting herself from a post-traumatic pattern of avoiding full-time employment.

Residual flickers of old views and feelings could be expected to occur at times, but she was now well positioned to deal with such moments.

It is noteworthy that her symptom of abrupt, involuntary suppression of any happy, energetic feelings was being generated by three distinct pro-symptom positions concurrently. These three positions, revealed by radical inquiry, can be linguistically characterized as follows:

1. "Feeling happy about current things pales in comparison to how unhappy I feel over something much bigger: my father doesn't love me; I've been left out and left behind." (This central emotional truth was dispelled by making it conscious, crying over it, establishing the new position "I'm right about the

problems in the family," and being willing to confront father with his failure to say, "I love you.")

2. "Sustained satisfaction and enthusiasm in work would lead to a 'career,' which would eliminate everything else I love doing, so enthusiasm is too threatening to allow." (Presupposing that "career" would be all-consuming reflected her own addictive need for the "high" of being totally consumed in work. This dissipated when she no longer needed that high to keep her out of depression and no longer needed to drive herself to live up to dad's standards, opening up the possibility of a relaxed approach to work and making the prospect of career safer.)

3. "Sustained satisfaction and enthusiasm in work would lead to full-time, long-term employment under some boss and to a repeat of my traumatic failure to perform adequately in that situation, so I mustn't let this good feeling stand." (This was diminished by developing a new construction of the meaning of the earlier work situation, seeing not herself but the boss as the cause of the problems and pain—an assertion of her new position, "I'm right about the problems in the family.")

As a protective action against actually feeling her immense loss and grief over her father, this woman had created and was maintaining a construction of hope or rectifiability, an unconscious plan to recover what was lost and set right the story by getting an unloving man (an emotional replica of her father) to become loving. A construal of rectifiability functioning as a protective action against experiencing a wound of profound loss generates repetition compulsion: an endlessly repeating, doomed attempt to undo the loss.

Resolution of this woman's low self-esteem and depression involved substantial fourth-order changes. She dissolved her construal of herself as fundamentally bad, insufficient, and unlovable and replaced it with knowledge of herself as fully worthy of love. She dissolved another fourth-order construal of herself as having a fundamentally deficient capacity to have accurate perceptions of family relationships, along with the associated fourth-order construal of intrinsic "weakness of character" as the explanation of why she felt so unhappy in the family. These she replaced with the knowledge that her intrinsic capacity to *know* is sound and trust-worthy ("I'm right about the problems in the family").

With so much change occurring at a very high level of super-ordinacy, it is not surprising that a wide range of spontaneous changes accompanied the elimination of the symptoms. Higher-order construct A was changed in order to change lower-order con-struct B, but of course then most other constructs subordinate to A also changed. The higher the superordinacy of A, the more numerous, visible, and significant will be these accompanying lower-order changes.

We can now define more precisely why DOBT's methodology of utilizing the emotional truth of the symptom rapidly produces change beyond symptom relief. The emotional truth of the symptom is a set of constructs that are superordinate to the symptom. Resolv-ing the symptom through change at this superordinate level pro-duces enhancement of well-being in the more deeply meaningful domain of that level as well as in the domain of the level on which the symptom exists and in the domains of all other levels in between.

Table 2.1. Orders of Position and Constructs of Woman Who Was Unhappy No Matter What.

Order of Position	Construct
Fourth Order: *Nature of self/others/world*	I am incapable and unlovable. I lack the capacity to understand what is happening in personal relationships. I cannot survive disconnected from my original bond to my father.
Third Order: *Purpose to be served by attributions of meaning*	Prevent disconnection from father at all cost. Get father to love me and confer lovability on me.
Second Order: *Attribution of meaning in concrete situations*	Men like dad are the attractive ones. Situations of work and love are sources of evidence that I am unable, bad, wrong, unlovable.
First Order: *Concrete thoughts, feelings, behaviors*	Dad's right—I'm a dilettante and a failure. Chronic low self-esteem, depression, workaholism.

The hierarchy of constructs generating this woman's low self-esteem and depression is depicted in Table 2.1. Therapy transformed her fourth-order constructs, which produced change in the fourth-order domain (a major enhancement of self-concept and core sense of well-being), a third-order change of purpose to be served by construing (the purpose changing from maintaining connection with dad through self-invalidation, to self-expression and separation-individuation), second-order changes (in how she construes current problems, friends, family, career, and partner), and many first-order changes (including elimination of workaholic behavior, depressed mood, needy behavior with friends, and repetition compulsion with men).

Summary

We have studied examples of rapidly resolving the presenting symptoms of lifelong depression and low self-esteem as well as the deep emotional wounds generating those symptoms. This was accomplished by carrying out the two top priorities in depth-oriented brief therapy: (1) *radical inquiry* to identify the hidden emotional truths necessitating the symptom, and (2) *experiential shift* to transform key constructions of reality comprising the client's unconscious, pro-symptom position. These two key processes alternate and interweave in the course of working with a pro-symptom construction of some complexity. The therapist freely pursues any part of the methodology of DOBT as needed, in any sequence, and the process becomes a nonlinear one and continues until all relevant pro-symptom positions are dispelled.

For dispelling low self-esteem, two types of experiential shift are needed: (1) Through position work, the client directly feels and knows his or her (third-order) *purposes served* by maintaining the negative construal of self and becomes aware of being unwilling to harbor positive self-worth, for the sake of those vital purposes. The realization of actually being the purposeful implementor of the state of low self-worth dispels both the plausibility of that construction and its seemingly involuntary nature. As a result, the client for the first time allows (2) changes in (fourth-order) knowledge of the nature of self, such that the self is no longer construed as hopelessly deficient.

As a way of conceptualizing how the construction of reality in a pro-symptom position is organized and how therapy alters that construction, we have applied and extended Bateson's scheme of the "logical types" or orders of change. We conceive of the constructs that make up a person's models of reality as having a four-level, hierarchical organization, with superordinate and subordinate roles in defining reality. It becomes apparent that *therapy is most effective when change is carried out on levels superordinate to the level on which the presenting symptom occurs.* The two clients in this chapter changed as rapidly as they did *because* the therapist focused radical inquiry and experiential shift on creating change at high-order levels of the clients' pro-symptom positions. The perhaps exotic sound of "third-order" and "fourth-order" change should not in any way obscure the accessibility principle—the fact that unconscious constructions on these levels are immediately discoverable and available for change.

As the reader may have noticed in these first two chapters, most of the specific interventions used for radical inquiry and experiential shift are simple and transparent. How to inhabit the conceptual framework and the therapeutic stance in which such simple but exceedingly effective interventions naturally come to mind is the subject of the next two chapters.

Notes

P. 4, *Our remedies oft in ourselves do lie:* W. Shakespeare (1988), *All's Well That Ends Well* (Act I, Scene 2), New York: Bantam.

P. 67, *a similarity, though not an equivalence, of these ideas with, for example, those of Fairbairn:* W. Fairbairn (1974), *Psychoanalytic Studies of the Personality,* New York: Routledge, Chapman & Hall. (Original work published 1952.)

P. 91, *Bateson's scheme of the "logical types" or orders of change:* G. Bateson (1972), *Steps to an Ecology of Mind* (pp. 279–308), New York: Ballantine.

CHAPTER 3

The Emotional Truth of the Symptom

But such is the irresistible nature of truth,
that all it asks, and all it wants,
is the liberty of appearing.
THOMAS PAINE, *The Rights of Man*

When we use the phrase *emotional truth* with clients, they intuitively know what it means. This kind of vocabulary is of value in achieving deeply effective therapeutic results in the shortest possible time. It is evocative for clients, and using it actually helps them go deeper *into* emotional truth, experientially, in the session.

We believe that the technical language therapists use to conceptualize and to talk to each other about therapy should also be therapeutic for clients and directly useful in therapists' in-session responses. For us, this is a criterion for a psychotherapy that is fully congruent with its purpose of producing psychological well-being and emotional healing. This criterion requires a nonpathologizing paradigm, because to communicate to the client even implicitly a pathologizing understanding of him or her is to have the therapy work powerfully against itself.

The *intuitive* understanding of "the emotional truth of the symptom" is the most important kind of understanding to have of this central concept in depth-oriented brief therapy. However, DOBT is not only the practice of a subjective art. In this chapter we elaborate the conceptual definition and the structural mapping of the symptom's emotional truth, showing how it operates in the client as an unconscious, pro-symptom position. It is the discovery of the emotional truth in the client's pro-symptom position that is the goal of radical inquiry, itself the subject of the next two chapters. Having a clear understanding of what is being sought will serve as a useful foundation for the coming discussion of how radical inquiry is carried out.

We begin this chapter with a description of the symptom's emotional truth as a construction of meaning within a specific but unconscious context in the client's life. The nature of the pro-symptom position is then further clarified by noting how it differs fundamentally from the psychodynamic concept of secondary gain and from the family-systems concept of the function of the symptom. Next we describe a solution to a major epistemological problem that plagues constructivist psychologies: the problem of a human being's capacity for simultaneously knowing and not knowing something, which we propose to resolve with a conception of the unconscious that provides a unified epistemology of conscious (anti-symptom) and unconscious (pro-symptom) process.

This is followed by a systematic description of all of the types of constructs comprising pro-symptom positions. Here we map out the internal organization of positions in terms of the four orders of structure introduced in previous chapters. Lastly, we review how our clinically derived model of autonomously functioning, unconscious positions receives striking corroboration from developments in the fields of cognitive psychology, emotion theory, and, in particular, cognitive neuroscience, the experimentally derived mapping of brain structures involved in psychological functioning.

Emotional Truth and the Contextual Construction of Reality

You are a writer of science fiction. You are populating a world with intelligent beings who have a truly bizarre mental makeup. You are pondering the specific design of that mental makeup. Would it seem to you sufficiently strange to have each individual mind simultaneously harboring any number of different realities, different constructions of sense and meaning for any one perception or item of experience? To us this would be more than sufficiently bizarre for science fiction, but strangest of all is the fact that our real-life human mind operates in exactly that way.

However, this only begins to hint at the mind's truly creative troublemaking capacity. Trouble arises for several extraordinary reasons.

First, the mind not only harbors multiple meanings for the same item but also may *apply* two or more of these differing meanings *simultaneously.*

Second, it often happens that only one of these simultaneous attributions of meaning is conscious, while the other(s) are *un*conscious.

Third, a meaning that is unconsciously construed and attributed triggers behavioral actions and mood states no less readily than do consciously applied meanings.

Now the possibilities for our science fiction plot are both unlimited and truly strange. Welcome to planet earth.

An earthling in therapy is initially *conscious* only of how the presenting symptom figures in contexts in which the symptom interferes painfully and pointlessly with his or her functioning. We call these *symptom-negative contexts.* The client is *unconscious* of the symptom's great *positive* value in certain other contexts; these we call *symptom-positive contexts.*

Let's reconsider the agoraphobic woman whose therapy sessions were described in Chapter One. During her symptomatic moments while walking alone to a store, she would experience the delusion of having her caring former therapist nearby, and she would consciously construe only a symptom-*negative* context of psychiatric pathology to make sense of this delusion. In that context, she naturally attributed to her symptom dire meanings such as "psychotic," and it was this interpretation that was so fear-producing that she had started staying home. Through radical inquiry, the therapist found the unconscious, symptom-*positive* context in which the same symptom had great value to her: the context of emotional connectedness or belongingness. In that context, which the woman was unaware of *also* invoking as she walked along a street, the activation of a painful emotional wound of abandonment would unconsciously begin to occur, and the symptom was for her a much-needed and quite effective way of protecting herself from letting this happen. The delusion was for this reason more important to have than not to have, despite the considerable conscious distress that accompanied having it.

In the client's conscious, anti-symptom position, awareness is limited to symptom-negative contexts. From this position the client naturally regards the symptom as completely undesirable, valueless, senseless, an absolute obstacle to well-being. This anti-symptom position is not "wrong"; it is valid in relation to all contexts in which having the symptom genuinely torments the client. The client genuinely wishes to be free of the symptom *in those contexts.* It is vitally important for the therapist to indicate to the client ample understanding of, and accurate empathy for, how the symptom hurts in symptom-negative contexts.

However, the client harbors at least one other context, a symptom-*positive* context, in which the picture is decidedly different, where the symptom has intensely positive value. Yet the client is unconscious of this positive value and perhaps of the very existence of this context in his or her life.

Only by viewing the symptom in the symptom-positive context(s) does it become clear how the symptom is more important to have than not to have. Within that context the client has a specific construction of meaning, the pro-symptom position, that directly makes the presenting symptom vitally valuable and meaningful.

For example, the symptom may be a solution (or an attempt at a solution) to a problem existing in the symptom-positive context. In the always-fighting couple cited in Chapter One, the hidden value of each partner's symptom of readiness to fight was found in the symptom-positive context of autonomy or personal power. Within that context the symptom was made compellingly necessary by a construction consisting of the emotionally urgent, self-protective rule "avoid being controlled in personal relationships" plus the unconscious presupposition that "if I am in harmony with my partner, I am being controlled." This does not deny the fact that "being happy together" was also an important priority for each of them, but preserving autonomy was an even higher emotional priority, though neither of them was aware of this at the start of therapy.

To summarize: Within the client's emotional reality in the unconscious, symptom-*positive* context, the symptom is critically necessary and valued by the client, or it expresses imperative needs, the specifics of which are the emotional truth of the symptom, the unconscious, *pro*-symptom position of the client. Within the client's emotional reality in the conscious, symptom-*negative* contexts, the same symptom is hated and seen as a curse, an involuntary affliction to be cast away, the specifics of which are the client's conscious, *anti*-symptom position. All of our clinical cases in earlier and later chapters can be understood in these terms.

In essence, then, *living as though the symptom's emotional truth isn't the case is what generates the symptom in the first place.* Symptoms arise precisely because of unawareness of the meaningful, coherent personal themes that are generating them in the client's symptom-positive contexts.

A context itself proves to be an internally held construction of meaning that the individual invokes in response to perceptual cues rather than an external, objective reality, as it is usually regarded to be in the social sciences. A context is a large collection of specific meanings of situations, thematically related. Examples of distinct contexts include social relationships, work life, couple or marital relationships, parent-child relationships, sibling relationships, physical health, financial concerns, morality, sexuality, spiritual life, physical survival, creativity, politics, recreation, athletics, self-esteem, autonomy, belongingness, emotional safety, intellectual ability, and so on. Obviously these contextual zones of experience may overlap or be nested within one another, as, for example, when themes of autonomy are active in family-of-origin relationships, or when self-esteem is entangled with creativity.

A person's constructions of context can be his or her carbon copies of cultural and family (that is, consensual) constructions, as emphasized by the social constructionist movement, or may be more idiosyncratically created by the individual, as emphasized by the radical constructivist movement. In either case, whether a version of reality is received or personally created, it is ultimately the individual who installs it in his or her own mental makeup, implements it in concrete situations, and has the capacity to *un*make it. To implement or invoke a particular construction is to inhabit a particular subjective reality, which then *seems* objective. Usually, people are unconscious of the internal act of invoking humanly invented constructions, and instead they have the (largely illusory) experience of existing within externally imposed, nonarbitrary patterns of living.

When we describe a therapy client's governing, symptom-generating construction subjectivistically—that is, when we are emphasizing the subjective experience of the meanings and feelings comprising the construction—we refer to it as the emotional truth of the symptom. When we describe the same construction objectivistically, wishing to focus on it as a formation of certain psychological components, we refer to it as the client's pro-symptom position, or the "hidden structure of the symptom," or other such phrases referring to structure. Except for this difference in emphasis, the two phrases *emotional truth of the symptom* and *pro-symptom position* are synonymous.

The emphasis on emotional truth in depth-oriented brief therapy is to be clearly distinguished from merely encouraging the client's emotionality. With many clients the symptom *is* their habitual emotionality, and they need to be brought out of it. The emotional truth of the symptom is not the emotional state the client already consciously experiences, but rather the initially *unconscious* formation of emotional, cognitive, and somatic meanings and knowings that make the symptom (including symptomatic emotionality) compellingly important to produce.

A fundamental feature of this conceptual picture is the fact that the client's unconscious positions have autonomy. Despite being unconscious, a pro-symptom position is highly responsive to any current situation that appears to challenge its purposes, and it autonomously asserts its response. The response implemented by a pro-symptom position—such as delusion, depression, self-depreciation, or compulsive working, to name examples we have already considered in detail—always serves to protect the client or strives to secure well-being in some specific way that is construed necessary within the experiential reality of that position. Since this autonomous response happens to be troublesome or painful for the conscious self (or to others), it is termed a symptom, and it mystifies the client because his or her conscious position provides no way to make meaningful personal sense of it or of why it cannot be stopped by an effort of will.

The autonomy of a person's unconscious positions means that he or she does not merely *have* such positions but is, in some real sense, actively and simultaneously *in* all positions at once, though not consciously. The individual is ever scrutinizing current circumstances through the lens of each position simultaneously, and every position is ready to activate should circumstances appear to warrant it.

The pro-symptom position is a kind of subself of the client, an experiential reality narrowly and passionately preoccupied with certain highly focalized themes and possessing its own knowledges, memories, emotions, attitudes, and actions relevant to those themes. The "subpersonalities" or "parts" conceptualized by various experiential psychotherapies (such as Gestalt and Jungian therapies, transactional analysis, and neuro-linguistic programming) correspond more or less to what we term unconscious positions. In order to bring about an interaction and integration among these unconscious formations and the conscious self, these therapies employ many techniques that are directly applicable in DOBT. We emphasize, however, that DOBT desists from stereotyping or personifying unconscious positions or theoretically defining or naming them for the client, relying rather on the fully phenomenological approach of radical inquiry to discover *from the client* what the specific characteristics of his or her pro-symptom position(s) are, including such personifications as "inner child," "critical parent," "warrior," and so on.

Once a client has experienced and grasped the emotional truth of the symptom, we generally prefer to speak about his or her previously unacknowledged *position*, because it unmistakably yet blamelessly connotes the client's active, potent, purposeful involvement in generating the symptom. For example, by saying to a client, "So it seems you also have this other *position* that you didn't realize you had, a position in which you feel very strongly that . . ." the therapist fosters integration and an empowering experiential realization of being the author-creator-implementor of the symptom, rather than the victim of a reified "part" or "subpersonality." This is not a dogmatic point, however, and there are times when the term *part* is useful, provided it is not used in reifying ways that support the client's victim position.

The Pro-Symptom Position and the Concept of Secondary Gain

The concepts of the pro-symptom position and the emotional truth of the symptom are to be distinguished from the familiar psychodynamic concept of *secondary gain*. This concept rests upon the view that the presenting symptom in its *primary* nature is a form of defectiveness or pathology, but a pathology through which the client secondarily is deriving benefit in certain ways. In Freud's own words, "These are the certain uses the patient can make of his illness which have nothing to do with the origin of the neurosis but which may attain the utmost practical importance." This view is incompatible with the constructivist paradigm of depth-oriented brief therapy. In DOBT the symptom's aspect as a gain is not secondary to some primary aspect as a pathology, because the *primary* psychological significance of the symptom is the gain or success it achieves for the client, within his or her subjective world of meaning, conscious and unconscious. The symptom is never seen as a pathology or defect that can be identified according to external, "objective" diagnostic criteria of mental health. From the constructivist viewpoint, for a psychotherapist to "objectively" assess the client's symptom as a pathology or defect is virtually the same as an anthropologist from the United States regarding another people's ways as defective because they deviate so greatly from U.S. norms.

There may indeed be several types of gain associated with the same symptom in various symptom-positive contexts, with some of these gains being of less emotional weight than others. It may even be necessary to find and transform the pro-symptom position involved in each form of gain, in order for the symptom to cease occurring. However, this situation is not to be confused with the conceptual baggage of the phrase "secondary gain."

The Pro-Symptom Position and the Systemic "Function of the Symptom"

The "function of the symptom" is a phrase used widely in systemic family therapy to denote a situation in which the problem behavior of one or some family members is hypothesized as protecting the family from having another problem that the family would experience as even worse, and that would develop if the problem behavior were to stop.

The systems-theoretical function of the symptom cannot be located in any particular individuals. In DOBT, however, the function of the symptom is viewed as located in the intrapsychic, pro-symptom constructions of one or more individuals in the family and as being experientially discoverable and verifiable using standard DOBT methodology. (Chapter Six details a family session illustrating this.)

The family system is viewed in DOBT as consisting of no more and no less than an interaction among the family members' individual constructions of reality—essentially the "ecology of ideas" approach of Gregory Bateson and the "perspective, metaperspective, and meta-metaperspective" approach of R. D. Laing. In these views, how any one family member currently understands the others appears to that family member to be confirmed by the others' behaviors. This locks the system into its current, symptom-generating, mutually adversarial, reactive, or alienated configuration. The critical emphasis that DOBT adds to the picture is the fact that the "understanding" that one family member has of the behavior of another is often unconscious—an unconscious interpretation of the meaning of the others' behaviors, triggering an unconsciously generated behavioral response. The others then construe this behavior according to their *own* private and largely unconscious worlds of meaning, and they respond accordingly, possibly in ways that inflame the problem further, and the cycle of adversarial reactivity and miscommunication grows.

We prefer the phrase "ecology of meanings" to Bateson's "ecology of ideas." "Ecology of meanings" avoids the assumption as well as the implication that cognition ("ideas") is the sole home of meaning. Since Bateson wrote, a virtual revolution has occurred in cognitive psychology, establishing full parity between affect and cognition as coequal and interdependent modes of knowing, and recognizing even that "affective experiences and judgments take place or can take place prior to any conscious conceptual processing (thinking)." Our adjustment of Bateson's phrase is intended simply to preserve its accuracy and not to change what we believe was already his intended meaning.

However, as therapist Lynn Hoffman points out, "The weakness of Batesonian systemic views is that they offer no language in which to describe experiential events." DOBT fills in this gap with its central focus on clients' experiential events and with its methodology for actually discovering and verifying individuals' unconscious constructions of meaning. This completely obviates the need for inherently undetectable explanatory entities such as "the systemic function of the symptom." If the family's presenting symptom is protective in some way, this protective purpose and function *cannot exist independently of the discoverable positions of individuals in the family.*

The field of systemic family therapy, in shunning work with emotions and the unconscious (see Introduction), divested itself of the therapeutic approaches most effective for accessing and transforming the family's largely unconscious ecology of meanings. The methodology of depth-oriented brief therapy, being designed exactly for the purpose of rapidly discovering and reprocessing unconscious emotional truths, is well suited for dispelling the divergence of private, isolated realities and creating common ground among family members' constructions of meaning, thereby dispelling symptoms. The therapeutic potency of family members accessing and revealing their symptom-related emotional truths or constructions of meaning in the presence of each other cannot be overestimated (see clinical examples in Chapter Six). If an unexpressed personal meaning and feeling is largely unconscious, as is often the case, accessing it and bringing it into communication between family members requires, on the part of the therapist, skill with radical inquiry and comfort with emotional process.

Conscious and Unconscious Knowing

As easy as it may be after one hundred years of psychodynamic theory to take for granted the existence and activity of the unconscious mind, we confess to being genuinely intrigued by its autonomous intelligence. That the involvement of a conscious "I" is wholly unnecessary for carrying out complex constructions and strategies is a haunting mystery, made no less so by mechanistic, reductionist analyses of behaviorist and cognitive theorists. It is this freedom of the unconscious psyche from any constraint of coordinating with a conscious "I" that allows for multiple autonomous realities relevant to the same item of experience. Within the domain of the conscious "I" the tolerance for inconsistent versions of reality is relatively limited, but outside that domain there is no limit on divergent, coexisting constructions.

When an unconscious, pro-symptom position gets activated and is asserting its autonomous response, it takes control away from the conscious position. The reasons for this pro-symptom "possession" are simple: First, within the experiential reality of the pro-symptom position, circumstances now urgently require the response that is this position's job to carry out. Second, pro-symptom positions invariably are, at core, emotionally urgent constructions, because they involve crucial needs or desires. The habitual conscious position is no match for this double dose of intensity once a pro-symptom position is activated.

The extent of the displacement of the individual's usual, conscious state by the pro-symptom position can range from the minimal degree of simply noticing a discrete, fully dissociated symptom (such as a facial tic); to the intermediate degree of being subjectively drawn into some of the emotions, cognitions, kinesthetic sensations, and overt behaviors of the pro-symptom position (the familiar, conscious "I" is still present enough to be aware of being strangely possessed, as in anxiety attacks or depression); to the maximal degree of total immersion in the reality of the pro-symptom position, with no trace of the usual conscious identity remaining (as in fugue states or dissociative identity disorder).

If the mind harbors any number of different realities having very different views, feelings, and responses in relation to the same event or perception, then what does it mean to say, for example, "I feel angry" or "I now want a divorce"? Am "I" *this* experiential reality or *that* one?

For purposes of the conceptual framework of DOBT, we cast all these considerations in the following way: As both Bateson and Maturana centrally emphasize in their biological theories, all activity of the psyche is epistemological, a "whole-being embodiment of knowing," in Mahoney's evocative phrase. In other words, *all human psychological activity consists fundamentally of the activity of knowing, which occurs with or without the involvement of the conscious "I."*

Independently of any involvement of a conscious "I," the mind's fundamental operation is to know (just as the human infant continuously is engaged in active knowing even if there is no "I" present). Where *in addition* there occurs an awareness or knowing of this knowing, this extra or meta-level awareness constitutes "I," or reflective awareness. In other words, the conscious "I" itself consists of a particular kind of knowing: the awareness of being present as a knowing attention. For example, the graduate school procrastinator in Chapter One *knew* not to do his course work in order to refuse an unwanted path in life, but he did not *know* he knew this until the therapist called his conscious attention to this knowing. *It is this meta-awareness, or knowing-of-knowing, that is the "I," not the content of what is consciously known.* This definition differs from the popular usage of the term "I" in which it *is* the content of all conscious knowings that constitutes the personal, subjective identity of the "I"—contents such as "I own a car" and "I love my spouse." Note, though, that an amnesiac with total forgetfulness of the knowings comprising personal identity still says "I," showing that, actually and essentially, *"I" refers to the knower's awareness of being present as a knowing attention, not to the content of what is known.*

What is conventionally termed *unconscious* is, in this view, anything a person knows without the involvement or awareness of the conscious "I." All such unattended knowing—including the formation of elaborated, unconscious positions and their activities—proceeds autonomously. To say that an emotional, cognitive, or somatic item is unconscious means simply that the knowing constituted by this item is present without the meta-level awareness of this knowing. In contrast, to say that some item is *conscious* or is *in awareness* means simply that the person *knows* the knowing constituted by this item—that is, has attended to it.

Psychotherapists and psychologists generally understand *unconscious* inherently to mean a state of "unknowing." That is, if something is unconscious, then the client is regarded as devoid of knowing with respect to it. We take a different view and regard unconscious constructs and processes of all types—unconscious emotions, kinesthetics, and somesthetics—as being in fact knowings, though unattended by the conscious "I."

In the course of daily life, one unconscious position after another becomes activated and "seizes the microphone," temporarily bringing its particular set of meanings, feelings, and responses to bear and, as we noted earlier, displacing the familiar version of self (the habitual conscious position) to one degree or another. Knowings normally held in the conscious position as constituting "I," such as "I love my spouse," can then be lost temporarily (as in "splitting"). The "I" of popular usage, being the *content* of whichever position is currently active and at the microphone, therefore goes through drastic changes and is experienced as unstable, unreliable, or defective, because according to cultural norms one is *supposed* to be a single, monolithic self. However, "the central 'I' is not a fact, it's a longing—the longing of all the selves within the psyche that are starving because they are not recognized," as writer Michael Ventura observes in his insightful exposé of the "fiction of monopersonality." Assisting a therapy client to come to grips with that fiction occurs naturally within the methodology of depth-oriented brief therapy.

The above formulation of the types of knowing—known or attended-to knowings and unknown or unattended-to knowings—provides a basis for a consistent, constructivist epistemology that encompasses the heterogeneous (multi-reality) structure of human psychology. The lack of such an inclusive epistemology has led to both conceptual gaps and methodological errors among constructivist clinicians. Consider, for example, this classic situation: "the case of a mother of a juvenile delinquent who displays two very different attitudes towards her offspring: an 'official,' punitive, censoring one, which verbally demands good behavior and respect for society's rules; and a non-verbal, seductive one, of which she may honestly be unaware, but *which is very noticeable to the outside observer* and especially to the delinquent, who is only too alert to the gleam in her eye and her secret admiration for his questionable exploits" (italics in original).

Commenting on this description of the mother-son interaction, theorist Jan Cambien writes, "People can simultaneously know and not know something. In this case, mother 'knows' that she admires her son's questionable exploits, for there is a gleam in her eye and she does seduce him to persist in his wickedness. If she didn't know, there would be no gleam and no seduction. Yet one can accept that she may be honestly unaware of this. . . . How can we be 'blind,' that is, both know and not know a certain reality? What kind of epistemology could serve us if we are confronted with . . . such mind-boggling problems?"

Cambien's conundrum is created by his presupposing the conventional notion that "unaware" *means* "devoid of knowing." The solution to this conundrum is the simple one we have defined above—namely, adoption of the view that "unaware" does *not* mean "devoid of knowing," because unconscious knowings are indeed knowings, though unattended by the conscious "I." In this view there is no paradox in the person having a conscious position containing no knowledge of something that the person's behavior shows he or she knows. That is, unattended knowings have direct access to the body and are not dependent upon cooperation from the conscious "I" in order to express themselves behaviorally ("seductiveness," "gleam in the eye," posture, voice tones, and so on). Evidently, the psychophysical capacity to know and to act is independent of the central executive function of the conscious "I" to a far greater degree than is presumed in our ego- and rationality-worshipping, scientistic culture. Cambien's conundrum typifies how we underestimate the sophistication of the knowings that occur without any "help" from the "I" at all.

In this picture, the conscious "I" finds itself in the unique position of noticing, over time, the discrepancies between the realities of all the various positions, as detected through their autonomous manifestations and their perturbation of the habitual conscious state. The conscious "I" can become interested in fathoming or coming to terms with these discrepancies (even if only in an attempt to rid itself of the inconveniences or sufferings they cause it), opening up the process of a true dialectical interaction of these many versions of reality as they come into mutual contact through the agency of the "I."

This sort of consistent epistemology encompassing conscious and unconscious constructions is needed as a corrective for the tendency in some psychotherapeutic frameworks to view human consciousness as unified and monolithic, as though all presenting symptoms stem from material already accessible to and controllable by the conscious "I." An important example of this error (which has afflicted much of constructivist thinking in the 1980s and 1990s as well as behaviorism, cognitive psychology, and family systems theory since the 1950s) is the view, widespread among constructivist *narrative* psychotherapies, that all presenting problems exist entirely within language, as creations of the client's linguistic self-narrative. An expert narrative psychotherapist who claims that all problems are formed in language is much like an expert farmer who claims that our planet is entirely covered by soil. The claim only reveals an exclusive focus upon one domain and a remarkable unawareness of the presence and influence of an even greater domain. Many of a person's emotional knowings and all of his kinesthetic and somesthetic ones exist in other than linguistic form.

Let's note more concretely how this is so. To fully heed an experience of emotion is to be richly informed of important personal knowings, meanings, perceptions. If on an ordinary day I notice myself feeling distinctly sad but have no idea why, I am immediately informed by the heavy feeling itself that there exists *something* I am sad about. The emotional region of my mind already knows what this something is—hence the sadness, which is the felt knowing of a loss—but "I" do not. By attending to this feeling and finding and cognizing the already-present knowings that are generating this feeling of loss, "I" come to know these knowings and realize suddenly, for example, that I am having an anniversary depression.

Emotion is, in its essence, the experience of knowing that something of relevance to personal need, desire, or values is occurring. The therapist welcomes the emotion as a valuable carrier of important knowings and meanings involved in the problem. We do not see emotion as an aftereffect or an epiphenomenon of cognition, nor do we carry out DOBT by using reason and evidence to "correct" cognitive errors or irrational beliefs and thereby control emotion, as characterized the early view in cognitive-behavioral approaches. Rather, we regard emotion and cognition as complementary ways of knowing, operating concurrently. While fundamentally different in experiential quality, emotion and cognition are not separately or independently functioning, but rather often mutually influence each other's formation—a view we share with more advanced developments in cognitive science and emotion theory.

Kinesthetic and somesthetic sensations and actions likewise are knowings in the domains of physical movement in space and immediate personal and interpersonal conditions, such as expansiveness or contractedness, violations of psychological boundaries, and connection or disconnection with others. They are not in themselves cognitive or emotional, though they may be accompanied by knowings of either type. Specific kinesthetic and somesthetic *states* may be implemented by the individual for various purposes. A forty-year-old woman described her problem as intense, sharp pains in her throat whenever she began to strongly feel and express anything of an emotional nature, negative or positive. She was describing the sensation created by her own unconscious contraction at the base of her throat, a somesthetic act that was itself a knowing of how to rapidly prevent herself from doing what would bring violent abuse—as occurred many times throughout her childhood in response to showing her feelings. An example of the kinesthetic knowing involved in symbiotic attachment is described in Chapter Five.

Cognitions are knowings that are internally represented either in verbal form (sometimes as inner dialogue in the auditory perceptual mode) and/or in visual form (imagery in the visual perceptual mode). The cognition of highly abstract relationships (as in mathematics and physics) generally involves a joint effort or synthesis of visual capabilities and a palpable, kinesthetic representation of the relationship in question.

Why is it important in depth-oriented brief therapy to appreciate that all constructs are knowings? The therapist *must* appreciate the epistemological nature of all constructs in order to recognize their emotional truth, their essential quality of being coherent, cogent, and constructively purposeful and adaptive, rather than seeing them às defects, errors, and pathologies.

The Structure of Positions

Next we turn to the specific types of knowings that comprise the emotional truth of the symptom, the stuff that radical inquiry reveals the client's pro-symptom position to be made of. Here our discussion will be largely structural or objectivistic rather than subjectivistic, in the sense that we will describe constructs—the components of positions—more as mental objects having certain properties than in terms of how the client subjectively experiences them.

The Components of Positions

As clinical examples in previous chapters have illustrated, an unconscious pro-symptom position is a formation of three major components:

- Emotional wounds

- Presuppositions
- Protective actions

Each of these in turn is made up of any or all types of knowings: emotional, cognitive, kine/somesthetic, and perceptual/motor.

Emotional wounds or *traumas,* of course, consist primarily of emotional (nonlinguistic) meanings stored somesthetically in the body and linked to perceptual memory, and secondarily are also comprised of any language-based cognitions by which the individual understood or made sense of the emotionally wounding or traumatizing experience. Such cognitions include, for example, views of what caused the experience and the formation of strategies or intentions for preventing any future occurrences of this kind. All of these elements may be unconscious. Therapists who have been present as a client experiences the emergence of a previously unconscious, purely somesthetic/emotional memory of trauma will have a vivid sense of the existence of such nonverbal knowings. The term "memory" is somewhat misleading here because the body carries the trauma currently and unconsciously, so that the accessing of an emotional memory is a true reexperiencing of the original emotional state in the present, not merely a remembering of the past. Likewise, readers who have received psychotherapeutic bodywork and have had the experience of a powerful emotional state, pregnant with clear, coherent meaning, suddenly pouring into awareness nonverbally from the body, know most directly how potent these nonverbal, noncognitive representations of reality are. Such experiences leave no doubt whatsoever that emotional knowledge can be stored in nonlinguistic forms. All emotional wounds involve emotional memories that act as nonverbal presuppositions of how a certain type of situation will develop once key behaviors have occurred.

Protective actions utilize any type of construct or behavioral act to avoid the occurrence of any unwanted event or experience, including the experience of emotional truth. Both examples in Chapter Two involved key protective actions: one woman's construal of "I'm ugly" in both the cognitive form of inner dialogue and the somesthetic form of a shard of glass cutting her in the abdomen, and the depressed woman's workaholic "high" and repetition compulsion with men, always choosing an emotional replica of her father instead of grieving his failure to express love. As these examples show, very often the presenting problem *is* the client's protective action, disowned. Protective actions include interpersonal or family-systemic patterns of behavior that avoid dealing directly and openly with the emotional truths in the family or that covertly manipulate family members in order to prevent imagined disasters. During a visit to his parents' home, for example, an adult therapy client may go into depression as a protective action against the perceived dangers of confrontation, anger, or rejection that he expects and fears would result from staying in touch with his primary feelings and relating on that basis.

Presuppositions are unconscious, unquestioned assumptions about the nature of reality (the self, others, the world). The effectiveness of working with presuppositions in therapy is due to the fact that people's problems are generally not about events or circumstances in themselves, but about what these *mean* or what the *possible choices* are, as defined by their presuppositions.

Presuppositions are not necessarily cognitive-verbal in form. They may also consist of representations of reality held in unconscious emotional or kinesthetic memory, with little or no verbal-conceptual representation.

For example, consider a child, eleven months old and preverbal, who has on twenty-eight occasions since birth heard daddy angrily yelling and then heard mommy crying. This child's knowledge of how men are, how women are, and what is going to happen once a man starts speaking loudly is stored entirely in emotional, perceptual, and kinesthetic memory. This completely nonverbal knowledge constitutes reality-shaping presuppositions about what to expect from, and even how to be, a man or woman.

In this example, the child's preverbal stage makes obvious the formation of nonverbal knowings. However, even after the stage of verbal development is reached, emotionally powerful experiences still create nonverbal representations in emotional memory, which are stored in association with any verbal-cognitive representations that may also be formed in the experience. These emotional memories function as nonverbal presuppositions that inform the individual of the emotional meaning of what is taking place—or about to—in concrete situations.

An indication that a presupposition is of the noncognitive type is the client's very high degree of amazement and disorientation when finally the presupposition comes into awareness. This intensity of amazement and disorientation occurs because noncognitive presuppositions are even more divergent from the client's familiar, cognitive view of self and world than are cognitively held presuppositions.

An amusing example is a male client, age thirty, who came for therapy feeling very upset and oppressed by his mother's anxious overinvolvement in his life. Early in the first session the therapist became aware of this fellow's presupposition that whenever his mother goes into anxiety over him, it is immediately *his* emotional job to somehow get her out of her anxiety. This was not a subtle perception on the therapist's part. It was easy to see that this man was so oppressed by his mother's anxiety *because* he took it as his job to dispel it. But her anxiety was endless and certainly undispellable by him.

The therapist began doing the position work of having this man realize and own his position of having that job. Because of this chap's sturdy, spirited temperament, the therapist's first step in this direction was a challenging observation. She said, "It seems very important to you not to let her deal with her own anxiety. You seem very attached to having that job of getting rid of it *for* her. Is that a job you want to keep having?"

For the client, this was the first time the possibility of *not* doing that job had ever dawned on him, and it was a *stunning* insight. His mouth actually dropped open, he just gazed at the therapist for a few seconds, and then said, "That's *huge!*" He was truly amazed and visibly lifted by this undreamed-of possibility of liberation, and he *stayed* amazed for the rest of the session. He said, "That's huge!" at least three more times. He felt no need for a second session.

The naming into awareness of this man's presupposition of the emotional job he had to do for his mother had such an uncanny, world-changing effect because the presupposition was of the noncognitive, purely emotional type. As in the hypothetical example of the toddler cited earlier, this presupposition probably was learned preverbally from repeating patterns of family interaction.

Of course, bringing a presupposition into awareness and verbalizing it will not necessarily divest it of its power to define reality. A presupposition that "sticks" even after being rendered conscious is diagnostic of unconscious, higher-order purposes being served by maintaining the presupposition. Its existence is strategic in the sense that its purpose is not apparent from its content. The classic example is a presupposition of low self-worth unconsciously serving the purpose of preserving a positive image of parents who were in fact grossly abusive. A strategic presupposition will dissolve only if the entire higher-order purpose necessitating it is dissolved as well. The hidden purpose can be revealed experientially by temporarily disabling the presupposition (such as through the technique of viewing from a symptom-free position), at which point the unmet purpose flares into awareness. These points and methods are discussed further in Chapters Five and Six.

Whatever modes of representation constitute it, a presupposition is a standing, unquestioned assumption of how reality is or works, and it is unconsciously invoked to make sense of current perceptions to which it is relevant; it is a kind of hidden, personal epistemology or rule for knowing. Presuppositions by the hundreds are continually structuring our personal realities; some of them become components of positions that generate symptoms.

Here are the chief categories of personal knowledge that presuppositions inform, as we have encountered them clinically, each with an example of how an individual might verbally formulate such a presupposition after it has been brought to awareness:

1. *Teleology (construed intention or direction):* "My husband's lack of goals means he is in a bottomless downward spiral like my mother was."
2. *Roles (necessary behaviors, attitudes, and obligations):* "If my wife or mother shows emotional pain, I have to get her out of it immediately."
3. *Causality (what brings about or occurs with what):* "It's my fault he's been really closed and distant from me; I wonder what I did wrong." "She's raising her voice; she's going to reject me."
4. *Ontology (essential nature of self, others, or world):* "I'm fundamentally deficient." "There are two kinds of people: Creative, productive ones who are *never* thrown by adversity, and uncreative ones who let the world mire them down in adversity."

5. *Epistemology (how to know):* "The way to know if I'm being a good person is to see if others approve of me."
6. *Values (what is good and what is bad):* "Doing what others want or need is unselfish and good; doing what I want or need is selfish and bad."

It is obvious that unquestioned, unrecognized views such as these can be centrally involved in generating a client's presenting symptoms. Presuppositions powerfully structure what one takes to be reality, and they powerfully define what the possible choices are. When operating from a presupposition, it is not at all apparent that it is oneself who is supplying the meaning that appears to reside "*out there,*" in things themselves. This is why, when an important, high-order presupposition is suddenly brought into experiential awareness as being merely a changeable, personal *assumption* about the world rather than its intrinsic nature, the experience is uncanny. The individual is suddenly aware that she has invented the world she took as real—or a significant part of that world, anyway, and this puts all the rest in question. In addition, in such moments the conscious "I" becomes to some degree aware of itself as being distinct from the contents of its construings, a most unfamiliar and unsettling experience, and one we tend to extinguish as quickly as possible.

When the presuppositions involved in the presenting problem are altered or rendered obsolete, the entire nature and meaning of even a long-standing, painful problem can sometimes be transformed in seconds, or the problem can actually vanish.

The Internal Organization of a Position

Now that we have reviewed the components of the pro-symptom position sought in radical inquiry—*emotional wounds, protective actions, presuppositions,* and their constituent elements—we next examine how these various components are organized within a position. General patterns of organization of constructs, or "core ordering processes," are important both in clinical practice and in constructivist theory and research.

Actually, previous chapters have already sketched the scheme we have developed for depth-oriented brief therapy. We have described our clients' positions (particular constructions of reality) as a set of interrelated constructs existing on four levels or orders. These constructs may in general be conscious or unconscious, although all orders of a *pro*-symptom position are as a rule unconscious (except, of course, for the presenting symptom itself, this being the aspect of the pro-symptom position's activity that has been consciously noticed). We define these orders of position as follows, with each exemplified by the corresponding construct from the pro-symptom position of the woman with the cutting shard of negative self-image described in Chapter Two:

- *Fourth-order constructs*: The domain of ontology, the person's construings of the fundamental nature of the self, others, or the world ("My essential deficiency as a female is plainly visible and will inevitably bring slashing rejection"). Ontological constructs are the basis from which third-order governing purposes arise.
- *Third-order constructs*: The domain of governing purposes ("I must create an acceptable cover to prevent traumatic rejection"), in pursuit of which one generates second-order meanings for what is occurring in specific situations.
- *Second-order constructs*: The domain of meanings attributed to particular perceptions in concrete situations ("Social situations mean: I am repulsively ugly; I must never attempt a romantic or sexual overture; I must present my cover of intellectual competence"), which then give rise to first-order cognitions, emotions, kinesthetics, and actions.
- *First-order constructs*: The domain of concrete responses— cognitions, emotions, kine/somesthetics, and actions, including the presenting symptom—aimed at coping with the immediate situation in light of its second-order construed meaning (body language giving no signals of sexual candidacy; displays of intellectual competence; psychogenic cutting shard in stomach; inner dialogue expressing that "I'm ugly"; anxiety in social settings).

The construction of a client's positions can be captured in one clear, unified picture by means of the *position chart* we have devised for this purpose, as shown in Figure 3.1. The chart depicts the four orders of position along its horizontal span, and along its vertical span are the two major levels of awareness examined earlier: unconscious pro-symptom constructs and conscious anti-symptom constructs.

The specific constructs of the client listed above are entered into the chart. In any one box the therapist enters a verbal indication of any and all constructs (emotional, cognitive, kinesthetic, and behavioral; presuppositions, emotional wounds, and protective actions) that are involved in the presenting symptom at the order of position and level of awareness of that box. The entries in the four boxes of the lower horizontal row then together make up the client's pro-symptom position (which, subjectively experienced, is the emotional truth of the symptom). The specific constructs in the pro-symptom position make clear what the symptom-positive context(s) are. Similarly, the upper horizontal row makes up the client's conscious, anti-symptom position; symptom-negative contexts are readily apparent.

The filled-in chart in Figure 3.1 is a static view or snapshot of the therapist's knowledge at the point in the work when radical inquiry was complete enough to give the therapist the needed clarity into the emotional truth of the symptom. Such snapshots can also be created for other points in the process of therapy, showing, for example, the subsequent process of change and the final, resolution position of the client. By filling in the chart session-by-session from the start of therapy, adding newly discovered constructs, the therapist creates a comprehensive picture of the emerging structure of the client's constructions relevant to the presenting problem. Thus the chart provides an efficient, convenient way to make case presentations or to summarize therapy-in-progress when conferring with a consultant or supervisor. Such a picture is especially useful to the therapist in the process of learning depth-oriented brief therapy. It helps the trainee to stay oriented in relation to the body of information gained at any point (some degree of disorientation in the emerging material is natural) and to identify where in the four-level structure the therapist needs more clarity and should focus radical inquiry. We hasten to emphasize, however, that *during a therapy session, it is not theoretical considerations such as order of position that guide the therapist in pursuing the two top priorities, radical inquiry and experiential shift.* (How the therapist

Figure 3.1. Sample Chart of Client's Anti- and Pro-symptom Positions, Showing Constructs at Various Orders of Position.

LEVELS OF AWARENESS	ORDERS OF POSITION				
	FIRST ORDER Purpose enacted: concrete thoughts/ feelings/behavior	**SECOND ORDER** Attribution of meaning in concrete situations	**THIRD ORDER** Purpose to be served by attributions of meaning	**FOURTH ORDER** Construal of ontology: nature of self/others/world	
ANTI-SYMPTOM POSITION Conscious knowing	Inner dialogue: "I'm ugly." Cutting shard in body. Anxiety in social settings; confidence felt only in professional setting.	"I have no chance at all with men. I've got to be seen as impressively competent intellectually, or my personal repulsiveness will no longer be overlooked."			
PRO-SYMPTOM POSITION Unconscious knowing	Automatic behavior: no overtures of sexual candidacy; displays of intellect and competence	Meaning of social interaction is that I am repulsively ugly, I must not attempt to be a romantic/sexual entity, and I must use intellectual cover.	I must prevent: further trauma of slashing rejection, sexual sinning, alienation from mother. I must create an acceptable cover.	My essential deficiency as a female is plainly visible. I am gashed to the core by others' harsh rejection.	

approaches these two priorities is the subject of the remaining chapters of this book.)

The chart also gives an especially clear view of the hierarchical organization of the constructs comprising the position. Any construct in the hierarchical network is by definition *subordinate* to (existing within the context created by) higher-order ones and *superordinate* to (serving as the context and ground of) those of lower order. A construct is simultaneously a *context* of meaning within which lower-order constructs have their existence, and a *particular content* within the context of higher-order constructs.

These complex-sounding terms describe a principle that is intuitively obvious: If I make an assumption about what's so, this initial assumption directly gives birth to other assumptions or actions that *derive from* the first one and that can exist only *because* of the presence of the first one. In that sense, these derivative or resulting assumptions are subordinate to the initial one, which is superordinate to the derivative ones. For example, a client assumed her older brother was an unscrupulous manipulator. When he invited her to dinner at a restaurant, her derivative assumption was that this dinner meeting would be in some hidden way dangerous for her.

The principle operating here is the mind's fundamental need to preserve consistency among constructs at all orders *within the same position,* but not *between* positions. Characteristic of its extraordinary richness of function, the mind both insists upon internal consistency of reality (within a position) and simultaneously is completely free of that requirement (between positions), hence the great disparity between anti- and pro-symptom positions.

We mentioned above that any construct serves as a context or field of meaning within which lower-order constructs can exist. In other words, higher-order constructs involve a more abstract and inclusive scope of meaning than do lower-order constructs. Consequently, changing a higher-order construct involves a far more sweeping and fundamental change of the client's familiar reality than changing a lower-order construct. People automatically and tenaciously resist high-order change. When perceptions contradict our construction of reality, forcing a modification in that construction, we strive instinctively to accommodate the contradiction by modifying constructs at the lowest possible order, so as to minimize the extent of change in our experiential reality. When new experience brings two of our own already-held constructs into irreconcilable conflict, "The idea that survives is the one that is more abstract and has therefore been used successfully more often than the idea that does not survive," as psychotherapist Jeffrey Bogdan explains. The construct that is relinquished is the lower-order one whose loss does the least damage to the familiar structure of reality. One clinical implication of these ideas, which we elaborate further in Chapter Six, is that clients who are least likely to reach a lasting resolution briefly are those whose presenting symptom is generated by *multiple* high-order constructs.

The conceptualization in DOBT of the four orders of position structuring experiential reality is an extension of the seminal ideas of Bateson, who has had a profound influence on the development of constructivist as well as systemic psychotherapies. Calling attention to the hierarchy of constructs (an application of Whitehead's logical types) is one of Bateson's most important contributions to the field of psychotherapy. However, it has been adopted by therapists in the limited form of the concept of second-order change. As we described in the Introduction, this phrase has become widely used to denote any problem-dispelling change in the context that the client uses to define the meaning of the presenting symptom. This stands in contrast to first-order change, in which attempts are made to dispel the symptom with no such change in contextual meaning.

However, when orders of construction higher than the second order are recognized and are involved in therapeutic changes—as in depth-oriented brief therapy—then the phrase *second-order change* becomes inadequate and misleading as a general label denoting problem-dispelling transformations of context. Phrases such as *superordinate change, contextual change,* and *third-* and *fourth-order change* are more appropriate indicators of the full range of change processes and of structure involved in a comprehensive constructivist psychotherapy.

Unconscious Positions: Corroboration from Scientific Disciplines

In conceptualizing and working with the heterogeneity of the client's construction of reality—the presence of any number of unconscious, autonomous positions in addition to the conscious one—DOBT is consistent with important developments in the fields of cognitive psychology, emotion theory, and cognitive neuroscience (also known as psychoneurology, the field of experimental research into how the structural, anatomical organization of the brain corresponds to subjective psychological experience). We will note the first two very briefly and focus more on the biological results supporting our clinical model.

In all three fields, a major conceptual and empirical development over the past twenty years has been the discovery of the modular organization of meaning and information processing in human psychology.

In cognitive science, mental functioning is being seen as occurring through parallel distributed processing, in which many distinct information-processing modules, each handling a particular, relatively narrow domain of information, operate simultaneously without requiring conscious attention. Furthermore, the view of cognition and emotion as separate or even opposed functions has become a quaint relic of an earlier era, replaced by an understanding of the *emotion scheme,* a module of experiential knowledge consisting of a multilevel integration of stored sensory, emotional, and cognitive information regarding a particular type of situation or theme of meaning. The activation of an emotion scheme by a perceptual cue generates the felt meaning of the situation as well as a predesigned response to it. In these formulations of cognitive science and emotion theory we see a strong corroboration of DOBT's unconscious, autonomous, pro-symptom position, a conceptualization that developed on the basis of our clinical experience.

The support from cognitive neuroscience is perhaps most striking. One of those at the forefront of this research is Michael Gazzaniga, whose early work in the 1950s and 1960s first revealed differences in functions carried out by left and right brain hemispheres. His subsequent findings evolved this initial, simplistic left/right model much further. Gazzaniga reviewed the extraordinary results of many of his studies in his 1985 book, *The Social Brain.* He explains:

Interpreting our behaviors would be a trivial matter if all behaviors we engaged in were the product of verbal conscious action. In that case, the source of the behavior is known before the action occurs. If all our actions consisted of only these kinds of events, there would be nothing to explain. . . . [*T*]*he normal person does not possess a unitary conscious mechanism in which the conscious system is privy to the sources of all his or her actions.* . . . [T]he normal brain is organized into modules and . . . *most of these modules are capable of actions, moods, and responses. All except one work in nonverbal ways* such that their modes of expression are solely through overt behaviors or more covert actions [italics added].

In the picture that emerges from cognitive neuroscience, any number of largely autonomous brain modules, each a group of neurons, operate outside of conscious awareness and "can compute, remember, feel emotion, and act"—strongly resembling the phenomenology of clients' unconscious, pro-symptom positions. The brain's single verbal module is a key component of the conscious self and "is committed to the task of interpreting our overt behaviors as well as the more covert emotional responses produced by these separate mental modules of our brain. It constructs theories of why these behaviors occurred and does so because of that brain system's need to maintain a sense of consistency for all of our behaviors. It is a uniquely human endeavor." The verbal module's concoction of conscious explanations in its effort to make sense of behaviors generated by nonverbal modules operating out of awareness corresponds precisely to the client's initial, conscious, anti-symptom position in DOBT. Likewise, our earlier definition of the conscious "I" as consisting of knowings-of-knowing seems to correspond to the interpretive activity of the verbal, reflectively construing module Gazzaniga describes.

Gazzaniga emphasizes that "brain modularity is not just a psychological concept. . . . Through [experimental] studies . . . it becomes clear that modularity has a real anatomical basis." The point is not the reductionistic one that consciousness has its source in the physical brain, but only that brain structures *carrying out* the operations of human psychology are being mapped with unprecedented precision. In more recent studies by other researchers using new technologies that give high-resolution, real-time imaging of brain activity, the performance of specific psychological tasks has been found to involve highly localized regions of the brain, corroborating Gazzaniga's model and DOBT.

Summary

To conclude this chapter, we will use the position chart (Figure 3.1) as a teaching device to make some final points. First, the chart makes it especially clear why DOBT's utilization of emotional truth tends to have the beneficial ontological effect mentioned earlier— that is, restored sense of self-worth and core well-being, whatever the presenting problem may be. In general, as our case examples have shown, bringing a client into awareness and conscious ownership of the emotional truth of the symptom includes awareness of his or her *purposes* for producing and maintaining the symptom—the *third*-order constructs in the pro-symptom position. Becoming aware of these third-order purposes is a change whose immediate ripple effect is the *fourth*-order realization by the client that his or her own mind has been full of sense and coherent functioning in producing the symptom, something that seemed at first to be evidence of defectiveness or pathology. This accompanying fourth-order realization of having a mind whose deep nature is of such intrinsic intelligence and coherence restores the sense of self-worth and well-being. This effect occurs even if the fourth-order realization remains entirely implicit and there is no explicit change in fourth-order content (such as a change from "I am unlovable" to "I am lovable").

Second, the filled-in chart (shown in Figure 3.1) serves as a map that gives visible form to a region of the client's architecture of reality that the therapist has induced the client to discover. Mental constructs are, of course, created out of human imagination, but once installed by the owner in his or her experiential reality, they operate as enduring, detectable, identifiable mental objects with particular properties. In other words, a construct may be said to be *invented* when it is first formed and installed by the individual, but subsequently it is *discovered* by the owner to be present in his or her mental world. (The mental objects that we ourselves invent may be the *only* kinds of objects that we can know directly enough to discover.) In depth-oriented brief therapy, radical inquiry is a process of *discovering*, not *inventing*, the client's already-present network of constructs relevant to the presenting symptom. Any competent therapist should discover the same set of constructs (allowing for superficial, stylistic differences in how the constructs are verbalized, which should be determined by the client anyway). Processes of dissolving old constructs or creating new ones then may follow as part of the work of inducing experiential shifts.

Finally, we note that the inclusion in the chart of four orders of position, and not five or more, is based on the fact that constructs and changes of fifth and higher order are rarely involved in psychotherapy. These orders represent ontological constructs and states that are neither included nor, on the whole, recognized within present-day Western psychology. However, an important pattern organizing the orders of position is illuminated by considering the nature of the fifth and sixth orders, and for this reason we will briefly do that.

To define the fifth order of constructs of experiential reality, we must identify what we are presupposing as the tacit basis or context for our definition of the *fourth* order, and *that* will be the *content* of the fifth order. The fourth order of constructs is itself ontological, as we have already seen, but it consists of the particular ontological possibilities that are widely recognized in our culture. For example, regarding the ontology of the self, these conventional fourth-order possibilities are that the essential self is good or bad, lovable or unlovable, whole or fragmented, intact or defective, connected to or disconnected from a greater whole, pure or sinful, wise or ignorant, eternal or mortal, and so on. What all such ontological possibilities share as a presupposition is the existence of the essential self as a *separate, limited entity* that therefore can be viewed as having this quality or that. Thus the fourth order represents the *domain of separate-self construals*. The fifth order, it then follows, is the *domain of purposes for construing oneself a separate being.* Specific fifth-order purposes determine which specific fourth-order attributes of separate self are activated out of the latent background of all possible self-construals.

Here the reader might notice the pattern that is emerging in the sequence of orders of position: an alternation of *domains of discrimination* and *domains of purpose for discriminating.* The discriminative construals made in one domain derive from (are motivated and defined by) the *purposes* that comprise the next higher domain, which in turn derive from the discriminative construals in the next higher domain, which derive from *purposes* at the next level, and so on. By extending this pattern, we can see that the *sixth* order is a domain of discrimination that is prior to any separate-self-construal but that gives birth to fifth-order purposes for construing a separate self. This sixth-order experiential reality involves no sense of separate self, but it does involve a type of knowledge that spawns purposes for construing separate existence.

Although some conceptual definition can be given to the fifth and sixth levels, their unitive experiential nature is hardly imaginable by conventional standards of reality. Actually, even throughout the first four orders of position relevant to psychotherapy, each step up (or down) is a very big one, an exponential expansion (or contraction) of the field of meaning—a kind of Richter scale of reality.

Some clients describe significant change-promoting effects from numinous or transcendent experiences in dreams or waking life, which may represent experiential contact with fifth- or sixth-order constructs. Note that the unconscious constructs at *any* order of position can, in the autonomous manner of such material, at any time transiently and partially come into the awareness of the conscious "I" as imagery and/or as direct, lucid apprehension of meaning.

Having considered the fuller meaning of the emotional truth of the symptom as described in this chapter, the reader is ready to explore the methodology of DOBT for discovering it: radical inquiry.

Notes

P. 93, *But such is the irresistable nature of truth . . . :* T. Paine, "The Rights of Man (Part 2)," in E. Foner (Ed.) (1995), *The Collected Writings of Thomas Paine* (p. 548), New York: Library of America.

P. 97, *the social constructionist movement:* See, for example, P. Berger and T. Luckman (1966), *The Social Construction of Reality,* New York: Doubleday; K. Gergen (1985), "The Social Constructionist Movement in Modern Psychology," *American Psychologist, 40,* 266–275.

P. 97, *the radical constructivist movement:* See, for example, E. von Glasersfeld (1984), "An Introduction to Radical Constructivism," in P. Watzlawick (Ed.), *The Invented Reality* (pp. 17–40), New York: W. W. Norton; E. von Glasersfeld (1987), *The Construction of Knowledge,* Salinas, CA: Intersystems.

P. 99, *"parts" conceptualized by various experiential psychotherapies:* See, for example, R. Schwartz (1987), "Our Multiple Selves," *Family Therapy Networker, 11*(2), 25–31; R. Schwartz (1994), *Internal Family Systems Therapy,* New York: Guilford.

P. 100, *"These are . . . utmost practical importance":* Quoted in O. Fenichel (1945), *The Psychoanalytic Theory of Neurosis* (p. 126), New York: W. W. Norton.

P. 100, *The "function of the symptom":* See, for example, L. Hoffman (1981), *Foundations of Family Therapy,* New York: Basic Books; M. Selvini-Palazzoli, L. Boscolo, G. Cecchin, and G. Prata (1978), *Paradox and Counterparadox,* New York: Jason Aronson.

P. 101, *the "ecology of ideas" approach of Gregory Bateson:* G. Bateson (1972), *Steps to an Ecology of Mind,* New York: Ballantine; J. Bogdan (1984), "Family Organization as an Ecology of Ideas: An Alternative to the Reification of Family Systems," *Family Process, 23,* 375–388.

P. 101, *the "perspective, metaperspective, and meta-metaperspective" approach of R. D. Laing:* R. D. Laing, H. Phillipson, and A. Lee (1966), *Interpersonal Perception,* New York: Perennial Library.

P. 101, *"affective experiences . . . prior to any conscious conceptual processing (thinking)":* L. S. Greenberg and J. D. Safran (1984), "Hot Cognition—Emotion Coming In from the Cold: A Reply to Rachman and Mahoney," *Cognitive Therapy and Research, 8*(6), 592. See also R. Zajonc (1980), "Feeling and Thinking: Preferences Need No Inferences," *American Psychologist, 35,* 151–175; R. Zajonc (1984), "On the Primacy of Affect," *American Psychologist, 39,* 117–123; S. Rachman (1984), "A Reassessment of the 'Primacy of Affect,'" *Cognitive Therapy and Research, 8*(6), 579–584; L. S. Greenberg and J. D. Safran (1987), *Emotion in Psychotherapy: Affect and Cognition in the Process of Change.* New York: Guilford.

P. 101, *"The weakness of Batesonian . . . no language in which to describe experiential events":* L. Hoffman (1990), "Constructing Realities: An Art of Lenses," *Family Process, 29,* 7.

P. 103, *As both Bateson and Maturana centrally emphasize:* G. Bateson (1972), *Steps to an Ecology of Mind,* New York: Ballantine; G. Bateson (1979), *Mind and Nature: A Necessary Unity,* New York: Dutton; H. R. Maturana (1980), "The Biology of Cognition," in H. R. Maturana & F. J. Varela, *Autopoiesis and Cognition: The Realization of the Living,* Boston: D. Reidel.

P. 103, *a "whole-being embodiment of knowing," in Mahoney's evocative phrase:* M. J. Mahoney (1991), *Human Change Processes: The Scientific Foundations of Psychotherapy* (p. 395), New York: Basic Books.

P. 105, *insightful exposé of the "fiction of monopersonality":* M. Ventura (1985), *Shadow Dancing in the USA,* Los Angeles: Tarcher.

P. 105, *"the case of a mother . . . for his questionable exploits":* B. Speed (1984), "How Really Real Is Real? Rejoinder: Mountainous Seas Are Also Wet," *Family Process, 23,* 514.

P. 105, *"People can . . . such mind-boggling problems?":* J. Cambien (1989), "Reality in Psychotherapy," *Journal of Family Psychology, 3*(1), 34–35.

P. 107, *as characterized the early view in cognitive behavioral approaches:* See, for example, A. T. Beck (1976), *Cognitive Therapy and the Emotional Disorders,* New York: International Universities Press; A. Ellis (1962), *Reason and Emotion in Psychotherapy,* New York: Lyle Stuart.

P. 107, *a view we share with more advanced developments in cognitive science and emotion theory:* See, for example, L. S. Greenberg, L. Rice, and R. Elliott (1993), *Facilitating Emotional Change: The Moment-by-Moment Process,* New York: Guilford; H. Leventhal (1984), "A Perceptual-Motor Theory of Emotion," in L. Berkowitz (Ed.), *Advances in Experimental Social Psychology* (pp. 117–182), New York: Academic Press.

P. 110, *emotionally powerful experiences still create nonverbal representations in emotional memory:* See, for example, L. S. Greenberg and J. D. Safran (1984), "Integrating Affect and Cognition: A Perspective on the Process of Therapeutic Change," *Cognitive Therapy and Research, 8*(6), 559–578; H. Leventhal (1982), "The Integration of Emotion and Cognition: A View from the Perceptual-Motor Theory of Emotion," in M. S. Clarke and S. T. Fiske (Eds.), *Affect and Cognition: The 17th Annual Carnegie Symposium on Cognition* (pp. 121–156), Hillsdale, NJ: Erlbaum.

P. 113, *General patterns of organization of constructs, or "core ordering processes," are important both in clinical practice and in constructivist theory and research:* See, for example, V. F. Guidano and G. A. Liotti (1983), *Cognitive Processes and Emotional Disorders,* New York: Guilford; V. F. Guidano and G. A. Liotti (1985), "A Constructivist Foundation for Cognitive Therapy," in M. J. Mahoney and A. Freeman (Eds.), *Cognition and Psychotherapy* (pp. 101–142), New York: Plenum.

P. 118, *"The idea that survives . . . that does not survive,":* J. Bogdan, "Family Organization as an Ecology of Ideas," p. 387.

P. 118, *an extension of the seminal ideas of Bateson:* G. Bateson, *Steps to an Ecology of Mind* (pp. 279–308), New York: Ballantine.

P. 118, *an application of Whitehead's logical types:* A. N. Whitehead and B. Russell (1913), *Principia Mathematica,* 3 vols., Cambridge, Cambridge University Press.

P. 118, *the concept of second-order change:* P. Watzlawick, J. Weakland, and

R. Fisch (1974), *Change: Principles of Problem Formation and Problem Resolution*, New York: W. W. Norton. It was these writers who influentially applied the phrases "first-order change" and "second-order change" to psychotherapy, having transferred them from the systems theory of W. R. Ashby. See W. R. Ashby (1952), *Design for a Brain*, New York: Wiley.

P. 119, *parallel distributed processing:* See, for example, J. A. Fodor (1983), *The Modularity of Mind*, Cambridge, MA: MIT/Bradford Books; P. Johnson-Laird (1988), *The Computer and the Mind*, Cambridge, MA: Harvard University Press.

P. 119, *replaced by an understanding of the* emotion scheme: See, for example, U. Neisser (1976), *Cognition and Reality*, San Francisco: W. H. Freeman; J. Pascual-Leone (1991), "Emotions, Development, and Psychotherapy," in J. D. Safran and L. S. Greenberg (Eds.), *Emotion, Psychotherapy and Change* (pp. 302–335), New York: Guilford; F. C. Bartlett (1932), *Remembering*, Cambridge, MA: Cambridge University Press; J. Piaget (1970), *Structuralism*, New York: Basic Books; J. Piaget (1985), *The Equilibration of Cognitive Structures: The Central Problem of Intellectual Development*, Chicago: University of Chicago Press.

P. 119, *Gazzaniga reviewed . . . in his 1985 book*, The Social Brain: M. Gazzaniga (1985), *The Social Brain*, New York: Basic Books.

PP. 119–120, *"Interpreting our behaviors . . . or more covert actions":* Gazzaniga, *The Social Brain*, p. 74.

P. 120, *"can compute, remember, feel emotion, and act":* Gazzaniga, *The Social Brain*, p. 86.

P. 120, *"is committed to the task of interpreting . . . It is a uniquely human endeavor.":* Gazzaniga, *The Social Brain*, p. 80.

P. 120, *"brain modularity . . . has a real anatomical basis":* Gazzaniga, *The Social Brain*, p. 128.

P. 120, *In more recent studies by other researchers:* See, for example, M. I. Posner and M. E. Raichle (1994), *Images of Mind*, San Francisco: W. H. Freeman; M. E. Raichle (1994), "Visualizing the Mind," *Scientific American, 240*(4), 58–64.

CHAPTER 4

Radical Inquiry: The Stance

> *. . . the inquiry of truth, which is the love-making, or*
> *wooing of it,*
> *the knowledge of truth, which is the presence of it,*
> *and the belief of truth, which is the enjoying of it,*
> *is the sovereign good of human nature.*
> FRANCIS BACON, *Of Truth*

The goal of radical inquiry is for the therapist to very efficiently gain lucid clarity into the emotional truth of the symptom—that is, the client's unconscious, pro-symptom position. With that clarity comes clarity into how the problem can be experientially transformed and resolved. The positions studied in earlier chapters were those of the *client*; now it is the position or stance from which the *therapist* works that is our focus. Chapter Five then details a wide range of specific techniques that presuppose the stance described here.

Stance refers to the presuppositions and intentions that a therapist brings to each session, defining what therapy is, what it can achieve, how to carry it out, and how long it will take. The therapist's stance is, in other words, his or her construction of psychotherapy.

The stance of radical inquiry has a number of defining features that operate together as a methodology:

- Assumption of immediate accessibility
- Active intentionality
- Powerlessness
- Assumption of coherence

- Experiential-phenomenological discovery and verification of constructs
- Anthropologist's view
- Freedom to clarify

These components of stance developed in our work as an evolving synthesis of many influences. The first three of these items, as well as the attention to stance itself, reflect most importantly the influence of Robert Shaw, M.D., director of the Family Institute of Berkeley. His insistence upon responding to clients from self rather than from theory, upon grappling with the therapist's own limiting presuppositions, and upon the possibility of rapidly restructuring the client's experience of the problem, along with his view that therapy should be noneffortful and nurturing for the therapist, helped shape our early therapeutic vision into one that developed over time into the approach we now call depth-oriented brief therapy.

Assumption of Immediate Accessibility

Unconscious material and unconscious process are much more close at hand and accessible than is commonly believed—even by many therapists. The fact that a person always avoids looking at something does not mean that this something is inaccessible or far away. Fully unconscious constructions that have been generating symptoms for decades can be brought to light quite rapidly, often in a single session of highly focused, experiential work, as examples in previous chapters have shown.

However, a therapist will not try to accomplish something that he or she does not believe is possible. The therapist will do what it takes to gain rapid experiential access to a deeply unconscious pro-symptom position *only* if the therapist presupposes the immediate accessibility of this unconscious construction. The rapid resolutions demonstrated in earlier chapters were possible only because of the therapist's assumption of immediate accessibility.

The traditional view in depth psychotherapy is that the cause of the client's symptoms are experiences and conditions in the dark past, in childhood, and that successful therapy therefore requires an objective, factual reconstruction and analysis of these conditions. The constructivist view in depth-oriented brief therapy is that in response to childhood experiences, the client formed constructions of reality that he or she still carries and applies, so they are *present* constructions of reality, and they are therefore accessible. In this view there is nothing underlying a client's problems but a phenomenology of *present* cognitions, emotions, and somesthetics, conscious and unconscious. The therapist does not need to find out factually what happened in the past in order to accurately elicit these current constructs.

In DOBT this is not just a semantic or philosophical position. It is a view that profoundly expands the therapist's perception of what is actually within reach right here, right now, in this very session. From this perspective it becomes natural to approach every session—in fact, every response to the client—as having the very real and immediate potential to produce deep change in the problem, because the psychological elements necessary for such a transformation are always present and available. The therapist's conviction regarding this *principle of immediate accessibility* is perhaps the most fundamental basis for carrying out radical inquiry.

With this stance, what the therapist is assuming can happen in the present session will be much more, and of a much deeper or substantive nature, than what the client is assuming can happen. In gentle but persistent ways the therapist invites the client to take another step, and then another, down into previously unattended emotional truths and constructions of personal meaning relevant to the problem, at all times remaining highly sensitive to any signs from the client that his or her tolerance for contacting new or difficult material is being reached. What we stated in Chapter Two bears repeating: it should always be the *client's* current capacity, not the therapist's assumptions, that limits what can happen in the session.

From the start of therapy, then, the therapist is *always* on the lookout for possible signs of a pro-symptom position and actively inquires into each possibility that appears. The therapist's assumption of immediate accessibility operates as though he or she is constantly guided by these questions: Given what I now know of the client's worlds of meaning, what is the unacknowledged area or theme of meaning that seems most likely to be requiring the existence of the symptom? What next move could I make that would most directly draw the client into attending to that area of meaning, experiencing it consciously, and finding out for himself whether, and how, that region of meaning makes the symptom important to have?

An example is the therapist's response to a thirty-year-old woman who was plagued by continuous restlessness and compulsive activity, which always destroyed any sense of satisfaction in her interests or relationships. The therapist learned in passing in the first session that at age six there was the sudden death of her father, whom she dearly loved and who was her only source of palpable affectional warmth. No outward process or expression of grieving occurred in the family. At eight she gained a stepfather who was emotionally abusive, and in her teens she nearly killed herself through drug abuse. The therapist, thinking from the start in terms of finding the pro-symptom reality in which the symptom is purposeful and necessary to have, immediately understood this woman's restlessness and manic activity as a protective action—but protecting against what emotional wound or vulnerability? The strongest candidate, given what had so far emerged, certainly was the death of her beloved father, though the client in no way emphasized this or identified it as a focus of therapy. The therapist felt most interested in seeing if her manic patterns were her lifelong protective action against feeling her enormous, disallowed pain over the loss of her father. Guided by the spirit of the questions in the preceding paragraph, the therapist devised a simple experiential probe, intended to bring her directly to the emotional truth of the symptom: he asked her to visualize her father and, when his image was sufficiently evoked, to try out saying to him, simply, "Daddy, I miss you."

Doing this, the client immediately precipitated the most intense feelings of grief, anguish, and anger, the avoidance of which had formed her personality and divorced her from her interior life for twenty-five years. In the next session she described unexpected relief in a long-standing jaw problem, saying, "I've always just had that pain and figured, just learn to live with it. I never had an even bite. Well, in this last week I finally have an even bite. It's amazing . . . my jaw has released." The full processing of the father-related feelings and meanings, and the reorientation to sweeping changes in her experience of self as a *feeling* self, required twelve sessions spanning almost nine months. Her tormenting restlessness and compulsive activity completely subsided (manifesting, for example, in the emergence of a genuine desire—instead of the prior manic disinclination—to spend "quality time" with her two-year-old daughter). In addition, a wide range of unexpected changes spontaneously occurred, including the emergence of a "rock-solid self-confidence" at work, the cessation of extreme and childish moodiness and neediness with her husband, and an entirely new empathy and emotional responsiveness to her two sisters.

As this example shows, assuming immediate accessibility means knowing that seemingly buried constructions are actually close at hand, and seemingly locked constructions open easily and immediately when a fitting key is used.

Active Intentionality

Beyond assuming that powerful, unconscious, symptom-generating material can actually be contacted and transformed in this very session—from the first session—*active intentionality* is the therapist's total readiness and *intention* for this to happen.

The reason this needs to be stated explicitly is that within the practice of psychotherapy there are numerous sources of motivation *not* to bring rapidly to light the full emotional truths generating the client's symptoms. The fact is, many therapists are deeply ambivalent over the prospect of doing rapidly effective work that ends in five, ten, or fifteen sessions.

Contrary to the widespread assumption in many schools of psychotherapy that emotional work necessarily makes therapy long and messy, our experience is that engaging the emotional aspects of the presenting problem accelerates the work and helps rapidly produce effective, lasting results. Conversely, *not* working with the emotional construction of the problem can result in therapy that is prolonged and not decisively effective.

Therapists have many different kinds of blocks to doing rapid, deep, effective work with clients. We have listed them below (our elaboration of other such lists previously published) to assist the reader in undertaking the position work of identifying and owning any unwillingness to work deeply and briefly.

- Belief that a therapeutic alliance cannot be formed rapidly

- Belief that working with the client's emotional wounds is a necessarily lengthy process
- Fear of the client's emotions
- Belief that having the client attend fully to painful emotion would be harmful
- The assumption, shared with the client, that the presenting symptom is completely valueless and undesirable, and that therapy should focus on empathically fostering the client's wish and ability to keep the symptom from happening
- Belief that longer therapy is intrinsically more effective than shorter therapy ("more is better") because brief is necessarily superficial and incomplete
- Belief that success in psychotherapy means thorough restructuring of character
- Overestimation of the role of character disorder in the client's presenting problems, combined with the belief that character disorders can never be changed quickly
- Overreliance on analysis and interpretation and underutilization of other therapeutic methodologies; overestimation of the therapeutic value of cognitive insight
- Belief that pathologizing is therapeutic, that categorizing the client according to pathology schemas can be healing
- Attachment to the aura of esoteric knowledge and power and to the stature conferred upon the therapist-priest, who is presumed to hold the keys to the "dark mysteries" of mental pathology
- Belief that patterns of cognition, emotion, and behavior that were formed over many years of developmental history necessarily take years to undo
- Belief that the unconscious is by its very nature too inaccessible and impenetrable to allow significant change to occur in brief therapy
- Unwillingness to let go of the client for financial reasons
- Unwillingness to let go of the client for emotional-countertransferential reasons (e.g., the therapist's need to be needed, fondness of client, desire to know the client's whole story, perfectionistic need to "finish" the work, fear of being seen as rejecting, and so on)

- Unwillingness to make the greater effort of sustaining the level of therapist activity and focus required in brief treatment
- Aversion to the greater visibility in brief treatment of the therapist's skill or lack of skill in assisting the client to alleviate the presenting symptom(s)
- Loyalty to mentors and training experiences supporting a longer-term paradigm
- Belief that being active and directive is necessarily too leading and impinging and results only in transferential compliance, hostility, or resistance
- Belief that without the therapist's mostly silent, impassive, nondirective acceptance, the client cannot project a full transference, and therefore there can be no corrective emotional experience
- Belief that the transference and its interpretation provide the only reliable way to access the client's real issues
- Belief that clients do not already possess the capacities or resources needed to dispel the presenting problem and that the therapist must supply them

We will not elaborate here on the fallacious nature of many items in the list, because the material we present throughout this book serves as our refutation of them. However, one of the items—fear of clients' intensely felt emotional states—warrants comment here because of its prevalence.

If you fear your clients' emotions, you will not conduct radical inquiry. You will not head straight for emotional truth. That is what radical inquiry is: heading straight for the full emotional truth of the symptom. Emotional truth does not *necessarily* show up in the form of florid, overpowering emotion, but it might, or it might contain extremely dire, seemingly unworkable content having to do with themes of hopelessness, hate, intensely felt worthlessness, anger, grief, terror, despair, and loneliness.

If you fear your clients' emotions, you will also not do position work. In position work, when an important element of emotional truth is found and felt by the client, the therapist keeps the client right there, rooted to the spot, and stays *in* it with the client, *without trying to make anything else happen.* The therapist does nothing except saturate the client's awareness with the meanings, atmosphere, and feelings of this previously unconscious position. What to do next in the work becomes clear by *staying there* and taking stock of the emotional landscape *from* this new position, not by dashing off of it. To allow the client's attention to come up and away from a newly contacted emotional truth too soon is to have a lapse in active intentionality and to collude with the client's wish to avoid the experience.

For some therapists, dread of clients' emotions stems from the presupposition that intense, dire emotions are irrational and too refractory to change and would therefore be more powerful than the therapy is. The therapist fears not being able to respond effectively to such emotions and failing as therapist. Also, the therapist may carry the prevailing cultural view that attending fully to painful emotion is destructive, when in fact it is healing when done properly.

All such fears indicate that the therapist needs focused training in experiential emotional process. Many therapeutic modalities that developed in reaction (we would say overreaction) to psychoanalytic and psychodynamic approaches threw out the gold with the sludge and removed emotion from the focus of therapeutic attention. Consequently, many therapists, prepared neither by professional training nor by their own families of origin to be at home in the emotional process, are understandably anxious and avoidant in relation to it. However, to work without facility and comfort with the emotional component of therapeutic change is to severely limit the efficiency and effectiveness of the work, as well as the depth of resolution achieved. This deficit of skill is not only remediable but also most rewarding to remedy, both professionally and personally.

We are aware of only one adverse effect that could follow radical inquiry. This occurs with some clients who are survivors of severe childhood abuse *and* who have an unconscious position that is fiercely dedicated to preventing awareness of the memory of the traumas. To protect against these terrifying and extremely painful memories becoming accessible, this position may respond to initial steps of inquiry (whether radical or conventional) by inflicting severe disincentives to any further incursion toward the emotional truth, in the form of intense psychogenic pain, self-mutilation, or compulsive behaviors that produce emotional oblivion (binge eating, drinking, manic activity, and so forth). Any such responses to radical inquiry are important signals to the therapist to first establish communication and a working alliance with the protective position before proceeding further toward the central emotional truth of the abuse.

Bear in mind that radical inquiry does not mean *aggressive* inquiry, as is quite clear in our many clinical examples. It is active and persistent but never pushes beyond the client's current capacities or limits. The therapist is fully responsive to all such signals. (In Chapter Five we focus on how the therapist responds to client resistance during radical inquiry.)

Many clinicians are skeptical of the two basic requirements for making in-depth use of the emotional features of the problem in *brief* therapy: rapid trust building and rapid evocation and transformation of relevant emotional states. Many do not believe that trust can develop in the therapist-client relationship quickly enough for brief therapy to include meaningful emotional work, and many believe that even if trust *could* be developed quickly, there still is not enough time in brief therapy to carry out a process of deep emotional work.

Arguing theoretically about these biases is futile. With the great majority of clients who come through our doors, neither of these conditions is a problem. Chapters One and Two gave detailed examples of emotionally deep work occurring very rapidly. Certainly, with some clients this will not be possible, but for the great majority it *is* possible to do deep, transformative emotional work briefly. For the therapist's beliefs to rule this out is a great disservice to clients.

We know of only two ways to make sense of any therapist's insistence that, in general, it is not possible for trust to develop fast enough to allow for deep emotional work in brief therapy: either the therapist is a hyperpathologizer who believes all clients in fact have character disorders, or the therapist's personal qualities and manner are exceptionally anticonducive to emotional openness and trust, resulting in the observation that it regularly takes many sessions before clients trust enough to get near their feelings. (In a remarkably candid and valuable self-exposé, psychotherapist Richard Schwartz describes his discovery of how his therapeutic stance was having just such a trust-inhibiting effect; it is recommended reading.)

Clients are exquisitely sensitive to therapist fears. In DOBT, radical inquiry itself is the trust builder, the clear signal that we are ready to go to the emotional truth and have it emerge, whatever it is, and that we are safe presences for that to occur. In radical inquiry, the therapist's attitude is so respectful of the client's expression and demonstrates such palpable *interest* in the more deeply felt aspects of the client's lived experience that emotional trust develops readily in most cases.

As with the assumption of immediate accessibility, the purpose of active intentionality is to eliminate the barriers that the *therapist* might unknowingly place in the way of deep, transformative work occurring as rapidly as it could.

With active intentionality, the therapist forms every next response as a best effort at shaping the key that could access the emotional truth of the symptom and create a breakthrough.

The assumption that each session has the potential to transform the problem significantly—and the intention for this to actually take place—has a direct implication for the manner of scheduling sessions. When and whether to schedule a subsequent session can be decided only at the end of the present session, once therapist and client see what best suits the client's state and process in effect at that point. The therapist schedules no more than the next session, one session at a time, and at the end of each session makes a joint decision with the client whether to meet again in one, two, or more weeks or on an as-needed basis when and if the client calls, or to declare the problem resolved with no view toward future meetings. This arrangement helps prepare the client for the end of therapy from the start, and it communicates to the client the therapist's stance that every session can produce an important result that changes the situation substantially.

Powerlessness

Paradoxically, the therapist's base of effectiveness in DOBT lies in knowing that he or she has *zero* power to make the client change. It is the client who is the real agent of change, and for therapeutic efficacy the therapist is totally reliant on client motivation.

Therefore, requiring the client to be the source of his or her own motivation for change is another fundamental element of the therapist's stance.

The therapist shows full interest and involvement in the client's work but does not attempt to supply initiative or motivation. If a client appears to lack motivation for change, the therapist can overtly use his or her own powerlessness to therapeutic advantage with such comments as "A therapist can't bring about a change for someone who doesn't actually want it for himself. I have no power at all to create a change for you. *You* have that power, not me. I can help you make a change you actually want, but I *can't* help you make a change you *don't* actually want. I feel that whatever you want or don't want is a valid, legitimate choice. But we need to look at whether it makes sense for you to be here, seeing me."

Therapy will fail if a client does not have real motivation to change. The therapist must be absolutely clear about this and must require real motivation from the client as a precondition for beginning and then for continuing the therapy process. The therapist should be ready to resign, without blaming or judging the client, if he or she fundamentally lacks motivation to change—even if a couple's marriage falls apart, or somebody might start drinking again, or someone might go back to jail.

Furthermore, by staying on his or her own side of the motivational boundary—that is, by not trying to supply motivation that should be coming from the client—the therapist consistently maintains a noneffortful stance that avoids strain and burnout. If the therapist is unwilling to assume and maintain a zero-power position and is straining to supply the motivation for the work, this indicates that the therapist's own needs or anxieties are shaping the therapy in counterproductive ways.

Assumption of Coherence

The practical methodology for carrying out radical inquiry derives from this fundamental assumption of coherence: *Every activity of the mind, conscious and unconscious, occurs coherently, according to the mind's own current constructions of meaning, in a purposeful attempt to satisfy desires and interests established by those constructions of meaning.*

Here "every activity of the mind" means everything we experience and do, including, of course, clients' presenting symptoms. This assumption of coherence is the lens through which the therapist views the emerging picture of the client's various constructions of reality; it guides and organizes the therapist's understanding of the client's positions and how they operate.

The assumption of coherence provides the central logic for radical inquiry, as follows: To rapidly and accurately find the unconscious, pro-symptom position generating the presenting symptom, the shortest path lies through the central question, *What position or construction of meaning exists that makes the symptom more important to have than not to have?*

In this view, the presenting symptom does not signify that the client's psyche is out of control or defective. The psyche all along remains coherent and completely *in* control of producing or not producing the symptom. Furthermore, the nature and form of the symptom itself is coherently determined by the psyche; it is not random or chaotic in the least. The symptom seems senseless, out of control, and chaotic only from the client's *conscious* position. With real clarity into the version of reality in the client's unconscious, pro-symptom position, the symptom is revealed to be a coherent feature of that version of reality, and to be more important to have than not to have, even with the pain or limitation it brings. For the therapist to approach the client's problem with this understanding from the outset proves to be a "master key" for unlocking it.

The psyche behaves quite contrary to common sense, in that it adheres to its present solutions to perceived problems with indifference to the pain these solutions (symptoms) cause the conscious personality. The client's suffering due to the symptom should not in itself lead the therapist into believing that client's governing emotional position is to be rid of the symptom. The therapist, while empathizing accurately with the painfulness of the symptom for the client, knows a priori that a powerful part of the client's *unconscious mind regards the symptom as good, needed, meaningful.

Once the emotional truth and coherent personal meaning of the symptom are in plain view, the therapist accords full validity and dignity to the newly recognized needs and themes involved. In thus reframing to the emotional truth of the symptom, the therapist reframes to sense and valid personal meaning—the hidden sense of how the symptom has been the client's way of striving to meet those important needs and themes, though at a cost that motivates him or her to finding a new way to do this. Throughout this work, the therapist, knowing that it is the client's own formidable power to create, hold, and change positions that determines whether the symptom is maintained or changed, never views an adult client as *actually* helpless, even when empathizing with the client as *feeling* helpless.

We recognize one important exception to the stance just described—the case in which the presenting symptom involves overt harm done to another and an attitude consisting of malevolent intent, flagrant exploitation of a power differential, and/or absence of empathy for suffering inflicted. When these antisocial positions *are* involved, we *do* hold a value judgment of them as fundamentally unacceptable, although the degree and manner of expressing this to the client is decided on a case-by-case basis.

The concept of the symptom's coherence within the operation of the psyche is not a new idea in the history of psychotherapy. In various forms it can be traced back to Freud. More recently, family therapist and systems theorist Paul Dell made the case that a constructivist view of coherence should replace the conceptually flawed and *ad hoc* concepts of homeostasis and resistance. What is new in depth-oriented brief therapy is the very deliberate, pervasive, persistent, and precise use we make of our assumption of coherence, in every session, for working in depth to find the elements of meaning that are generating the presenting problem, and for getting rapid results.

In practice, the central question for radical inquiry into a pro-symptom position (*What construction exists that makes the symptom more important to have than not to have?*) gets more specific and branches into three guiding forms or variations:

1. What does the symptom do for the client that is valued or needed in the client's world? How, and in what context, does the symptom express or pursue a valid, important need or priority?
2. How is the symptom an actual success for the client, rather than a failure? To what problem is the symptom a solution, or an attempt at a solution?

3. What are the unwelcome or dreaded consequences that would result from living *without* the symptom? What happens if the symptom doesn't?

Seeing the symptom as having deep emotional value, as meeting important needs, as being a success or a solution to an important problem, or as preventing something unwelcome from happening is not a trick. This is seeing and acknowledging the symptom in its truest significance within the coherent psychic life of the client, which is why this approach accesses, engages, and transforms the deeper sources of the symptom so directly and effectively.

Collectively, these three lines of inquiry embody the assumption of coherence and they define, and keep the therapist on, the shortest path to the emotional truth of the symptom. Their utility cannot be overstated. *All radical inquiry into pro-symptom positions consists of the experiential pursuit of one of these lines of inquiry,* adapted to the immediate therapeutic situation in any way the therapist deems expeditious (specific techniques for this are the subject of the next chapter). The therapist starts from the presenting symptom and tracks down its pro-symptom emotional truth through one or more of these three lines of radical inquiry.

Experiential-Phenomenological Discovery and Verification of Constructs

As the clinical material in earlier chapters has indicated, there are many different techniques and types of therapist-client interaction that elicit the pro-symptom material that answers the above three guiding questions of radical inquiry, without ever asking those questions explicitly. Whether or not these key questions are explicitly asked, and regardless of which specific techniques are used to pursue them, what *is* necessary is to work *experientially* and *phenomenologically*. In DOBT, this commitment to working experientially and phenomenologically is as much a matter of basic stance as of technique.

To have a client *experientially* find an answer to any one of the three guiding questions is to have the client discover and reveal some part of the emotional truth of the symptom—not speculatively and not by talking *about* the problem, but through the client's direct, subjective encounter with his own previously unattended presuppositions, emotional wounds, and protective actions. As described in Chapter One, a step of radical inquiry is designed so that *the only way for the client to respond is to have an experience* of some aspect of the hidden constructions of meaning—the unrecognized emotional truths—involved in creating and maintaining the problem.

Experiential does not necessarily mean that something dramatic or emotional happens. In radical inquiry it means simply that the client encounters, experiences, and reveals his or her own constructs of reality involved in the presenting problem, as our clinical examples have illustrated. Even to encounter and own a predominantly *cognitive* construct, such as a previously unrecognized "belief," is an experiential event, because any such belief is not a dry, impersonal fact but is seeped with personal meaning and emotional significance.

In working with trainees who are making the transition to DOBT from a more traditional, interpretation-oriented approach, we find that a special emphasis on working experientially tends to be needed. To work experientially is to draw the client into focusing and keeping attention on his or her actual, in-the-moment experiencing, as distinct from having attention on ideas *about* present (or past) experiencing of the problem. For example, if a woman in therapy is talking about her problem of interacting with her boss at work, the therapist can ask her to imagine being there at work and to notice and describe what she is experiencing, in her body as well as emotionally and cognitively, as the boss walks into her office and the problematic pattern occurs. Doing this, she says, "I'm starting to feel *small* and *scared.*" She and the therapist now begin to have access to the problem itself. In the same way that a sculptor needs to have the block of stone in the room in order to work with it, and cannot do so by talking or thinking *about* the stone, a therapist needs to have the client's experience of the problem actually present in the room. This is what working experientially does. It is only through *experiencing* that the client *actually accesses the constructions of reality involved in generating the problem.* Constructions of reality are accessed by experiencing them, not by talking *about* them.

The key to being a therapist who can effectively *evoke experience* in clients is to stay very close to the current point of maximal poignance or felt meaning in the client's account of the problem. In attempting to follow as direct a trajectory as possible into the heart of the emotional truth of the symptom, at each step the therapist sensitively places attention into the most meaning-laden and/or feeling-laden elements of the problem currently in the field of view. A client with a presenting symptom of uncontrollable, violent rage mentions in passing in the first session that in childhood, the way parents and teachers always reacted made her feel she was "hit by a meteor." The therapist recognizes the intensity and importance of the emotional themes tacitly referenced by that casual phrase and begins to unpack them and make them explicit and central, saying, "A meteor comes with *tremendous* suddenness and force. One moment everything seems fine, and the next, you're violently smashed, cratered. Is *that* how it feels to you?" Then follows a pointed recognition that meteors out in space are random, but meteors between *people* seem aimed and hurled, so it feels like *attack*. Finally the therapist summarizes what he understands, saying, "So, as a girl you experienced the world of people as a very hostile, dangerous, frightening world of sudden, violent attacks that kept smashing you deeply." The client is significantly moved; even this much recognition of unattended emotional truth might in itself be a healing validation (and self-validation) for her.

The therapist deliberately uses a vividness, even a starkness, of phrasing that does justice to—yet does not exaggerate—the actual intensity and passion of the emotional truth of the client's lived experience. The client has a habit of attenuating and diluting these deeply dimensional emotional meanings in her life, and she needs the therapist to be unstinting in recognizing and bluntly naming the emotional truth of her experience. This close-in tracking of the themes of maximum meaning or poignance is experienced by the client as a deeply empathic interest on the part of the therapist, and it naturally moves the client toward *experiencing* important emotional realities rather than merely conceptualizing or talking *about* the problem.

A useful exercise for trainees is to undertake the practice of converting each in-session understanding or interpretation that they would normally state conceptually to the client into an evocative response that will elicit direct experience of emotional meaning in the client.

A somewhat more subtle requirement than the need for *experiential* work, but an equally stringent one, is the requirement that the work also be phenomenological. This means that the therapist works entirely within the terms of the client's own constructions of meaning and does not subordinate the client's constructions to any that the therapist brings, including psychological theories and diagnostic labels. DOBT's conceptual scheme—a scheme only of how the client's construction is internally organized—has no external explanatory content claimed to be senior to anything the client can experience as true for himself.

The therapist's attention during a session is fully absorbed in the client's present experiencing and in the moment-to-moment task of responding to the client in ways that bring about radical inquiry (revelation of structures of meaning) or experiential shift (transformation of structures of meaning). The clarity into the client's constructions of reality that is gained by the therapist in this absorbed mode of attention is not to be confused with the formulation of hypotheses from an "objective" theoretical standpoint. Jealousy of a sibling would not, for example, be interpreted as a competitive striving or as having a family-systemic function; instead, it is worked with strictly in terms of the person's actual feelings, images, losses, gains, and other construed meanings in relation to the sibling.

Of course, as we have said, there are moments in therapy when it is supremely valuable to the client for the therapist to voice what he or she understands of the client's emotional truth. Whether this is done for the simple purpose of verification or as a way of inviting the client to place awareness into particular constructs of meaning, this articulation is always presented (1) free of any references to theoretical or diagnostic categories and labels and (2) in a way that makes it clear that *the therapist is submitting this view to the client for his or her experiential verification of accuracy.* In depth-oriented brief therapy, it is the client who is always the judge and jury regarding emotional truth. The therapist never imposes his or her concept of the client's emotional truth. It is the *client's* governing construction that the therapist is attempting to articulate, and so it is only the client who can experientially recognize the accuracy of that description and subjectively endorse it as "true." Therefore, the therapist checks with the client frequently regarding the accuracy of the therapist's understanding and the fit or tailoring of in-session activities suggested by the therapist. When the client indicates that the therapist has the wrong idea, the therapist is glad to be set on the right track by the client's corrective feedback. The therapist's willingness to be corrected is very important to clients, because it signals respect for the fact that only the client could possibly be the final authority as to what is true for him or her.

To rely on interpretation is to rely on the client's capacity for conceptual insight, which can be a severely limiting factor. Experiential-phenomenological work, in contrast, does not encounter this barrier. While only some people are conceptually insightful, *everyone* lives and moves in some experiential reality and is subjectively reachable through the medium of that experiential reality. Everyone who has a symptom also has a pro-symptom position, and the client's own pro-symptom position is already, *through the symptom itself,* in an experiential relationship with his or her conscious position and can be *further* elicited experientially.

Working phenomenologically means becoming comfortable with the expectation that "everybody is an exception," in therapist William O'Hanlon's words, that idiosyncrasy of symptom production is the rule, that good psychotherapy is never formulaic. To embrace the fully phenomenological approach of DOBT is always to expect to have the client show *you,* the therapist, where the emotional truth of the symptom lies—not the other way around.

In DOBT it therefore becomes quite clear to the client that the therapist regards the client's own inner knowings as both reliable and highly important for resolving the problem. This in itself has much therapeutic impact for some clients, ushering them into trusting their own experience and their natural intelligence, and creating a sense that for them simply to be themselves in relationship is sufficient, viable, and gratifying.

Anthropologist's View

In therapy, the client's behavior—including verbal expression—always contains hidden doorways that open quite directly onto the unconscious, pro-symptom position(s) sought through radical inquiry. However, these doorways are perceptible to the therapist only if he or she is observing in the way an anthropologist does:

with no assumption of already knowing what anything means. Maintaining the stance of *anthropologist's view* means that when you first hear your client utter familiar-sounding words and phrases such as "angry," "happy," "having a shared direction," or "depression" you do not assume that you know what these words *mean* to your client, or that the meaning is inferable. You are aware that you must pursue more specific information about what your client means by these familiar-sounding words. That is an anthropologist's view, and it is vitally important for radical inquiry. A simple example will illustrate why.

In a session of couples therapy, a woman client describes her husband's behavior and then says, "When he talks to me like that, it really hurts." Suppose that as therapist, I then have a vivid sense that how he talks to her would really hurt *me,* too. Now I am assuming I know what she means by "hurt," and *because* I am assuming I know what she means, right there my inquiry stops going deeper. Actually, I am now just one question away from a breakthrough in the problem, but I never ask that next question because I am assuming I know what she means by "hurt."

However, if I am maintaining an anthropologist's view, I am aware that I do *not* yet know what she means by "hurt," despite how strongly *I* relate to that word in this situation. So I *ask* her what she means. I say, for example, "What about the way he talks to you is hurtful for you?" My aim in asking this question is this: Right behind that familiar-sounding word are the specific cognitive, emotional, and somesthetic structures that comprise the state she calls "hurt." Suppose in unconscious, perceptual-emotional memory she has a construction of reality in which a man talking to a woman that way *means* he will then leave her. Suppose this emotional template is closely linked to unhealed, unconscious emotional wounds in relation to her father, wounds that flare with pain and fear when her husband talks to her that way.

All this being the case, this woman used her word "hurt" to refer to exactly those hidden structures of meaning and feeling, as if everyone has those particular constructs and as if everyone is referring to those when they use the word "hurt" in this sort of situation. As the therapist I do not yet know *what* constructs she is implicitly indicating when she says "hurt," but I do know that she *is* referring to a private world of meaning in that utterance. And I know that revealing those hidden constructs and their operation is usually the beginning of a breakthrough or resolution. The question "What about the way he talks to you is hurtful for you?" directs her to *find and reveal* those hidden keys to what she experiences.

I persist in that inquiry until it is completely clear to me what goes on in her in response to her husband's words that results in the state she calls "hurt." Then I work directly with these emotional and other constructs driving her response to her husband.

In order to resolve a presenting problem rapidly, deeply, and effectively, the initially hidden substructure of the problem needs to be made clear very quickly. To that end, maintaining an anthropologist's view is crucial, because then the therapist is in a position to open doors that appear, fleetingly, in the guise of familiar-sounding words like "hurt" and then unpack the important, reality-forming constructs from the dark room right behind that door.

Anthropologist's view is the *sine qua non* for accurate empathy. Without this, the therapist is experiencing a pseudo-empathy based on projecting his own meanings onto the client's nominalizations and is empathizing only with these therapist-generated meanings. This actually is the therapist's *self*-empathy, a kind of counter-transference in the guise of empathy for the client's experience, an actuality still unknown to the therapist.

Anthropologist's view is based on the therapist holding a constructivist conception of how people know to say what they say. In the example just considered, the therapist's entire approach is based on understanding that there is nothing to be taken for granted in how the woman arrives at saying "hurt" from hearing her husband speak to her in a certain way. She (unconsciously) processes that perception in specific, idiosyncratic ways that add up to how she *knows* to feel "hurt." This use of language to provide access to how a presupposition is creating perception is a distinctive feature of constructivist approaches, as theorist Robert Neimeyer observes:

> For the orthodox cognitive therapist, the meanings of the client's verbalizations are typically treated as unproblematic and literal. . . . Emotions are understood in equally straightforward fashion, as the result of one's cognitive appraisal of situations. . . . Influenced by a hermeneutic, phenomenological perspective, constructivists

characteristically inquire closely into personal meanings that form the subtext of the client's explicit statements (Kelly, 1955), making extensive use of metaphor . . . and idiosyncratic imagery.

Anthropologist's view may be summed up as a defining feature of radical inquiry in this way: During a therapy session, if that which is presented seems easy to understand and familiar, do not assume you already know what it is. Look closer. Have "beginner's mind." Do not assume your client's words mean what they mean to you. Burrow into meanings; get specific; require the client to get very specific, until the client's own meanings are clear, with nothing being read into them by you.

Anthropologist's view operates in close conjunction with the next and last element in the stance of radical inquiry: *freedom to clarify*.

Freedom to Clarify

As we begin describing each of the defining features of radical inquiry, we are tempted to write, "It's *this* one that is most important," which must mean that each is indeed indispensable. *Freedom to clarify*, however, *is* the most important, at least for therapists new to DOBT, because if the therapist does not assume this element of stance, none of the other aspects of radical inquiry will get a chance to operate.

Freedom to clarify means simply that in doing radical inquiry, you feel free to do *nothing* but seek the clarity you need—clarity into the hidden emotional truth that will make lucid sense of how and why the symptom or problem (1) makes complete psychological sense to have and (2) remains needed and therefore stuck.

Freedom to clarify means that as you persistently seek clarity, *you are unconcerned with changing the client, fixing the problem, or making the symptom stop happening.* You are attempting none of that. You are only going after the clarity you need into the hidden structure generating the presenting symptom. You are getting the client to lead you into his or her hidden architecture of meaning, and you are not trying to *change* that architecture, only to know it. Attempting to make the symptom stop happening before reaching clarity into its emotional truth short-circuits both radical inquiry and the achievement of experiential shift (a process that becomes a blind, hit-and-miss, lengthy, and ineffective attempt to change or override the client's pro-symptom position). In short, freedom to clarify is freedom from preoccupation with changing the client or the problem.

The client has already been trying hard to make the symptom *stop* happening without knowing *why* or *how* it happens. The proof that any overt, direct attempt to make the symptom stop isn't likely to work is the fact that the client is in your office. As was discovered over twenty years ago at the Mental Research Institute in Palo Alto, California, doing "more of the same" in that sense will actually have the effect of maintaining the symptom you are trying to help dispel. When the therapist fully accepts and embraces the fact that the path of greatest efficacy is *not* through trying to make the symptom stop, he or she goes a long way toward firmly establishing the freedom to clarify.

In DOBT the therapist regards the symptom as the visible point of access to some very important, very meaningful area in the client's experience. DOBT is highly effective at rapidly dispelling symptoms, yet the therapist's attitude is never one of rushing to get rid of the symptom but rather of wanting very much to receive the important message that the symptom is sending—the message being its emotional truth. So there is never an inclination to use a technique as a blind attempt to stop or block the symptom. (In cases involving real danger of great harm—violence, child abuse, or suicide—where a symptom *must* be stopped at once, we take gross, overt measures that are not "techniques," including when necessary physical separation, hospitalization, involvement of police or a child protective service, or massive intervention with extended family and friends.)

The underlying principle here is that by pursuing real clarity into the precise structure of the problem, effective ways to induce change will become apparent at the earliest possible moment.

When learning this approach, one of the main things that frees therapists to drop their habitual stance of attempting to make the symptom stop, and to take instead the stance of freedom to clarify, is the discovery of the richly therapeutic effects of the radical inquiry itself. Even though the therapist is not yet intending to produce important shifts for the client, radical inquiry is profoundly therapeutic. We conduct an extended dyadic exercise in freedom to clarify in some of our DOBT workshops, and in the debriefing after the practicum, invariably the comments from participants include surprised accounts of the therapeutic impact experienced by the "client" in being on the receiving end of the therapist's pursuit of nothing but his or her own clarity.

We find in our consultation work with therapists that the most common cause of the therapist feeling the work with a client is somehow *stuck* is the therapist's attempt to produce a change and get rid of symptoms without having first obtained enough clarity into the client's hidden position driving the symptom. When the therapist then shifts gears and focuses simply on getting sufficient clarity, *that* is the breakthrough, and the work with the client takes on a whole new character. The following short excerpt from a therapist's DOBT consultation session shows the contrasting stances very clearly. The therapist, consulting about her work with a couple, first described how the woman spent most of one session in an "emotional tantrum," which to the therapist seemed to be a very childish state. The consultant then had the therapist resume the session in imagination, with the couple in chairs in front of her. The consultant then coached the therapist.

Consultant: Ask her how old she feels.

Therapist: She says four.

Consultant: What do you want to say next?

Therapist: [Pause] I don't know. I'm at a loss.

Consultant: What are *you* feeling right now?

Therapist: A tense, almost urgent need to get her to be able not to go into being four. I want to stop her from doing that.

Consultant: What's it to you?

Therapist: I'm her therapist! I'm somehow failing if she keeps being four and acting like that!

Consultant: No you're not.

Therapist: I'm *not?*

Consultant: How about asking *her* if that pattern of reacting and feeling like she's four is something *she* wants to change?

Therapist: Oh. Right. God, what a relief.

Consultant: What's the relief?

Therapist: To remember that it's not up to me to *make* her change, or to want to. I was trying to get her *away* from her emotional truth of being four as fast as I could, but you reminded me just to stay right there *with* that emotional truth, and let *her* come to terms with it.

Consultant: Yes. Let's do a short role-play. You be her, I'll be the therapist. [To therapist who is now in the role of the female client] So, since you say that when you feel this way it feels like four, does it seem true to say that there's a four-year-old side of you that sometimes emotionally comes to the front?

Therapist: Well, I've never thought about it that way, but it seems true.

Consultant: Is that something you can live with, or is it something you want to change?

Therapist: I guess I ought to change it.

Consultant: Well, I'm asking if you *want* to change this pattern of how you sometimes react.

Therapist: Well, I don't know; it's such a new idea. I've never looked at this and seen it like this, or thought it *could* change.

Consultant: So then let's try something. Like many people do, you seem to have some old emotional hurts from childhood, from around four, that sometimes flare up in the present. I'm wondering if there's some-thing important you've believed or hoped your rela-tionship would do for this side of you. So, would you be willing to just *imagine* something for a minute or two? *Imagine* that you never again went into being four with your husband. *Imagine* that you stayed at your actual age, even when arguing and being very upset.

Therapist: [Pause] Ugg. That's hard. I couldn't carry on. Then it's between grown-ups.

Consultant: Good. Keep going. Keep seeing your husband. He's just said or done something that you're pretty upset about, and you stay grown-up as you feel this and respond to him.

Therapist: [Slowly, with eyes squinting] If—I stay grown-up—then he's—as right as I am, or I have to listen to *his* side, and he *might* be right, or at least as right as I am, and then I won't get to have my way. That's it: I don't want to let there be *any opening at all* for him having his way and me not having mine. I don't *want* it to be between equals.

Consultant: What makes that really important for you, to have him do just what *you* want?

Therapist: [Pause] 'Cause nobody ever did. Nobody ever did, and it's not fair, and actually I'm really angry about that.

Consultant: Does that mean that something you've really hoped for from your marriage is for your husband to set right that unfairness that you feel so angry about, that you suffered as a child, by him taking *seriously* what you want and *doing* what you want?

Therapist: [Popping out of the client role] You know, at that point, I couldn't keep being her. What you just said completely undid her ability to stay in her familiar view of reality.

Consultant: Yes. And what did I do, as the therapist, that had that effect?

Therapist: Let's see. [Pause] You know, I think all you did was ask me to see what it's like for me if I *don't* go into being four. And then what came up was—why I do it, because I could tell what I'm losing if I *don't* do it. And then you asked about setting right what happened as a child, and I felt like you'd gotten *under* me, like I was being scooped up.

Consultant: Yes, exactly. And I was just freely inquiring. I wasn't trying to make her change any of this, and yet look at how effective that was.

Therapist: But didn't you ask her to stop being four by asking her to stay grown-up?

Consultant: No. I was never trying to get her to be finished with the symptom. I was doing nothing but trying to make sense *for myself* of why the symptom is important to have. For that purpose I asked her to see what happens if she temporarily suspends it. So my experience was of zeroing in on what might be going on. If she then said, "Look, I *insist* on trying to get some man to give this four-year-old what she never got," that's OK with me, because it's *her* experiment with life, isn't it? I wouldn't feel I'd failed to change something I should've changed.

This transcript shows the difference between the stance of effortfully trying to stop the symptom and the stance of freedom to clarify, as well as the therapeutic effect of the therapist's clarity-seeking in itself.

Freedom to clarify allows the therapist to return to clarity-seeking as needed throughout the work with a client. The fact that the therapist is persistent and purposeful in pursuing the needed clarity in no way implies a hurried, aggressive, or businesslike manner. Usually our own styles are relaxed and gentle, but we stay very much on purpose. When clients ramble into detailed narrations that are not serving our need for clarity and are of unclear personal significance or relevance, we soon ask how this information is important or connects to the work. If it does not, we bring the focus back to genuine relevance, or focus on identifying the client's current need to ramble.

Freedom to clarify involves a kind of open space of inquiry, a capacity to approach and move through the session in a state of not-yet-knowing, or at least free of any fixed preconception of what will happen or how to understand the symptom. There is a degree of existential uncertainty in this not-yet-knowing that the therapist needs to be able to tolerate. The therapist's not-knowing is only on the level of *content* and is not a state of directionlessness, since the therapist is always working within DOBT's directional framework of moving from the symptom to the pro-symptom position that certainly is there to be found. During radical inquiry, the three shortest-path questions always serve as the therapist's orienting framework. However, the therapist does not pursue them in a linear attempt to *change* anything. They are the route to clarity only—insight into how the symptom is in fact more important to have than not to have.

The therapist also needs to feel comfortable in letting his or her not-yet-knowing be plainly visible to the client. The therapist's expertise does not depend on maintaining an image of all-knowing doctor or sage, but on being expert at discovering. For the therapist to allow his or her own efforts to achieve clarity to be visible to the client is in itself highly therapeutic in many cases, as an example of being fully at home with being only human. Overall, DOBT is a highly transparent psychotherapy. With few exceptions, generally all of the therapist's conceptualizations and methodology are visible or can be made visible to the client with no detriment to therapeutic efficacy, which is in marked contrast to strategic and transference-centered therapies.

Depending upon the work setting, the therapist may be working with a treatment plan or some diagnosis or theoretical view of the problem. This need not actually conflict with an in-session stance of not-yet-knowing. The therapist simply makes use of his or her own innate capacity to hold several different positions at once, and holds all such plans and labels lightly enough so that they do not prevent the pursuit and the emergence of a new clarity in this very session—a clarity that could revise everything and lead directly to a breakthrough.

What about moments when the therapist has no idea what to do next? If you do not know what to do next, it means only one thing: you are lacking clarity about something. Therefore, you drop down into your freedom to clarify: you *sit back* in your chair, you relax and pay attention to your own subjective sense of where you need more clarity. There is a faculty of your own mind that is always feeding you a felt sense of where to focus for the clarity you need—a kind of homing signal, a sense of psychological direction. However, that prompt or signal is lost in the noise of anxiety over finding a way to stop the symptom from happening, or over performing impressively as therapist.

About twenty years ago one of us attended a two-day workshop with James Simkin, one of the founding figures in Gestalt therapy. Right after he worked with someone on a very long, complex dream, another participant asked how he chose which among the many elements of the dream to work with. One expected Simkin to give some Gestalt-theoretic scheme for identifying the important elements. What he actually said was completely unexpected, producing a kind of shock, a little revolution in the mind. He said he followed his sense of interest. He managed somehow to convey that as the therapist, you can trust your own psyche to sense and let you know where the real action is in the client's process. You *feel* your interest, your attention, go to certain elements, and you follow that.

So, when at a loss in a session, that directional antenna, that nameless feeling of interest, will point you right into the area where it is important for you to get more clarity. It is necessary, though, to have full freedom to clarify, in order to be relaxed and attentive to this internal compass.

The therapist's subjective experience of interest, pointing his or her attention to certain areas of inquiry, can be understood as the therapist's use of self in the relationship with the client. This is an integral aspect of the freedom to clarify in radical inquiry. In this way the therapist can sometimes know to focus radical inquiry on key areas without cognitively knowing how he knows to focus there and can then converge very rapidly upon the emotional truth of the symptom.

There are two criteria for knowing when the needed degree of clarity, the terminus of radical inquiry, has been reached: (1) the emotional truth and psychological sense of the presenting symptom within the client's world is now transparent, and the creation of the symptom is no longer a mystery; (2) based on this clarity into the network of constructs that make the symptom important to have, one or more ways by which the client could resolve the problem are also now clear, and the stage is set for a process of experiential shift.

Summary

Without the assumption of immediate accessibility, the therapist would not attempt the rapid discovery of the client's hidden, symptom-generating constructions.

Without active intentionality, the therapist would not in fact do what it takes to meet the client in the emotional truth of the symptom time-effectively.

Without the stance of powerlessness, the therapist would attempt to provide motivation that must come from the client, interfering with the client's own relationship to change—a setup for ineffectual therapy and a sense of "failure" on the part of the client.

Without the assumption of coherence, the therapist would have to resort to external theories to make sense of the client's material and would miss its truest significance in the client's life.

Likewise, without experiential-phenomenological discovery and verification of constructs, the therapist would impose meanings from without, complicating and obstructing the therapeutic process in many ways, and would not usher the client into felt knowledge and direct possession of the meanings within.

Without anthropologist's view, the therapist would miss many easy openings and opportunities for quickly accessing the hidden constructions of meaning involved in the symptom.

Without freedom to clarify, the therapist would attempt to fix, cure, and change the client before reaching clear knowledge of how to do so, resulting in ineffectual, drifting, or coercive therapy, based more on therapist guesswork, theorizing, or countertransference than on having an accurate map of the client's construction of the problem.

With all these defining features of the stance of radical inquiry, the techniques detailed in the next chapter emerge as natural actions.

Notes

P. 127, *The inquiry of truth . . .:* F. Bacon, *Francis Bacon: The Essays or Counsels, Civil and Moral, of Francis Ld. Verulam, Viscount St. Albans* (p. 9), White Plains, NY: Peter Pauper Press.

P. 131, *other such lists previously published:* See, for example, M. F. Hoyt (1985), "Therapist Resistances to Short-Term Dynamic Psychotherapy," *Journal of the American Academy of Psychoanalysts, 13,* 93–112.

P. 134, *focused training in experiential emotional process:* Live training in the basic techniques of Gestalt therapy is of inestimable value for experiential emotional work.

P. 135, *before proceeding further toward the central emotional truth of the abuse:* See R. Schwartz (1992), "Rescuing the Exiles," *Family Therapy Networker,* 16(3), 33–37, 75.

P. 135, *In a remarkably candid and valuable self-exposé, psychotherapist Richard Schwartz . . .:* See previous citation.

P. 139, *coherence should replace the...concepts of homeostasis and resistance:*

P. Dell (1982), "Beyond Homeostasis: Toward a Concept of Coherence," *Family Process, 21,* 21–41. A more controversial, "radical constructivist" view of coherence is the concept of *structure determinism,* which is central to the biological theory of Humberto Maturana and Francisco Varela. Structure determinism emphasizes that the particular, coherent structure of the individual's knowledge-organizing system is the *sole* determinant of the individual's experience and response in all interactions with the environment. See, for example, H. R. Maturana & F. J. Varela (1987), *The Tree of Knowledge: The Biological Roots of Human Understanding,* Boston: New Science Library; and P. Dell (1985), "Understanding Bateson and Maturana: Toward a Biological Foundation for the Social Sciences," *Journal of Marital and Family Therapy, 11*(1), 1–20.

P. 144, *the expectation that "everybody is an exception":* W. H. O'Hanlon (1990), "Debriefing Myself," *Family Therapy Networker, 14*(2), 68.

PP. 146–147, *"For the orthodox cognitive therapist . . . and idiosyncratic imagery":* R. A. Neimeyer (1993), "An Appraisal of Constructivist Psychotherapies," *Journal of Consulting and Clinical Psychology, 61(2),* 224.

P. 147, *(Kelly, 1955):* G. Kelly (1955), *The Psychology of Personal Constructs,* New York: W. W. Norton.

P. 148, *maintaining the symptom you are trying to help dispel:* P. Watzlawick, J. Weakland, and R. Fisch (1974), *Change: Principles of Problem Formation and Problem Resolution,* New York: W. W. Norton.

CHAPTER 5

Radical Inquiry: Techniques

In sooth I know not why I am so sad.
It wearies me, you say it wearies you;
But how I caught it, found it, or came by it,
What stuff 'tis made of, whereof it is born,
I am to learn . . .
WILLIAM SHAKESPEARE, *The Merchant of Venice*

The client's presenting symptom is itself the first point of access to the unconscious constructions of meaning creating it. Radical inquiry therefore starts from the symptom as the chief "clue" or signpost of emergent meaning and tracks down the hidden position producing it.

The techniques that we describe in this chapter are those we have found, within our own styles of working, to be most often useful and effective for radical inquiry. Some of these techniques have been invented specifically for depth-oriented brief therapy; others are applications or variations of methods developed in other modalities of psychotherapy. As is true of constructivist approaches in general, depth-oriented brief therapy can integrate and coordinate the use of a wide range of therapeutic techniques. We emphasize, however, that taking the stance of radical inquiry (discussed in Chapter Four) is a far more important condition for success with DOBT than applying any specific techniques. We will often comment on how the use of a technique embodies the stance. There is no limit to the ways in which a therapist who has positioned him- or herself in the stance of radical inquiry can work for rapid, experiential discovery of hidden constructions of meaning.

In this chapter we also address resistance—how it is conceptualized in DOBT and how the therapist utilizes its occurrence as a valuable opening for radical inquiry.

By definition, all techniques for radical inquiry into a pro-symptom position are specific ways of finding answers to radical inquiry's central question or to any of its three concrete variations, which comprise the shortest path to the emotional truth of the symptom, and which we reproduce here for easy reference.

The central question or central logic is, What position or construction exists that makes the symptom more important to have than not to have? Its three variations are as follows:

1. What does the symptom do for the client that is valued or needed in the client's world? How, and in what context, does the symptom express or pursue a valid, important need or priority?
2. How is the symptom an actual success for the client, rather than a failure? To what problem is the symptom a solution, or an attempt at a solution?
3. What are the unwelcome or dreaded consequences that would result from living *without* the symptom? What happens if the symptom doesn't?

These questions serve more as internal guides for the therapist's attention and understanding than as point-blank questions to ask clients. The client's problem exists for the very reason that the answers to these questions are unconscious, and so clients tend to flounder or offer unuseful responses if asked such questions too soon, too directly, and too cognitively. If the therapist does wish at some point to ask one or more of these questions explicitly, it should be done in broadly suggestive terms, avoiding any one slant of meaning that rules out many others. For example, in a mock session a therapist-in-training asked question three of the client in this narrow form: "If you no longer got depressed, *what would go wrong?*" The arbitrary and too-specific phrasing "what would go wrong" did not capture the particular way being without depression would pose a difficulty for this client, and so she could not relate to the question. It proved more fruitful when the therapist revised the wording to "It will feel much better when you no longer feel depressed anymore, but at the same time, is there any way there might be some new, *unwelcome* effects, or some difficult side to it, when you no longer go into being depressed anymore?" (Notice that the therapist said "*when* you no longer" rather than "*if* you no longer," because *when* more effectively evokes imaginal experiencing, while *if* tends to invite intellectual speculation.) The client reflected and said, "Well, actually, now that you put it that way, I guess I'll have to do all kinds of hard things that now people don't expect me to do." The question in this form allows her pro-symptom position to begin to emerge. The therapist would now continue with radical inquiry to find out what about keeping others from expecting her to do "hard things" is so vital that it is worth being depressed.

However, most of the techniques described throughout this chapter are *implicit* ways to experientially evoke the answers to the shortest-path questions above. The names of these techniques and methods are:

- Creating collaboration
- Experiential questioning
- Serial accessing
- Imaginal interactive techniques
- Experiential dreamwork
- Sentence completion
- Viewing from a symptom-free position
- Inviting resistance
- Utilizing unexpected resistance
- Utilizing the client-therapist relationship
- Mind-body communication
- Focused examination of personal history

Creating Collaboration

In order to gain a new client's readiness and willingness to collaborate in radical inquiry, the most effective first step the therapist can take is to attend sensitively to the client's conscious, anti-symptom position. To the client it is crucially important to feel that the therapist precisely understands and empathizes with her experience of the problem and the features of her anti-symptom position—why or how the problem is troublesome, painful, undesirable, irrational, not controllable, involuntary; and what it means about self or others, as the client views it. This anti-symptom position is the arena in which the therapist must demonstrate that she will actively, sensitively, and reliably attend to what truly matters most to the client. Only then will the client tolerate the vulnerability of moving into feelings and contacting unconscious material. When the therapist begins radical inquiry, this will be from the client's point of view a natural continuation of the therapist actively placing attention upon what is of crucial importance to the client.

Attending to the client's anti-symptom position does not mean giving the client carte blanche to consume the available time with long narrations or descriptions. For working deeply and briefly, the therapist must keep the session efficient from the beginning. For example, to a talkative client who is rambling into a convoluted narrative, the therapist might interrupt by saying, "You know, I see how much you're wanting to help me understand the problem, and I *am* going to need your help as we work together, but right now, in order to get my bearings, I need to ask you about some specific things." In such ways the therapist actively maintains control of the session when necessary in order to keep it on purpose at all times. This also implicitly informs the client to expect the therapist to be quite active in shaping the work.

As indicated in previous chapters, it is always the client's capacities that limit the pace of radical inquiry, rather than the therapist's assumptions or fears. With clients who show extreme defensiveness, vulnerability, and marked instability or lability in their construction of interpersonal reality (the abrupt changes in experiential reality associated with "splitting"), the therapist's interest in finding a pro-symptom position may be interpreted as implying blame, badness, and pathology, and therefore radical inquiry needs to be broached more delicately than with other clients. One way we do this and still keep the therapy time-effective is by first sharing a story such as this one:

> I once knew a person who owned a small business and very much wanted to make the business grow successfully into a much larger business, and yet, she [he] wasn't doing that, and over time she

became very self-critical about what she viewed as her *failure* to do that. It felt very bad to blame herself this way, but it seemed true. But then one day she realized that, even though she wanted her business to grow, there was another part of her that *didn't* want the business to grow, because this part of her believed that, if it grew as she wanted, she'd be so overwhelmed with work that she wouldn't have nearly enough time for anything else, such as her family or her other interests and enjoyments. She realized that she had this *other* side of her feelings, this other set of feelings that had its own very good reasons for *not* wanting the business to grow, and *this* was why she wasn't doing it. Previously she saw it as only a *bad* thing that she wasn't making her business grow, but then, when she realized this other side of her own views and feelings, she saw that in fact there was something very *good* about not making the business grow. And this made sense in a whole new way of why she wasn't doing it. It certainly wasn't just a failure on her part, as she had thought at first. And it's often this way with people. We generally do have different sets of views and feelings operating at the same time. That's the normal way our minds work, and that's why I'm interested in looking at whether there might be something *good* to discover about having the problem *you're* describing, something that might never have occurred to you before.

Experiential Questioning

There is a class of questions that induce actual experiential discovery of constructs rather than speculative intellectualizing. Our term for the use of such questions is *experiential questioning*. In DOBT such questions are particularly designed to prompt the client to place attention where he or she has habitually not done so, focusing directly on previously unconscious constructs involved in the problem, bringing into awareness presuppositions, emotional wounds, and protective actions along with the specific emotional, cognitive, kine/somesthetic, and behavioral elements comprising them. It is the *experience* of the discovery or coming-to-awareness of a meaning-laden construct that makes these questions experiential in their effect.

On the written page the questions may seem deceptively simple, and in many cases their potency for experientially carrying out radical inquiry is not immediately apparent. However, if pursued phenomenologically and with full freedom to clarify, they can reach directly into the hidden structure of the presenting problem.

Experiential Questions for Radical Inquiry

- "What would it mean about you [or your life, your marriage, and so on] if the problem never changes?"
- "You've said that the change you want from therapy is [X]. What is it that makes having [X] as important to you as it is? What would having [X] mean about you, or about your life?"
- "To whom else does it matter most that this problem change, and why?"
- "Is there something important that [the symptom] does for someone else?"
- "Specifically, what about that is [client's term: hopeless, frightening, hurtful, angering, saddening, depressing, and so on] for you?" [Iterate with each new item produced by client until presuppositions and/or emotional wound are identified.]
- "How would you teach me to have the problem exactly as you do?" Variation: "How do you know exactly when, or with whom, to start having the symptom happen?"
- "Why have you chosen to get help on this problem now?"
- "What would you actually have to do, or feel, or believe, for this to change?"
- "What does it *mean* to you about [A] that [B] is the case?" [For example, "What does it *mean* to you about your husband that he refuses to have a child?"]

An experiential question is implicitly both a request and an instruction to the client to have a specific experience in which the living answer to the question is subjectively encountered, not intellectually figured out. The therapist's manner and voice tones in asking these questions should indicate that merely conceptual, speculative answers are not being sought, and they are not accepted if offered.

Below, we illustrate the use of several of these questions in detail, in order to make it unmistakably clear how the asking of any one of these questions is, in every instance, a unique event, a creative interaction with the client in which the wording and the pursuit of the question is sensitively tailored to the moment. To ask any of these questions in a routine, mechanical way would certainly fail.

> "You've said that the change you want from therapy is [X].
> What is it that makes having [X] as important to you as it is?
> What would having [X] mean about you, or about your life?"

This question draws the client's attention to unconscious meanings that he or she attributes to the hoped-for change. The application of the "What makes [change X] important?" question was pivotal in the work with a thirty-eight-year-old woman who sought help because she intensely wished to have a child while her husband, who in a previous marriage had two children (now adolescents living with their mother), just as intensely wanted not to have another child. She initially said she wanted therapy to help her decide whether or not to divorce her husband, but she then said this wouldn't really be a solution, since "I still wouldn't have a child." She said she wished the therapist could tell her how to get her husband to want a child. She was, finally, painfully unable to answer the therapist's opening question, "What difference do you want therapy to make for you?" The therapist then began to use the "What makes [change X] important?" question.

Therapist: I can see what a painful quandary this is for you. What I don't yet understand as fully as I'd like to is this: *What makes having a baby as important to you as it is?*

Client: I just feel very, very strongly that I want to be a mother. My husband and I aren't a real family by ourselves. It doesn't feel solid somehow; we're just floating. There's no center.

Therapist: So, what I'm starting to understand is that you're describing a certain *problem,* which is that you have this feeling of unrealness and unsolidness, like you're floating in a way, in your marriage and in general. And you're also describing what you see as the *solution* to that problem, which is to have a baby. But perhaps the problem itself is that you experience this lack of realness in your couple relationship and in your life. Is that accurate so far?

Client: [Pause] Well, I mean, I do want a baby, too, but actually, yes, what you're saying is true, too. I hadn't thought about it quite that way.

Therapist: Mm-hm. And this problem of feeling a lack of solidness and realness in your life, has it been around for a short time or a long time?

Client: Oh, that's been around for quite a while.

Therapist: And for dispelling that problem you have this plan—which I can see you've put so much hope into—a very definite plan for how to create this realness and solidness that you feel is so lacking. And your plan is to have a baby, because you see that as bringing the realness and solidness you want. Is that right?

Client: Well, now that I hear it said out loud, I guess that *is* my plan.

Therapist: [Pause] You know, I'm curious about whether you're feeling that lack of realness and solidness right now.

Client: [Pause] Actually, I do feel realer and solider right now, from talking like this.

Therapist: What's "like this" mean?

Client: Well, I don't often tell what's so personal like this.

Therapist: So it sounds like you're noticing that from talking really personally like this and from saying what you truly feel, you start to have some of that realness and solidness that you want.

Client: Yes, but I could feel like this *all* the time with a child—my own child.

[The therapist at this moment understands that her unconscious "plan" is to relieve the unrealness and the floating unconnectedness she feels through a connection with a baby with whom she could safely be herself, and that she has been hiding emotionally from adults and plans to continue to do so.]

Therapist: I see. Yes.

Client: [Laughs] A baby's always real. They're always just themselves. A baby's the best! [Laughs]

Therapist: Yes, a baby's the best. [Pause] Remember we talked about the *problem,* on the one hand, and the *solution,* on the other? I'm getting a sense that the *problem* that you're dealing with is that there's nobody in the world you feel safe enough to really be yourself with, and you very much want and need to be your real self with *someone,* so you feel you have to actually *create* a safe person, a baby, as the solution.

[Until now the client's knowledge of the real problem—the unsafety of being emotionally real with adults—was located only in her unconscious, pro-symptom position, which has all along been carrying out its solution to that problem: suppression of her realness. This resulted in the unreal, unsolid feeling in her ongoing experience, itself a problem that she naturally was trying to solve by arranging for the only conditions she knew that would safely allow for realness: relationship with a baby. Her husband's refusal to have a baby therefore appeared to be the problem. Using the "What makes (change X) important?" question and viewing the situation through the constructivist lens of DOBT, the therapist has been able to identify these structural components during the first twenty minutes of the session.]

> *Client:* Well, wanting to be a mother is such a normal thing, isn't it? I mean, this is something I really want. You're a woman—you can understand that.
>
> *Therapist:* Yes, it's a completely normal thing, completely normal for you to want to be a mother and for you to have a baby. But what we're finding is that an important part of the problem that brings you here, if I understand you correctly, is that *it doesn't feel safe to be your real self with the grown-ups in your life.*
>
> *Client:* [Softer, lowered voice] I guess it doesn't. That's true. And it never has.
>
> *Therapist:* You know, if something doesn't seem safe to me, then naturally I hold back from doing it. I wonder if that's how this works for *you.* Feeling and expressing your real self has always felt unsafe, so you hold back from doing it, and as a result you go around feeling unreal and unsolid in your life.
>
> *Client:* [Nods. Eyes tear up.]

Therapist: Yes, it's felt necessary to hold back from being real in order to be safe, even though the cost is this terrible lack of realness in how it feels to be you.

[The therapist has just named the emotional truth of the symptom.]

Client: [Cries] So how do I get back to feeling real?

Therapist: What are those tears telling you about that?

Client: [Pause] That I need to somehow be real whether or not I have a baby with Dan [fictitious name]. [Cries]

Therapist: [Pause] Is *that* the difference you want our sessions to make for you, so that you finally get some of that realness and solidness you want?

Client: Yes, but it seems so big. It's pretty overwhelming, actually.

Therapist: Well, if that's the difference you want from our sessions, then we'll make sure that at every point the steps we take are just the size that seem right to you.

Client: OK.

> "To whom else does it matter most
> that this problem change, and why?"

This question, well known to systemically oriented therapists, is adapted in DOBT to probe for how the client's relationship to another person may be the symptom-positive context—the domain in which the symptom is more important to have than not to have.

For example, early in the first session with a woman whose presenting symptom was her weight, which she very much wanted to reduce, the therapist asked this question and learned that her husband had for a long time been exerting considerable pressure on her to lose weight. Probing further into how she construed their interaction on this issue, it emerged that as she perceived it, to lose weight under that kind of pressure is to submit to being profoundly controlled and to feel herself "cease to exist." This in turn brought out the fact that this same intense, determined struggle for autonomy was a dominant theme throughout her childhood, in relation to both her mother and her older sister. By the end of this first session it was transparently clear that autonomy in primary relationships was the symptom-positive context, and that within that context, the emotional truth of the symptom was that not losing weight was a vital success and expressed her "determination to preserve *me.*"

> "How would you teach me to have the problem
> exactly as you do?" Variation: "How do you know
> exactly when, or with whom,
> to start having the symptom happen?"

Another question that can be highly useful for identifying the unconscious structure of the problem is this one, devised by the creators of neuro-linguistic programming. This question begins a detailed phenomenological scrutiny of the elements that together constitute "the problem's" happening, without recourse to speculation, interpretation, or history about the problem. The question implicitly communicates to the client that the problem is a constructed or assembled configuration of elements, which therefore can be unconstructed.

The indicated variation on this question was used in the following example to reveal and dispel the unconscious phenomenology of a compulsive symbiotic attachment problem. The client was a thirty-three-year-old woman whose presenting problem was a repeating pattern of relationships in which she became, in her own words, "obsessive" and "dependent" on someone extremely charming, smart, and self-confident. She reported losing her capacity to know and assert her own feelings and views and becoming completely preoccupied with getting this person to regard her as "special." Radical inquiry and position work in previous sessions had revealed that the emotional truth of this overpowering pattern had much to do with suffering a permanent emotional abandonment by her mother at age three, when an infant brother was stillborn. Mother's emotional withdrawal left her forevermore feeling that her very survival depended on her father's love. Later, perceiving her father become emotionally rejecting toward her older sister was highly anxiety producing. Father was, yes, extremely charming, smart, and self-confident—and alcoholic, and had had a psychotic break when the client was thirteen, during which he raged around the house brandishing a butcher knife.

In the session before the one from which the following transcription comes, she said her mother's emotional disconnection from her was like losing a kidney, and that her father's love was her only remaining kidney, her only remaining life support. Throughout childhood she was therefore desperate to be special to him, so that she would not lose this vital connection. Her unconscious, pro-symptom position was one of spotting an emotional replica of her father (male or female) and instantly, powerfully forming an umbilical connection with that person, enjoining the familiar struggle to be seen as special. Consciously, she had been baffled over the compulsion to obsess, merge, and lose herself in this way.

In the following transcript the therapist makes much use of experiential questions that have her discover how she constructs and skillfully carries out her method for symbiotically connecting with a father replica, "Alex," she recently met. (This was followed by position work [see pp. 212–214] to complete her conscious ownership of this protective action.) The main experiential questions used in this session are, "How do you know exactly when, or with whom, to start having the symptom happen?" and "Is there something important that the symptom does for someone else?" Experiential questions are preceded by the symbol >.

Therapist: > If you can picture Alex when you first saw him, how did you know that he was the kind of person who can give you life support?

Client: I don't know. I was sure it wouldn't happen again, that I wouldn't become a heat-seeking missile again for that kind of person.

Therapist: Let's look at how this marvelously perceptive part of you recognizes the target so well.

Client: Well, it can't be just that he's so attractive and brilliant. It's more than just that. It has something to do with the way he talks. [Pause] I feel like I'm being given the role of an audience, with him. It's not a balanced give-and-take, like with other friends that I feel relaxed with.

Therapist: > How does that *very* quality make *him* the important person who can be your kidney?

[This question appears merely cognitive on the written page, but in the room it had the quality of a request for a fully experiential scan of her own early response to Alex. The client's facial expressions and her voice tone in her next response distinctly indicated that she was trying to find words for the nonverbal experience she was accessing in order to answer the question.]

> *Client:* [Pause] Something about me feeling needed and valuable to him, as his audience.
>
> *Therapist:* > And what are you doing for *him,* by being his rapt audience?
>
> *Client:* [Pause] Somehow I can tell that he needs to be heard and seen. My balanced friends don't need me to see and hear them in order for them to be OK. But Alex *does* need it in order to be OK.
>
> *Therapist:* Sounds like what you are describing is your sense of a wound in him.
>
> *Client:* Yes! Aha! Right! OK, OK, right. 'Cause I'm attracted to *fixing* somebody, like I did with Jeff. "I'll heal you with my love."
>
> *Therapist:* So you sense his woundedness, his neediness.
>
> *Client:* *Right.*
>
> *Therapist:* Was it anything like this for you with your father?
>
> *Client:* Oh yes, yes. I mean, the details were different, but that doesn't matter.
>
> *Therapist:* Because what *does* matter is . . . what?
>
> *Client:* [With a distinct, pleasurable tone of relishing the idea] That I can *fix* them, and I *want* to.
>
> *Therapist:* So it's that wonderfully attractive wound that's how you knew Alex was the right person?
>
> *Client:* Yes.
>
> *Therapist:* > So can you feel any connection between fixing the person's wound and the person being a kidney for you so you'll stay alive?
>
> *Client:* [Pause] They'll *need* me, and if they need me, they'll stay around.
>
> *Therapist:* They'll be *dependent* on you, very dependent on *you.*
>
> *Client:* Yes, right.
>
> *Therapist:* Would you be willing, right now, to imagine being at

the moment of first spotting someone who's the right kind of person?

Client: OK. [Closes eyes; silence] I keep having this image I talked about two weeks ago, of me having this *hole* in my middle, and so I see somebody else who has this hole in *their* middle. And like I can instantly shape-shift—*fffft!*—and I'm magnetized to that hole in him. I zoom over and fill it. Yes, I can sense this hole in the middle of the other person's being, and it's a magnetic field. I'm sucked into it—*fffft!*—really fast. And that's why it feels like there's no choice, because it feels so magnetic. And also it feels quite pleasurable, at least initially.

The preceding transcript shows how experiential questions are used in such a way that in order to answer them, the client has to do experiential inquiry into his or her previously unexamined constructs and positions. The questions, combined with the therapist's active intentionality, do not permit a merely speculative or cognitive answer. The client answered these experiential questions by accessing several important emotional and kinesthetic knowings, initially nonverbal whole-body knowings that were key facets of the symptom's emotional truth. Later in the same session, position work was carried out in order for the client to integrate these newly conscious feelings and knowings (see continuing transcript on pp. 212–214 in Chapter Six). The result was a permanent change in her previously automatic attachment response.

Serial Accessing

As we described in Chapter Three, the emotional truth of the symptom—the client's pro-symptom position—is in general a multicomponent construction, a set of coherently linked, unconscious constructs of meaning that we can describe as spanning various orders of position. If the therapist guides the client into subjective immersion in the experiential reality of any one of these component constructs, a process of *serial accessing* can readily unfold, in which each construct in turn is experienced and serves as a station of awareness from which the next directly linked construct becomes subjectively evident and accessible.

(Serial accessing is to be distinguished from the constructivist technique known as *laddering* devised by Hinkle. Laddering, as we understand it, consists of sequentially eliciting linked constructs that are already familiar to or at least readily identifiable by the client, being compatible with the client's conscious awareness. Serial accessing is a more deeply experiential process that elicits *unconscious* constructs that are not already familiar to the client, are not accessible to the client's unassisted conscious awareness, and may be markedly incompatible with the client's conscious position.)

Serial accessing is possible because of the fully phenomenological nature of radical inquiry and because of the internal coherence of the pro-symptom position. The therapist, while maintaining a grounded sense of separate identity, extends his or her psychological vision empathically into the client's pro-symptom construction of reality as currently known to the therapist. This vicarious reach into the client's experiential world has been referred to in some psychotherapeutic literature as "shared trance." In this empathic state the therapist, while carrying out radical inquiry, has a distinct, experiential sense of accompanying the client in subjectively encountering his or her constructs and of trying on the client's reality.

This ultra-phenomenological (yet nonpassive, non-Rogerian) way of working is advantageous because it gives the therapist an especially clear, almost firsthand knowledge of the experiential reality in the client's pro-symptom position. It enables the therapist to explore the client's constructions of reality from within—a kind of psychological spelunking, in which the therapist brings the searchlight of his or her own awareness into the client's unlit architecture of meanings and literally perceives how this reality is assembled.

What we are describing here can be clarified with the help of the position chart (introduced in Figure 3.1 in Chapter Three) for depicting the full architecture of clients' positions. The chart shows numerous, specific compartments of meaning linked like adjoining rooms in the client's unconscious, pro-symptom construction of reality. Just as within physical architecture, one can see into and step into certain rooms only by first positioning oneself in a nearby, adjoining spot. That is, positioning one's awareness subjectively in any one construct of reality within the client's psychological architecture brings other, linked structures of meaning into subjective accessibility, elements that could not be known from other vantage points. This *state-specific accessibility of constructs* becomes a very real and practical matter as the client and therapist are working their way from one linked construct to another, spending as many minutes in each newly discovered construct as needed to assimilate the experience emotionally and cognitively, reorient, and move on.

The therapist can closely accompany the client in this subjective discovery of one compartment of meaning after another by letting go, temporarily but completely, of all "objective," theoretical knowledge—which pins the therapist to a position external to the client—and by trusting his or her own inherent capacity to recognize the coherence of meaning, sense, and structure of the client's experiential world. The therapist, being less emotionally involved in each emerging construct, is often first to broaden the field of attention and become aware of other structures of meaning that are now subjectively accessible, and so is in a position to prompt the client's attention toward whatever important construct is linked to the presently realized one.

As an example, the following list summarizes the set of linked, unconscious elements of emotional truth that were serially accessed by the woman in the preceding transcript, working on her problem of compulsive symbiotic attachment in a previous session.

1. *Beginning:* To the image of three men with whom she previously became attached and dependent, she overtly voices for the first time her feeling of desperately needing a man like her father to bestow aliveness on her by regarding her as special.
2. *Spontaneously accessed:* A felt state of being at age seven.
3. *Accessed with prompting by the therapist:* "I feel dead" (at age seven). (This is accessed by being seven and confronting her image of her father with the emotional truth, "If you don't make me feel special, I don't feel alive.")
4. *Spontaneously accessed:* A sudden, intense fear about the possibility that feeling dead means feeling depressed, which is sharply incompatible with her habitual, conscious position of being the happy-go-lucky bright spot in the family.
5. *Spontaneously accessed:* Being depressed means being "damaged."

6. *Spontaneously accessed:* A childhood memory of wanting to die in her sleep.
7. *Spontaneously accessed:* The urgent, anxious position of "I *can't* be damaged."
8. *Spontaneously accessed:* The experience of desperately needing to appear "perfectly fine" in her family of origin in order not to be the same as her depressed, unstable sister, who (as perceived by the client) *was* regarded as damaged by her parents and consequently lost her father's love.
9. *Spontaneously accessed:* New imagery of her father relating to her as being fundamentally different from her sister and accepting her unconditionally. (This is accessed by *attending to the autonomous response of the image* after confronting the image of her father with intense, spontaneous emotion: "If I'm not really good and special and happy and really *on,* then you'll *abandon* me—and that's *terrifying!"*)
10. *Spontaneously accessed:* A sudden, new knowledge of herself as being fundamentally distinct from her sister even if depressed, and as lovable even if depressed.

In this serial accessing sequence, items one through eight represent encounters with fully unconscious (not merely preconscious) material. The immersion of her awareness in these constructs, one after another, was a significantly altered state, and integration of these new experiences required additional, subsequent work. As a result of arriving at item eight, the experiential shift of items nine and ten spontaneously occurred, a transformation at the ontological (fourth-order) heart of the whole father-symbiotic construction. A transcript of steps nine and ten is provided in the next section as an example of attending to the response of the image.

Imaginal Interactive Techniques

The session transcripts earlier in this chapter illustrate techniques from Gestalt and Jungian therapies that utilize a person's ability to visualize people, objects, or scenes as well as aspects of one's own mind and to engage in a spontaneous interaction with what is visualized. The original Jungian term for this is *active imagination,* and the basic technique has been applied in any number of subsequent psychotherapies in various forms. These include Gestalt empty-chair dialogues and two-chair work, experiential dreamwork, inner child work, all techniques in which some aspect of the client's psyche is personified and visualized, and all techniques of guided visualization. These can all be applied very fruitfully within the methodology of depth-oriented brief therapy.

Having the knack for this kind of process consists of relating to what is visualized as though it has complete autonomy of response, making no attempt to exercise control over what happens, but only watching to see and sense what response the image makes after each of the client's communications to it. The image itself forms in the same way: autonomously, not consciously designed by the visualizer. When allowed such autonomy of response, the visualized image is a direct, in-the-moment manifestation of an unconscious position or construction of meaning, and it provides direct contact between that unconscious formation and the client's conscious position. In the same way that the therapist's work with the client is completely experiential and phenomenological, so, too, is the work with the image. All understanding of the image is derived from what the image itself reveals or from the client's direct apprehensions of its meaning. Any stereotyping or manipulation of such images based upon externally applied interpretations merely signals to the unconscious position involved that it will not be heard on its own terms, and the process closes down.

The interaction between the client's conscious position and the image is a two-way communication: the unconscious realities get an opportunity to express themselves directly to the client; the client gets an opportunity to express emotionally important but never-before-voiced material to whomever or whatever is visualized, as in confronting a visualized parent with his or her abusiveness. Such two-way interactions are *real* in that they transform the relationship of conscious and unconscious constructions involved in the problem. This is the basis of the therapeutic effectiveness of these techniques. Of course, skillful execution is required. Some of these techniques have become popular methods of self-help, and in that context their effectiveness is unpredictable.

In order to apply these techniques for radical inquiry, the therapist coaches the client in creating and then interacting with the visualized image in two ways described below: (1) confronting with emotional truth and (2) attending to the response of the image.

In *confronting with emotional truth,* the client explicitly and bluntly voices previously unexpressed emotional truths to the relevant, imaged figures. The emotional truth voiced may have arisen in a previous piece of work with the therapist, after which the therapist suggested this imaginal encounter, or it may emerge in the moment, during the encounter, in response to the imaged figure. For example, the therapist might say, "And as you see your two sisters there in front of you, you might let yourself begin to feel, and to know, things that you never said to them, things that need saying, feelings that need expressing. [Pause] And what do you begin to feel, that wants to be expressed?" The therapist then coaches the client in articulating a very explicit, emotionally complete, accurate, and vivid statement of the client's emergent emotional truth.

Once the client opens in this way to the subjective experience of any new element of emotional truth, a process of serial accessing then often spontaneously occurs in which other, linked emotional truths that had been unconscious come into awareness and can be expressed. Confronting with emotional truth creates a kind of radical inquiry snowball effect.

In *attending to the response of the image,* the client perceives the image autonomously responding to her statements, expressing the specific unconscious position that it personifies, revealing emotional themes or wounds, views of reality, and/or protective actions. The position represented by the image is part of the client's own heterogeneous construction of reality, and becoming aware of its content can be pivotal. A striking instance of this occurred at the end of the example of serial accessing provided in the previous section. Recall that in childhood this woman perceived her father as emotionally rejecting her overtly depressed, emotionally unstable older sister "Jeanne." The implicit possibility that father could cut off from her, too, was a source of great and chronic anxiety, since he was her "only remaining kidney," her only possible supply of love since mother's emotional shutdown when the client was three years old. During serial accessing, one of the constructs that she entered into and vividly felt and realized was the protective action that she was urgently struggling to carry out in her family of origin (item eight in the previous section's list), a strategy of appearing "perfectly fine" in order not to be seen as being the same as her depressed and unloved sister. The therapist then had her visualize her father and bluntly tell him the emotional truth of her desperate need of his love and her terror of losing it (item nine). The following two-minute transcript segment begins in the midst of the ensuing, intensely emotional process, which centers on what happens when she attends to the response of the image.

Client: [To visualized father, and crying copiously] If I'm not really good and special and happy and really *on,* then you'll essentially *abandon* me—and that's *terrifying!*

Therapist: And how does he respond?

Client: [Sobbing] Sort of like, "That's not true, you *are* special, I love you no matter what." Just very comforting and "I love you whatever you are. I would never abandon you." He's very soft.

Therapist: It seems authentic to you?

Client: Yes, but—I don't know if I believe it.

Therapist: OK, so what do you need to say to him about *that?*

Client: [To father] You say that, but if I were like Jeanne, look how you treat *her.*

Therapist: And what does he say to that?

Client: "That's different. Don't mix apples and oranges."

Therapist: Do you know what he means? Do you know what difference he means?

Client: [Pause] Actually, I do. He means I'm not Jeanne. Actually, I do sense—I'm not her. So I do sense a difference.

Therapist: And does your awareness of that difference give you a new sense of trust in his affection?

Client: That's a good question. Why don't I trust in his affection? It kind of does, actually, 'cause I'm not—I'm not her. His relationship with Jeanne is independent of me.

Therapist: Yes.

Client: And even if I were depressed, I still wouldn't be Jeanne.

[This sudden new awareness of being "not Jeanne" is a significant breakthrough, an experiential shift of individuation and separation from the identity of her sister. Throughout childhood she was attempting to prove to father that she was not Jeanne, all along feeling as though in essence she was the same as Jeanne because she was secretly depressed and could be found out and rejected at any time. Note that what triggered this ontological (fourth-order) shift was the unexpected, autonomous response of the visualized image of her father.]

Therapist: Yes.

    Client: What makes her, her, is not just that she's depressed.

Therapist: Good, good. I'd like you to again now see the other three men [with whom she had become obsessed and dependent] and tell each of them, "I'm not Jeanne, even if I'm depressed."

    Client: Say that to each? All right. I'm not Jeanne, even if I'm depressed. They kind of say, "Well, we know that." Which is sort of what dad says: "Yeah, you're not."

Therapist: Would you try saying to them, "I don't have to prove to you that I'm not Jeanne, do I?"

    Client: I don't have to prove to you that I'm not Jeanne, do I? They say, "No, you don't."

Therapist: And how did it feel to you to say that?

    Client: Sort of liberating.

Serial accessing had brought her consciously into her emotionally true position of being depressed at age seven (as well as at thirty-three), which until now was too frightening to recognize because it had the fourth-order meaning, "I am damaged and unlovable, like Jeanne." Positioning herself consciously for the first time in this emotional truth of depression, however, immediately stimulated a spontaneous and surprising creation of new, fourth-order meaning that arose by attending to the response of the autonomous image of her father. What developed was a construction of herself as an individual who has her own distinct identity and is lovable even if depressed. This is a transformation in her superordinate, fourth-order, core construction of self. Since these constructs had been deeply unconscious, she was in a thoroughly altered state while subjectively experiencing them, and so she would not easily retain awareness of any of these themes of meaning. The therapist therefore gave her an index card on which he had written, "I now know that I'm not the same as Jeanne, even if I'm depressed." She was to read this twice daily, morning and night, to foster the position work of retention and integration. This woman subsequently began reversing patterns of dependency and submissiveness in relation to her highly intrusive and dependency-demanding father, actively and very substantially asserting healthy boundaries even though doing so risked her sizable inheritance.

The full versatility and potency of these imaginal techniques are tapped by appreciating that in the interaction between the client and an imaginal figure, the client can locate her consciousness in, and experience being, either participant. For example, in the session transcribed just above, the therapist could have had the woman *be* her father and visualize and interact with the client, his daughter. In this way the client experiences firsthand the subjective construction of reality represented by either figure.

Experiential Dreamwork

The same principles used in imaginal interactive techniques form the basis of experiential dreamwork in DOBT. The technique involves asking the client to reenvision a specific scene of the dream, not as a memory of the dream but as a present experience of again being in that same scene. The therapist directs the client to inhabit and experience being a particular figure or object involved in the scene and, as that figure or object, to interact with other figures or objects in the scene, including the figure of the client. The client is able to inhabit and access the experiential reality of anyone or anything she imagines, from waking life or from a dream, because every such figure is actually the visual appearance of a construction in the client's own mind. Experiential dreamwork can be a very fruitful arena for radical inquiry, because unconscious positions often appear in dreams in personified or objectified form. There is far more accuracy and far more therapeutic power in the client's own, direct, experiential discovery of the emotional truth(s) represented by the dream than in speculatively or theoretically interpreting the meaning of the dream with, or for, the client.

Sentence Completion

Sentence completion is an extremely simple and straightforward technique that can be surprisingly effective at eliciting hidden positions and their component constructs. We will review an earlier example and add a new one.

In Chapter Two the therapist asked the woman who was "unhappy no matter what" to visualize her father along with all the past boyfriends and lovers who turned out to be ambivalent or emotionally unexpressive like her father. The therapist then asked her to speak directly to them by completing this sentence, without pre-thinking the ending: "If I know that I'm OK . . ." After several rounds of this, each time with a spontaneous new ending, one arose that was the surfacing of a crucially important, third-order purpose: "If I know that I'm OK, I won't need to try to get it from *you* anymore." Accompanied by an emotional release of tears, this was a significant breakthrough into an awareness that she herself was actively maintaining the "I'm *not* OK" position in order to preserve her old role relationship with her father and carry out an unconsciously held plan of rapprochement.

The fact that unconscious, hidden positions readily surface through sentence completion is a striking phenomenon, and it is one of the most direct forms of evidence supporting the view that unconscious positions and constructs have an intrinsic desire or need to become conscious. They certainly seem unable to resist the temptation to complete a relevant sentence fragment.

To set up sentence completion, the therapist tells the client there is no right or wrong response, not to pre-think the ending of the sentence (repeating this point as needed during the process), and just to say the fragment supplied, reaching the blank at the end of it and seeing what ending arises by itself. From the beginning the therapist welcomes every ending that arises, never indicating judgments of irrelevance or unsuitability. Whatever ending the client first generates, the therapist says, "Good. Keep going; say it again and see what comes up next." Usually several rounds occur before unfamiliar, emotionally significant material begins to emerge. As a rule we do sentence completion with the same fragment until no new endings arise, which differs from how the technique has been described by some other writers. It is this repetition of the same fragment, clearing away endings comprised of already-conscious material, that allows unconscious constructs to emerge. It is sometimes necessary to ask the client to continue, especially when he or she prematurely thinks there are no other endings available. The only way to be sure the process is complete is to reach the blank two or three times and consistently find nothing arising. Occasionally it is necessary to prompt the client's attention toward certain general classes of response, such as, "I wonder if there are any endings that might have to do with your mother."

The therapist can switch to a new sentence fragment in order to pursue a newly emergent line of meaning that appears promising, but does so at the risk of leaving the original line before the most important material has appeared. For example, hearing the client say, "If I know that I'm OK, I won't need to try to get it from *you* anymore," the therapist might then ask her to complete the fragment, "If I don't need to get it from you anymore . . ."

At times the client may experience a nonverbal completion of the sentence in the form of emotion or a bodily sensation with no cognitive content. The therapist then assists the client to cognize and verbalize the felt meaning in such a response.

The offered sentence fragment should be custom-made by the therapist based on her or his most current knowledge of the phenomenology of the client's problem. The sentence fragment is an expression of the therapist's active intentionality, a best effort to elicit the emotional truth of the symptom right now. Working from lists of prefabricated sentence "stems," as published in some books on this technique, is inappropriate, because it amounts to a policy of *not* learning to develop the all-important subjective facility for meeting, engaging, and inquiring into the client's constructions directly, moment by moment.

The value of sentence completion in radical inquiry is well illustrated by how it was used in the sixth session with a thirty-year-old man whose problem was an almost ever-present, sharp fear of failure in all his creative efforts in his artistic career. Despite his artistic sensitivity and creativity, he was very much an intellectualizer, and he was profoundly ensconced in a construction of reality in which the core problem is the knowledge that to exist is to be hated and attacked and the only solution is to be invisible—the defining features of what we term a *schizoid construction*. At the start of this session the client had commented that the therapy work seemed thoroughly relevant, yet he felt as though it was about someone else. The therapist used sentence completion for the next steps of radical inquiry as a way to bring him into more intimate contact with his own elements of emotional truth.

The therapist had learned in the previous session that this fellow had a rigid presupposition about how the world works, an unquestioned belief that hard work and talent lead directly to success, as reliably and predictably as gravity leads objects to fall straight down. With this presupposition, lack of success in any effort meant inherent lack of talent (since he knew he worked hard). Since, like the rest of us, he was often having the experience of the world in one way or another obstructing success in some pursuit, small or large, over time his confidence in his talent had been quite undermined. This seemed to the therapist a factor in the presenting problem of chronically fearing and expecting failure. That presupposition, despite its costly effect on his confidence, presumably was an important, coherent part of some larger position or construction of reality.

In order to probe that construction, the therapist first invited this man, here in the sixth session, to consider the possibility that the world works differently than he thought—that many other factors in addition to talent and effort are involved in the outcome. He said that while of course he was willing to entertain this idea intellectually, it meant nothing to him; it was an utterly foreign idea. Here the therapist used sentence completion in order to have him entertain the idea experientially. The therapist said, "Well, just *suppose* for a minute that it's *true* that success is *not* determined only by talent and effort." Then, after giving the instructions for sentence completion, the therapist asked him to complete the sentence, "If *that* is how the world is . . ." The client sat forward, closed his eyes, and the following endings emerged with each successive utterance of those words:

" . . . then there is no justice."

" . . . then I can do everything right and still things can go wrong."

" . . . then is there any way I can guarantee success for myself?"

" . . . then the *only* thing to do is to do my best at any given moment."

" . . . then there is no path that I *should* take."

" . . . then no one's going to judge me as harshly as maybe I think they would."

" . . . then anyone who understands that would look at me and say, 'He had a run of bad luck,' without judging me."

As evidenced by soft sniffling, moist eyes, and nostrils flaring with feeling, at some point during this process he dropped into his feelings, something he did not readily do in general. What is especially striking is that in spite of saying he saw no way at all to step out of his rigid, long-standing presupposition, in minutes he *did* step out of it and began contacting the new possibilities that open up in a world not defined by that presupposition—just from completing a well-chosen sentence fragment. Of course, further work was needed to integrate those new possibilities, but here were the pivotal moments of his contacting them.

The therapist anticipated that even if this man were receptive to these new knowings, he would also necessarily have a position of unwillingness to let his familiar, world-organizing presupposition be changed. In other words, the therapist supposed that this presupposition was part of a pro-symptom position that had not been fully addressed as yet. In order to elicit more of that position, about five minutes later in the session the therapist said, "Could I hear from the side of you that's *un*willing to see the world in this new way?" On his own the man spontaneously used the sentence completion format to find his answers to this question. He again leaned forward, closed his eyes, and said, "I'm unwilling to see the world this way because . . ." and he came up with the following endings:

" . . . it means I have to admit myself vulnerable."

" . . . I can't take as much pride in my successes, because I wasn't 100 percent of what was behind them; I have to acknowledge the luck that went into those, too."

" . . . I'm unwilling to feel like a pinball being buffeted around by forces I cannot control."

" . . . if the world is that way, it makes me feel a lot smaller."

Here important emotional and presuppositional structure, as well as new alternatives to that structure, came to light in less than ten minutes of work, and with very little effort.

Viewing from a Symptom-Free Position, or Inviting Resistance

The technique we term viewing from a symptom-free position was introduced in Chapter One and was also utilized in a variety of ways in the case studies in Chapter Two. Actually, this is not a single technique but a strategy that can be carried out through any number of specific experiential techniques. Sentence completion, guided visualization, and experiential questions can all be used.

The purpose of viewing from a symptom-free position is *not* to get the client to be free of the symptom permanently, but only to experience for a few minutes what happens if the symptom does not occur in a situation where normally it would. Being without the symptom in a situation where actually it is needed results in a conscious experience of discomfort or difficulty that reveals how the symptom is important to have.

The strategy of viewing from a symptom-free position is a quintessentially constructivist one, because it makes direct use of the client's fundamental ability to construct an experiential reality, inhabit it, and know firsthand how it works.

As the earlier clinical examples showed, the therapist instructs the client very explicitly to (1) imagine being in a situation in which the symptom predictably would occur, (2) imagine being without the symptom in that situation, and (3) notice the new experience that then develops. The therapist ushers the client through this creative, experiential process, repeating the instructions as needed, and prompts the client if necessary to notice the cost, disadvantage, or discomfort that results from being without the symptom. If the client has difficulty imagining being free of the symptom, the therapist simply coaches the client by verbally evoking very concretely the specific features of not having the symptom. In this way, even clients with lifelong low self-esteem can temporarily inhabit a position of knowing they are good, worthy, lovable beings and from that position view their parents or partner, for instance, and experience what happens to the felt emotional bond. In nearly all cases the client will spontaneously notice and describe a previously unrecognized, valued effect of the symptom that has been lost (such as the "incredible shrinking parent" experience—the attenuation of the emotional bond that is often reported by clients with low self-esteem).

We illustrate the technique here with a short example involving the mother of a molested child. At the time of learning about the molestation seven years earlier, she responded very protectively and called the police, pressed charges, and arranged for years of therapy for her then eight-year-old daughter and for herself. She did everything at the time that could be done, and yet:

> *Client:* I feel so stuck in suffering over my daughter's molest. Years and years are going by, and she's now fifteen, and I'm still under a dark cloud almost as much as ever. Is this how a mother has to feel forever? I need to get my life back. I don't know if there's really any way out of feeling tormented.
>
> *Therapist:* I wonder what you would start to experience if you weren't parked there, in that unhappiness. I mean, *imagine* approaching a single afternoon with a deliberate intention of seeing *what happens*, if you're not staying in that familiar base of suffering, under that cloud. What if you released yourself from that for a whole afternoon, and you went through your day actually finding out what it's like to live without it?
>
> *Client:* While you were saying that, somehow I could tell what would happen. It just became very clear. What got clear is that if I stop suffering, there'd be no chance for *me* of *ever* getting the caring I never got, as a child or ever. It's like I stay in misery so that maybe somebody will come and take care of me. It's like I don't want to give that up. [Pause] I never saw this before.
>
> *Therapist:* Are you saying that it feels to you that to stop suffering is to give up a secret hope you have, a hope of getting some of that real nurturing you never got?
>
> *Client:* [Softly crying] Yes.
>
> *Therapist:* [Pause] Yes, I see that. [Pause] What I'm understanding is that you have *both* feelings or both positions: you

want very much to get out from under this dark suffering, but at the same time, you have what might be an even stronger desire to stay *in* it as your key way to attract something you profoundly want, which is to experience being truly cared for and taken care of, in the way you *should* have been when you were a girl, but you weren't.

Client: [Crying] Yes.

Here a two-minute process of viewing from a symptom-free position, applied directly to the client's presenting symptom of unending misery over her daughter's being molested, brought to light the unconscious pro-symptom position maintaining that misery, a position centered on an emotional wound of severe emotional neglect in childhood. (The therapist then engaged her in the position work of having her knowingly take her stance of "I need to stay miserable in order to get somebody to finally take care of me. If I'm happy, nobody ever will." These words were written on an index card given to her as part of a between-session task of staying aware of trying to carry out this plan in her daily life. In the next session she reported that being so aware of how she was trying to "extract mothering from the universe" made her feel fed up with this strategy. "This will never work," she said. "I've got to start finding ways to really feel better." She began using therapy for real healing of her old wound. Her pro-symptom position had dissolved and she was now willing to grieve for the low level of nurturance in her childhood rather than covertly maneuver for its reparation.)

Viewing from a symptom-free position is not to be confused with the "miracle question" technique that is central to solution-oriented brief therapy. Although both techniques initially direct the client's attention to a symptom-free state, the ensuing therapeutic processes and strategies are completely different.

Now, what happens if the therapist in one way or another invites and prompts the client to view from a symptom-free position, and then the client goes blank, gets confused, intellectualizes, or looks up and says, "Something inside won't go along with this"? In other words, what if the client's response is resistance?

Resistance here turns out to be as useful a response as cooperation. An example follows. First, consider this: Which of the client's positions is it that is unwilling to allow her to take a symptom-free position and so resists? It is, of course, her *pro*-symptom position, in which the symptom is vitally important to *have*. That position is likely to protest or manifest resistance when the client attempts to assume the symptom-free position. The resistance, in whatever form it takes, is a protective action being executed in the moment by the autonomous pro-symptom position. Moments when the resistance is occurring are moments when the pro-symptom position is directly asserting itself in the room and can therefore be engaged and further elicited and drawn into awareness and expression. In effect, the client's pro-symptom position is "caught" when it shows itself through its resistance, as the following case example clearly shows. The final result is the same as if the client had instead cooperated and viewed from a symptom-free position: her pro-symptom position is found out.

Since resistance is as likely as cooperation when the therapist is setting out to have the client view from a symptom-free position, the name of the technique could instead just as well be *inviting resistance*. The two names—viewing from a symptom-free position and inviting resistance—denote the two ends of the same stick.

What follows is a transcript of segments totaling twelve minutes from a single session. Gaps in the transcript are indicated by four dots. The client is a fifty-year-old woman, a history teacher in a large urban high school, presenting a new problem for the first time to a therapist she had seen previously for other matters. All of the hidden, pro-symptom structure found in this session was also new to the therapist. The client first expressed her anti-symptom position, with which the therapist empathized. As a way to pursue radical inquiry into the emotional truth of the symptom—her pro-symptom position—the therapist caught an opportunity to invite her to view from a symptom-free position, which here turned out to be inviting resistance.

> *Client:* [Upset and angry] I've reached a level of real high anger because I'm being provoked by one of my students who has a lot of anger. And God, I can't say a word to him, but he flies off the handle and starts shouting at me and he's just unbelievably uncon-

trolled. . . . I don't know what was said—I can't remember exactly—but, um, his remark was, "I know somebody who should get hit in the mouth." He was talking to *me*. He meant *me*. So I turned to him and I said, "Do you mean me?" And he said, "No, I wasn't talking to you.". . . I'm just feeling really, *really* angry, because I feel like, you know, here's somebody threatening me and I gotta have him in my class, and I gotta sit and listen to this shit every day?

Therapist: Yes.

Client: I gotta have this kid mouthing off at me and talking to me like I'm something he'd like to squash under his foot 'cause I'm in his way? You know? I'm getting *sick* of that kind of stuff that we have to put up with!

Therapist: Really.

Client: I just feel like over *one kid* I'm losing my temper every day?. . . And these kids just tear a school apart, 'cause they don't care *what* they do. . . . I mean, this kid could drive me into a heart attack, 'cause I get really *angry,* and I'm trying to control my anger, you know. I would really like to take him and choke him. I mean, I really would like to get physical, because I feel like in a way that's what needs to happen to him, is somebody just punches him out—till he sees that he just can't do this? But I can't do that, of course. So I go home with all this fury, you know, or I spend the *day* feeling furious, and then I don't know what to do to *deal* with it. . . . And when I feel this angry I eat more, 'cause I feel really defeated. I feel made impotent, and I get really angry when somebody tries to make me impotent. . . . I don't feel good about being hooked into somebody else's anger.

Therapist: Do you want to focus here for a few minutes now on that hook? And see if we can do some work with that?

Client: Yeah, that's what I *should* do. 'Cause I wasn't sure, you know—I just felt, well, I could bring that much intense anger in here, 'cause that's what's important. . . .

Therapist: So again now, how to unhook . . . .

Client: It seems like, you know, I just can't perceive people like him the way I'm perceiving them.

Therapist: What's the new track, what's the new *frame* or way of perceiving him?

[When the client said, "I just can't perceive people like him the way I'm perceiving them," meaning that she could stop feeling rage if she found a different point of view, the therapist saw an opportunity for inviting her to view from a symptom-free position. The therapist is aware that in response to the experiential question he then asked, either she will find such a new position, or her attempt to take that symptom-free position will trigger resistance or protest from her unconscious, pro-symptom position, bringing that position into awareness. Note that this is an experiential intervention; the therapist's manner made it plain that he was asking her not merely to speculate intellectually but to actually construct and assume a symptom-free position.]

Client: [Closes eyes, reflects internally for several seconds, then opens eyes and speaks with an ironic tone] I've got a *lot* invested in keeping this opinion. You know, I just tried to see if I could shift it, and it went, "Nn-*nn!* Gotta hang *on* to this."

Therapist: And what's that 'Nn-nn!' protecting? What do you lose if you let go of that? Really, what's at stake, if you let go of that?

Client: [Pause; then speaks in a monotone as she gazes at the therapist] I couldn't keep living in kind of a crisis mentality. I'd have to give that up—and it's adventurous, and it's exciting.

Therapist: I see. I see. Adventurous and exciting.

[This is the turning point of the session. The therapist asked her to take a symptom-free position. As she tried to do that, she experienced the feeling, "Nn-nn! Gotta hang on to this." This is her pro-symptom position suddenly coming into her awareness through its resistance and revealing itself as valuing being "hooked" into this boy's anger and unwilling to have that stop. She experiences this directly, not through interpretation. This sudden activity of her pro-symptom position is an important opportunity for engaging it, and from the moment it makes its appearance the therapist rivets attention on it through inviting it to express itself further, on its own terms, in order to find what those terms are. And in response, that hidden position comes right out into the open. Since it is unconscious material that the client is now accessing, her voice becomes noticeably monotonic and her eye contact becomes more of a gaze as she voices the hidden position and says, "I couldn't keep living in kind of a crisis mentality. I'd have to give that up—and it's adventurous, and it's exciting." In this she is beginning to contact and articulate the emotional truth of the symptom. The therapist will now continue to elicit the symptom's emotional truth—the pro-symptom position—until it is completely clear why the symptom of staying in anger is more important to have than not to have.]

Therapist: So does the part that went, "Nn-nn! Gotta keep this!" fear a bland, boring existence if you give that up and disengage from this boy?

Client: Yeah, because that also means that I'm in control to some extent, too, I think. You know, I have a part to play in this adventure then? The other must mean more surrender and kind of—maybe more feminine way of looking at things. You know, this part of me doesn't like that.

Therapist: Likes to join the battle—engage the battle.

Client: [Laughs] Likes to be a *warrior.* I mean, really likes to go out there and *fight.*

[For the therapist, the client's last words clinched the case, unmistakably confirming the nature of her pro-symptom position. The therapist now feels finished with radical inquiry. It is also clear to him that reverse resolution will occur, since the client strongly values her pro-symptom position. He therefore will now focus entirely on the position work of drawing the client into inhabiting her pro-symptom position in relation to the boy in question, which will resolve the problem by transforming the meaning of her symptom of staying emotionally engaged with him (reframing to the emotional truth of the symptom). Note how the therapist arrived at his last words, which decisively elicited the pro-symptom position: he was already listening to the client's previous words with the one-pointed intention of finding signs of her pro-symptom position. She had just said, with spunk in her voice, that the part of her that was resisting being unhooked is opposed to "surrender" and loves the "adventure" and "excitement" of the struggle with this boy. The therapist, listening with pro-symptom ears, heard in this a love of battle and simply voiced that impression—and was ready to drop it if disconfirmed by the client; but she fully confirmed it.]

Therapist: So it sounds like from the point of view of *that* part of you, this problem is not a problem. In other words, it's—

Client: Yeah, it's provoking a fight! [Laughs]

Therapist: It's *good* to be in a battle. It gives a warrior—you know, a warrior lives to be in battle, right?

Client: Yeah.

Therapist: That's what a warrior's about.

Client: [With great spunk] I mean, there's always been a part of me that would like physical battle, where, you know, you end up shaking hands afterwards or something— you know, "Well, that was a *good* tussle, wasn't it!" You know? There *is* that part of me. 'Cause I can remember when I was in Cleveland a friend of mine said he used to like to wrestle with me. He said, "You really fight!" You know, and then—I would *really* put a lot of energy into it!

Therapist: [Slowly] So from this part of you, would you try out saying to me, right now, this sentence: "I *like* battling with this kid every day."

Client: [Laughs hard]

Therapist: From this *part* of you.

Client: All right. All right. This part of me. [Striking change of facial expression; face now appears suffused with pleasure and mischief.] I really *like* to battle with this kid, every day. It's exciting.

Therapist: Yes.

Client: And it's on the fringe. And it's on the verge of danger.

Therapist: Yes. I *get* it.

Client: And I like danger.

Therapist: I *get* it.

Client: I like adventure.

Therapist: Good. I see that look in your face. You really—this part of you really gets something out of that. *Loves* that.

Client: [Laughs]

Therapist: Yes. So there are parts of you that really hate the way this feels, but there is a more powerful part of you that really thrives in some sense on this battle. Goes for it.

Client: Well, there's a whole *code* in me of warriorship. You know, it's the whole thing of, you don't back off of a battle with somebody. . . .

Therapist: I'd like you to try something now. I'd like you to visualize him, this kid. In fact, I'd like you to visualize keeping him after class. So everybody else has left the class.

Client: Uh-huh. [Closes eyes]

Therapist: That's it. And he's standing there. And you walk over to him, and right into his face, you say [slowly spoken], "I want you to know—that I look *forward*—"

Client: [Laughs hard]

Therapist: "—to coming here every day—"

Client: [Laughs]

Therapist: "—and wrestling with you. I *love* it. And I really *don't* want you to leave my class, because then I won't have *this* to look forward to every day."

Client: [Laughs]

Therapist: "You make my day."

Client: [Laughs]

Therapist: Go ahead.

Client: Mmm.

Therapist: And see how he responds, as you say these things.

Client: [Closes eyes, is silent for a few seconds, then laughs] I think it would end up in laughing. Yeah, like, "That's a *good* fight. That's *worth* doing." [Long pause with eyes still closed] There's this part inside me that's sort of cowering watching this: "Aaahhh!"

Therapist: That's another part that hates the fighting and is scared of it?

Client: It's kind of scared of it. Not hating it, but kind of, "That's a really big person up there, towering over me."

Therapist: Scared of it, but not hating it.

Client: No, because I don't think the fighting energy is really malicious. It's not a malicious fighting energy, because it would take on the other person as an equal foe, I think, and—you know, the whole idea of a warrior.

Therapist: So does that mean it's more of a *sporting* energy?

Client: In the sense that you were talking about, *yeah,* I think it is. You know, it's like going to the joust, or something? See if I can knock you off your horse, or you knock me off. . . .

Therapist: So listen, I wonder if you could do an experiment, come Monday morning. I wonder if you could go into school deliberately positioned in the warrior part of you that's looking *forward* to today's joust. You walk into the room where you know he is, or he walks into the room where you are, and your senses just are *wide* open, *wide* awake—you gotta watch *every* move your opponent makes.

Client: [Laughs]

Therapist: You know, it's an intense, high thing, right from that point.

Client: [With a conspiratorial look and lowered voice] That would be fine if nobody else was involved. That's the *problem,* isn't it? That's exactly what I said earlier is, this kid is *consuming* all my *time.*

[In saying that "this kid is consuming all my time" she has suddenly returned to her original anti-symptom, victim position, as if it is this boy who consumes her attention, rather than her own great attraction to the joust. The therapist has to respond immediately and challenge this switch of positions, because the therapeutic strategy at this point is to arrange for her to stay in her joust-loving (pro-symptom) position and no longer be unconscious of it. The therapist will therefore immediately ask her to switch back to her warrior position's viewpoint.]

Therapist: I'd like you to again go into your warrior part and find out about this from that angle.

Client: It doesn't fuckin' *care* if it takes up all the time with one kid! [Laughs hard] I mean after all, that's the joust.

Therapist: That's right, the joust.

Client: It's very single-minded, concentrated. And meanwhile all these other poor kids don't know what the hell's going on! [Laughs]

Therapist: So how about doing this just for one day, or one class with him? In other words, to really, deliberately come into it from this position, this warrior position, and fully experience it, from that position. *Savoring* the joust—

Client: Mm-hm.

Therapist: —as your world. The main event. And accepting this part of you in one class with him. 'Cause you may not have many more classes with him.

Client: [Pause while gazing at therapist] What a pity, eh? [Laughs hard]

Here we have seen radical inquiry via the dual technique of viewing from a symptom-free position and inviting resistance; the session also involved an experiential shift via position work. In the next session, two weeks later, the client reported what then happened. The session above was on a Saturday. She went into school Monday morning in her "warrior" position and felt completely free of the old victimization or anger. She also spoke with the guidance counselor and got the counselor to agree to take the boy out of her class—something she said she could have done, but had not done, for many weeks, but now she did it on the next school day after the session. She could now *choose* to give up this boy as a jousting partner because she was now consciously owning her enjoyment of jousting with him. As we have seen in several other instances, having a client consciously take the position generating a symptom is the best way to enable her to vacate that position permanently. It had been so difficult to stay in her role as an effective teacher with this boy, not so much because of him, but because of her *own* great desire to go into her warrior position and joust with this kid—and to hell with teaching the other kids! But her warrior position and her desire to be in it had been unconscious, so the only way she could make sense of her difficulty staying in the teacher role was by seeing this *boy* as pulling her out of it and seeing herself as his victim.

Utilizing Unexpected Resistance

In depth-oriented brief therapy, as in other nonpathologizing, constructivist therapies, resistance is viewed simply as an expression of the coherence of the client's constructions of reality. As systems theorist Paul Dell pointed out, "The individual's . . . coherence is the lock—and the therapist's interventions are the keys. . . . It is always the lock that determines which keys will work." A wrong key indeed encounters resistance, but for the reason that it is a wrong key, not because the lock is "resisting." The lock simply has the structure it has and coherently behaves according to that structure. In precisely the same way, the therapist's experience of encountering resistance means one thing and one thing only: what the therapist is trying to do does not fit with the structure of the client's construction of reality. Therefore, the therapist should change keys rather than blame the lock. That is, rather than view the client as noncooperative, pathologically opposing health, or not yet ready for treatment, "It would be more accurate (and more honest)" according to Dell, "to say that the treatment is not yet ready for the patient."

More specifically, the therapist has the experience of encountering resistance when the client's coherence generates a protective action in response to the therapist's actions. The readiness for implementing this protective action is already present in the client's coherent construction of reality. Resistance is a protective action occurring in relation to the therapist, and it is a *routine* response of the client in the sense that it already exists within the repertoire of the coherence with which the client comes into therapy. In DOBT the therapist's genuine attitude toward the resistance is therefore to welcome it in the same spirit in which the therapist regards a protective action presented as a symptom, namely as a valuable point of access to key emotional truths and hidden positions, exactly in the manner illustrated in the preceding transcript. Resistance is the live appearance in the room of an important hidden position. Spotting resistance and viewing it as a protective activity of a hidden position gives the therapist an excellent opportunity to work from that protective action directly to that hidden position and to that which is being protected—usually an unhealed emotional wound and associated emotional themes and presuppositions. So the therapist immediately does radical inquiry into the resistance while it is occurring, without ever psychologizing or subtly blaming the client for it.

Let's look at how the therapist works from the resistance into its hidden structure. As a working example of resistance occurring in a therapy session, let's consider dissociation. The patterns of work we will describe apply equally to other forms of resistance, such as intellectualizing, emotionalizing, arriving late for sessions, and so on.

Many clients dissociate during sessions when the work gets near an emotional wound or trauma. The client's attention becomes diffuse and diverted from the requested focus, affect flattens, the voice becomes monotone, confusion sets in, a blank look develops, and so on. Some clients describe a kinesthetic "wall" that comes up or down around them, or a "fog" that rolls in suddenly, an emotional numbness, a sense of remoteness in which the themes under scrutiny seem to belong to someone else, or a cozy fatigue and overwhelming desire to sleep.

When a client manifests any of these signs of dissociation, a first step of response from the therapist is to comment on the client's specific manifestation and experience of dissociation, eliciting explicit acknowledgment of this from the client. A second step is to ask the client to deliberately *increase* the dissociation somewhat. This is a form of position work that both reduces the autonomy of the dissociated state and communicates the therapist's acceptance of this state as being what is emotionally true for the client right now.

The therapist then again acknowledges and accepts that the client is in the safety and the emotional distance of the dissociated state, and he or she proceeds to work with this state through either position work or what we call *distant viewing*.

The distant viewing technique consists of having the dissociated client *stay* dissociated and from that emotionally distant, safe state examine what it is protecting him or her from experiencing—in other words, what would have happened if the dissociation hadn't.

There are various ways to do this. One is through saying to the client, for example, "I'd like you to stay right where you are in that safe place in the fog and only *imagine* what would have happened here with me if you *hadn't* gone into that fog. Stay in the fog and only imagine how the scene was going to develop without the fog." In this approach, the client in the dissociated state visualizes himself having whatever experience was going to happen in the *non*dissociated state. Clients can actually do this and describe what they were going to experience if they hadn't dissociated. (In some cases, a client who dissociates will immediately be able to reengage the scene that activated the emotional wound and tolerate it if the therapist directs the client to view the scene from a distance and see herself "over there" in the scene, rather than viewing from a location *within* the scene.)

Another way a client can tolerate finding out what he would be experiencing without the dissociative protective action is through sentence completion—for example, "If I *hadn't* cut off when you asked me to picture my mother in that room . . ." Have him say and complete that sentence enough times and he will become aware of what he would have experienced and why it was necessary to keep that from happening.

For clients whose dissociated state during a session involves an image or feeling of a *wall* coming down around them, the therapist can frame that wall as a valuable, loyal friend that protects them whenever needed, which is an emotional truth and not a trick metaphor. The therapist encourages the client to stay inside the safety of that wall but invites her to step up on a rock or bench and just have a glimpse over it, or find a peephole *through* it, to see what's on the other side that she might need shielding from.

Once the client has identified the experience he or she is avoiding, the therapist asks, "What makes that so important to avoid?" and the work focuses there, to bring out whatever feelings or presuppositions necessitate and trigger the dissociation.

Position work is the other general method that can be applied to working with a dissociated state during a session. This consists of inviting the client to *overtly* assert his or her unwillingness to stay present for the work that the therapist was about to do.

The easiest way to do this is by offering the client a *trial sentence*. For example, the therapist says to the client, "Would you try out saying directly to me, in order to see if it's true, this sentence: 'I'm not willing to find out what you were asking me to think about.'"

(The reader may recall that a request of exactly this form was what produced the breakthrough in Chapter Two with the woman who viewed herself as repulsively ugly.) Since the therapist has already expressed complete acceptance of the dissociated state that has developed, usually it is not too hard to get the client to *overtly* acknowledge the unwillingness that *covertly* showed up as dissociation. Furthermore, in the trial sentence technique the therapist is asking the client only to "try on" the sentence to see "if" it fits.

Having the client try out saying, "I'm not willing to find out what you were asking me to think about" is position work because it has the client actually shift into that emotionally true position. The client says the sentence, then says it feels true, and what then usually happens is that as a result of openly, overtly expressing the unwillingness, the dissociated state immediately starts to disappear. The covert expression of the unwillingness—the dissociated state— is starting not to be needed at that point.

If the sentence rings true for the client but the dissociated state does *not* dissipate, the next step is for the therapist to express acceptance of *that* by saying, for example, "OK, I accept that you're unwilling to find out what I was asking you about. We won't pursue what I was asking you since you're telling me, 'No, not yet.' But tell me, *how come* that's something that's important for you to stay away from?" This is the same line of inquiry reached through the method of distant viewing, and *this* question usually gives the client a gradual, acceptable way to contact the material that he or she felt the need to avoid.

Utilizing the Client-Therapist Relationship

In depth-oriented brief therapy the therapist utilizes client transference much as he or she utilizes client resistance, as an expression of an unconscious position. Since a state of activated transference, positive or negative, tends to be richly imbued with feeling, it can be mined as an especially accessible vein into the unconscious position generating it.

Fundamentally, transference is no different than any other unconscious construal of meaning. All construing and attributing of meaning is projection. George Kelly, the originator of clinical constructivism, wrote, "Anything a person does can be interpreted as a projection of his personal constructs. Indeed, the whole system of the psychology of personal constructs might possibly have been called 'the psychology of projection.'" Transference is of course considered by many to be the master projection. However, DOBT does not hinge on its use. Nonetheless, the intentional depth-oriented brief therapist, always watching for corridors of meaning leading to the pro-symptom position, will capitalize on its expression, using the same methodology as for any other construction of meaning: radical inquiry and experiential shift.

Mind-Body Communication

It is also valuable in radical inquiry to focus on clients' somatic symptoms, including psychosomatic ailments, psychogenic pain, and kinesthetic sensations. The latter two—sometimes in the form of a headache; sharp pains in the throat, chest, or stomach; or a localized sensation of pressure, contraction, or energy—occasionally arise during a session in response to the experiential work under way. The following technique of body-mind communication, adapted from Gestalt therapy methods, is in our experience reliably effective for gaining access to the emotional truth of such symptoms.

1. Have the client fully focus attention on the sensation, with no attempt to change or stop it.
2. Still fully attending to the sensation, the client then visualizes the three-dimensional shape of the bodily region of the sensation.
3. Ask the client to describe this shape, including the type of surface it has (well-defined or fuzzy), whether it is stationary or moving and changing, and its coloration.
4. Have the client say to this visualized form in the body, either out loud or in silent internal dialogue (leaving the choice to the client), "I am very aware of you there. You have gotten my attention. Is there something you are trying to tell me?" Almost without exception, the client will experience an inner response from the body region, either in clear words or in an attitudinal or emotional meaning that the client can *put* into words.
5. If no response, invite the client to say to the region, "Are you quiet because you don't trust me to understand or care about what you want to say?"

6. If still no response, ask how the client is actually feeling toward this region right now. Does the client feel genuinely *willing* or primarily unwilling to hear what that region has to say? If the client is unwilling or closed, ask him or her to verbally express *that* to the region and then to explain to it specifically why. In response to this emotional honesty, the region will now trust the client's conscious position enough to make a response.

7. Coach the client through further dialogue with the body region in which the emotional message of that region is welcomed, received, clarified, and acknowledged.

This technique can provide direct access to key material. In psychosomatic conditions, often the afflicted body region locally can provide access to much or all of the emotional truth of the problem.

Focused Examination of Personal History

In DOBT the therapist explores the client's view of the past only as needed to discover the nature of present constructions of meaning. In some cases, all constructions relevant to the symptom are discovered without reference to the past at all. However, for many clients the emotions, cognitions, and somatics comprising the emotional truth of the symptom are unconsciously stored and represented most essentially in images and scenes of the past. Working directly with those current representations that the client regards as "memory of the past" is often the most direct and profound way to transform those constructions of reality and permanently eliminate the symptoms they generate.

The case examples in Chapter Two dealing with painfully negative self-image and with lifelong depression buffered by workaholism included this kind of work, so we will not further illustrate it here. We note only that in depth-oriented brief therapy it has to be the therapist, not the client, who controls how information on the past is obtained, according to the therapist's specific need to identify the symptom-positive context and the pro-symptom position in that context. Specific questions we use to begin to probe for relevant past experience are the obvious ones, such as: "Did you experience anything earlier in your life that felt similar to how you're now experiencing this?" "Did someone in the past respond to you in this way that you now expect others to do?" Subsequent work on relevant past experience is then experiential, with such questions as: "Would you be willing to imagine being seven, visualizing your mother, and seeing if this feeling is part of how you experience her?" "What do you want to say to him, that you never said at the time?"

Summary

Clarity into the client's pro-symptom emotional truth is what techniques of radical inquiry are designed to achieve rapidly for the therapist. We have reviewed many such techniques, including both linguistic and experiential methods that have construct-evoking impact, as well as techniques for utilizing client resistance, dreams, somatic symptoms, and the client-therapist relationship.

In keeping with the underlying stance of radical inquiry, all these techniques are *experiential* and *phenomenological*. Likewise, all operate as expressions of the therapist's *active intentionality* to meet the emotional truth of the problem and the therapist's *freedom to clarify* that emotional truth. The techniques are only means by which the therapist moves to enact the underlying stance. Once the techniques have become familiar and natural, the therapist does not think, "Now which technique should I use here?" just as he or she does not think, "Now which arm should I use to open this door?" If the therapist is inhabiting the stance of radical inquiry—holding the conviction that a pro-symptom position exists and can be significantly if not wholly accessed in this very session— the technique best suited to the moment simply comes to mind or can be invented on the spot.

Radical inquiry is one of the therapist's two main operational priorities for effectiveness in depth-oriented brief therapy. The other is experiential shift, the activity of transforming constructions of reality, and it is to these processes that we next turn our attention.

Notes

P. 157, *In sooth I know not why I am so sad . . .:* W. Shakespeare (1988), *The Merchant of Venice* (Act I, Scene 1), New York: Bantam.

P. 162, *reach directly into the hidden structure of the presenting problem:* We want to acknowledge Dr. Robert Shaw of the Family Institute of Berkeley,

California, for developing and teaching a way of questioning that elicits the implicit presuppositional structure of the presented problem, and that we have fruitfully adapted to the purposes of radical inquiry in DOBT.

P. 167, *devised by the creators of neuro-linguistic programming:* R. Bandler and J. Grinder (1979), *Frogs into Princes: Neuro Linguistic Programming,* Moab, UT: Real People Press.

P. 171, *the constructivist technique known as* laddering: D. N. Hinkle (1965), *The Change of Personal Constructs from the Viewpoint of a Theory of Implications,* unpublished doctoral dissertation, Ohio University.

P. 171, *"shared trance":* C. Tart (1969), "Psychedelic Experiences Associated with a Novel Hypnotic Induction Procedure: Mutual Hypnosis," in C. Tart (Ed.), *Altered States of Consciousness,* San Francisco: Harper. For a review of later literature, see G. Gleason (1992), "Mutual Hypnosis," *Whole Earth Review, 75,* 28–29.

P. 173, *active imagination:* See, for example, B. Hannah (1981), *Encounters with the Soul: Active Imagination as Developed by C. G. Jung,* Boston: Sigo Press.

P. 174, *Gestalt empty-chair dialogues and two-chair work:* See, for example, F. S. Perls (1969), *Gestalt Therapy Verbatim,* Lafayette, CA: Real People Press.

P. 179, *which differs from how the technique has been described by some other writers:* See, for example, N. Branden (1971), *The Disowned Self,* Los Angeles: Nash; for an application of sentence completion in working with couples, see J. M. Gumina (1980), "Sentence Completion as an Aid to Sex Therapy," *Journal of Marital and Family Therapy, 62,* 201–206.

P. 194, *". . . It is always the lock that determines which keys will work":* P. Dell (1982), "Beyond Homeostasis: Toward a Concept of Coherence," *Family Process, 21,* 35.

P. 194, *". . . the treatment is not yet ready for the patient":* Dell, "Beyond Homeostasis," 30.

PP. 197–198, *"Anything a person does . . . 'the psychology of projection'":* G. Kelly (1955), *The Psychology of Personal Constructs* (p. 202), New York: W. W. Norton.

CHAPTER 6

Experiential Shift: Changing Reality

People wish to be settled:
only as far as they are unsettled
is there any hope for them.
RALPH WALDO EMERSON, *Circles*

Actual change in the client's construction of reality, dispelling the presenting symptom, is the subject of this chapter. In depth-oriented brief therapy, the methodology of producing such actual change is termed *experiential shift,* one of the therapist's two top priorities. The reader has already encountered many specific examples of experiential shift in previous chapters. Our purpose here is to provide a more systematic overview, with clinical examples, of how the therapist guides the client into accessing, inhabiting, and transforming the version of reality in his or her unconscious, pro-symptom position.

As we have previously seen, symptoms are generated by living as though their emotional truth isn't the case. When the unconscious, pro-symptom position becomes known to the client, one of two kinds of resolution will occur. One possibility is that the client will want to be rid of both this position and the symptom it insists upon producing (direct resolution, as illustrated by the cases of low self-esteem and depression in Chapter Two). The other possibility is that the client will affirm both this pro-symptom position and the newly realized value of the symptom, in which case the status of the symptom immediately changes from unwanted to wanted and the anti-symptom position spontaneously dissolves (reverse resolution, as illustrated in Chapter One by the case of the graduate student whose "procrastination" was discovered to be his determination not to pursue an unwanted career).

The Ability to Change

In our constructivist view, psychotherapy can change a person's symptomatic experience and behavior because each person natively has the following two fundamental constructivist abilities:

1. *Control of illumination of constructs:* the ability to bestow consciousness on, or withdraw it from, a given construct. Since every construct is, as described in Chapter Three, a known or conscious knowing, or an unknown or unconscious knowing, this is the individual's ability to change the status of any construct from an unconscious to a conscious knowing and vice versa.

2. *Control of existence of constructs:* the ability to create, preserve, and dissolve constructions of reality. A construct is preserved by being regarded in *any* position as real, and it is dissolved by being regarded in *all* positions as unreal.

We define psychotherapy—any kind of psychotherapy—as an implicit or explicit agreement between client and therapist that they are interacting for the purpose of enabling the client to exercise his or her constructivist abilities so as to transform habitual constructions of meaning and thereby change satisfactorily the client's experience of, and response to, the presenting problem. The two fundamental constructivist abilities of human beings usually function in an unconscious, automatic, and reactive way and remain unrecognized and not choicefully utilized. Yet when cued or prompted by the therapist, most clients can readily perform constructivist feats that prove invaluable to them, though doing so would never have occurred to them on their own.

Once radical inquiry has given the therapist an understanding or map of the client's pro-symptom position or construction of reality within which the symptom is necessary, the process of experiential shift then consists of two basic aspects:

1. *Position work,* or guiding the client into inhabiting and inte-

grating the emotional reality in his or her unconscious, pro-symptom position. This process makes use of the client's ability to control the illumination of constructs.

2. *Coaching the transformation of pro-symptom constructs.* This process makes use of the client's ability to control the existence of constructs.

The next sections of this chapter describe and demonstrate these processes in detail.

Position Work

In position work, the therapist ushers the client into inhabiting the pro-symptom position, so that the client is actually experiencing the emotional and cognitive reality defined by it and is, in addition, integrating this reality—that is, accepting and including it as an emotional truth in the client's life. The intention is to permanently change the status of the pro-symptom position from unconscious knowing to conscious knowing. This in itself is a substantial experiential shift, and it is this shift that reframes the symptom to its emotional truth. In many cases this reframe, this lucid realization of the full emotional meaning or value of the symptom, itself achieves resolution. This reframe arises from within the client's own world of meaning and is therefore fundamentally different from the externally applied reframes used in certain other brief therapies.

Radical inquiry, in contrast, is an initial, more rapid pass through this same construction. It ordinarily does not integrate or render stably conscious the pro-symptom reality, serving only to reveal it to the therapist. The distinction between position work and radical inquiry may at first seem subtle. If we liken the client's unconscious, pro-symptom position to an arrangement of furniture and objects in a very dark room, radical inquiry is like looking around the dark room with a narrow-beam flashlight, momentarily illuminating one item at a time until the overall layout has become clear to the therapist. Once the flashlight is withdrawn, the room again goes dark for the client, even though each item was perfectly clear while it was illuminated. Later in the session, or in the next session, the client may again be unconscious of the very existence of that room, but the therapist remembers what has been found. Position work then generates for the client a consciousness of the whole configuration, like turning on the overhead lights of the dark room, permanently illuminating the whole. In radical inquiry the client has only briefly visited his unconscious constructs; in position work he moves in and lives with them.

The vital importance of position work for bringing about an experiential shift is that making the pro-symptom position a fully experienced, conscious knowing gives the client direct access to the constructs (feelings, beliefs, scenes, and so on) comprising it. This is the most powerful position the client can take for creating deep, lasting change, and yet it is usually the position the client least wants to take.

For clients (and for many therapists, too), the "intuitive" way to move toward freedom from the symptom is to follow the *anti-symptom* position's inclination to move *away* from the symptom as soon and as decisively as possible. This movement away from the symptom is an attempt to withdraw attention from the painful or troubling experience of the symptom, disclaiming and disowning the symptom and the emotional truths associated with it. Motivating this approach is the implicit and profoundly fallacious assumption that the client's dislike of or shame over the symptom in itself has the potency to prevent the symptom from occurring. With this assumption, the therapist follows the client's focus on his anti-symptom position, and gives empathy and support to what the client feels and sees in that position as an escape route from pain, and tries to develop that anti-symptom position to the point of prevailing over the symptom.

This is a strategy that produces ineffectual work. As natural as this kind of attempt may be, the focus on the anti-symptom position is precisely what locks the symptom in place: it maximizes the unconsciousness of the pro-symptom position, which also maximizes its autonomy, its freedom to produce the symptom. The client's anti-symptom position is not, in itself, the future symptom-free position, though initially the client thinks it is. The very attempt to be nonsymptomatic, rid of the symptom, is actually not a change at all, but is in fact more of the same unconsciousness of the emotional truth of the symptom that set up the production of the symptom in the first place. "As long as I attend to what I wish to be I need not attend to what I am," writes therapist Nancy Shuler. "As long as I do not attend to what I am, change is not possible. . . . [C]oncentrating [only] on change only serves to keep change from occurring."

Position work is a movement in the opposite direction, an experiential movement *toward* and down *into* the emotional truth of the symptom. For some clients and therapists, this at first seems counterintuitive, like running into a burning house instead of out of it. However, as our many clinical examples in previous chapters have shown, by bringing the client consciously into his or her pro-symptom position, position work rapidly gives the client direct access to the previously hidden-away phenomenology generating the symptom, making profound change an immediate possibility.

The guiding principle of position work, then, is this:

> Change is blocked when the client tries to move from a position that he or she doesn't actually have as a governing emotional truth. Therefore, for the client to be free to move to a new position that is free of the symptom, first have the client take the emotionally governing, pro-symptom position he or she actually has.

Let's quickly review a few instances of this that we have already seen:

The agoraphobic woman in Chapter One was trying not to have "psychotic" delusions from the position that she *didn't* want to have them, and so the symptom would not change, because that was not her emotional truth of the matter. When she recognized and took her position that she *did* choose to have this delusion as an effective way to avoid feeling a deep old wound of abandonment, she then found it easy to stop having the delusion.

The woman in Chapter Two with the cutting shard of low self-worth as a female became able to change this lifelong, painful view of herself as soon as she consciously took her unconscious, protective position of being actively unwilling to see herself as normally attractive.

The woman high school teacher in Chapter Five was trying unsuccessfully to stop reacting daily with impotent rage at an aggressive student. She was trying to make this change from the position that she *didn't* want to fight with him, when her unconscious emotional truth was that she *did* want to fight with him as a "warrior." By consciously taking that position, she immediately became able to change. She stopped reacting and disengaged from him.

Reality in the client's pro-symptom position—including the age and experiential identity of the self, the imaginal physical environment or home, and so forth—is the same reality that was being experienced at the historical time of the original formation of the emotional wound or trauma present in the position. The reality in the pro-symptom position does not contain any representation of other realities that the client later developed. In this sense, the client is unconsciously still living in the wounding or traumatizing situation. Time has not moved on there. The version of reality and the intentions and strategies formed by the client in the original wounding situation are still operating in the pro-symptom position; indeed, they *constitute* that position. The client may think of the original wounding situation as being in the past, but it is unconsciously a *present* reality in the psyche. The therapist needs to be sensitively aware of the emotional realness of what the client experiences on inhabiting a pro-symptom position.

When a client becomes aware of the version of reality and the purposes and strategies he holds in his pro-symptom position, he can become aware also of his own creative act of forming and implementing that position. This occurs when the client accesses and consciously experiences the very configuration of meaning and feeling that was (and still is) the motivating point of origin for forming the pro-symptom position. This point of origin may or may not be associated in memory with a specific historical moment; more primarily, it is a specific configuration of meaning and feeling, and in becoming conscious of it the client remembers creating his pro-symptom position and why he did it. The client comes into conscious possession of his actual capacity to create or uncreate that position, like finding control of a mental muscle he didn't know existed.

The goal of position work is for the client to assert to the therapist a statement of a *pro/anti synthesis* having the following form, as his or her own direct knowledge and emotional truth:

> I implement the symptom of _____ for the specific purpose of _____, and for me, achieving this purpose is worth the specific pain and troubles that accompany the symptom.

For example: "I think of myself as repulsively ugly in order to keep myself from ever again being a romantic candidate who could be utterly devastated by rejection, and for me, staying safe in this way is worth the emotional pain and shame of seeing myself as ugly."

In this form of statement there is a conscious synthesis of the client's pro-symptom position ("I implement the symptom for the specific purpose of . . .") and anti-symptom position ("the pain and troubles that accompany the symptom"). The goal of position work is for the client to experience and acknowledge not only his pro-symptom position but this complete synthesis of the pro- and anti-symptom realities. It is the client's clear, experiential awareness of the emotional truth of this synthesis that permanently alters the constructed reality of the problem and creates an experiential shift. By overtly linking the pro- and anti-symptom positions in this emotionally true way, neither can continue to function autonomously from the other, and the client in effect becomes lodged in a new state of conscious, purposeful implementation of the symptom.

Techniques of Position Work

It is within this understanding of the goal of position work as a pro/anti synthesis that the techniques detailed below are useful. First are five in-session techniques:

- Overt statement of position
- Cycling in and out of a symptom-free position
- Following the client a little bit ahead
- Confronting with emotional truth
- Traumatic incident reduction

These are followed by three between-session techniques:

- Index card tasks
- Daily review tasks
- Using the symptom as a signal to take the pro-symptom position

These techniques are ways of ushering the client into inhabiting his or her pro-symptom position, rendering it vividly conscious and experientially known, and forming a full pro/anti synthesis as described above.

Overt Statement of Position

Following the detection of an unconscious, pro-symptom position through radical inquiry, one of the simplest and most direct ways for the client to inhabit that position is for the client to deliberately make a simple, declarative verbal statement that voices the position in a blunt, clear way. Since this is an act of expressing meanings that until this moment have been unconscious, the first verbal version formulated is a trial statement: the client "tries it on" as an approximation that will be further refined for emotional accuracy, or discarded if too inaccurate. As always in depth-oriented brief therapy, accuracy is determined subjectively by the client, not by the therapist.

The therapist invites the client to come up with a succinct overt statement, but it often happens that the client is in confusion among the various components of meaning comprising the detected position, despite having experientially identified and verified the separate components piece by piece as they were discovered in radical inquiry. The client may be simply unable to synthesize the coherent meaning of the whole position. In such a case, in the interest of time-effectiveness, it is expedient for the therapist to formulate an overt sentence and invite the client to try out saying it. The statement summarizes and unifies what has been found during radical inquiry, and it begins position work. For example, the therapist says to the client, "Let's see if what we have found so far really is emotionally true for you. Would you try out actually saying it to me, in order to feel for yourself if it's true? Would you try out saying, 'When I start to feel all alone and abandoned while I'm walking down the street, it's so painful and so scary that dreaming up my old therapist to be with me is worth doing, even though I think that's crazy'?"

If the sentence is sufficiently accurate, or if the client modifies it to *be* accurate, after one or two voicings he or she will begin to experience the emotional truth of the sentence. This is not a merely cognitive exercise, despite being a verbal one. Once the client says, "Yes, this feels true," the therapist invites a deepening repetition by saying something like, "OK, since this feels true for you, would you say it again now, as being completely your own emotional truth?" Usually this brings the client quite fully into experiencing the emotional position expressed by the sentence. It is quite common for an important release of deep feelings to occur at this moment. This occurred, for example, with the "unhappy no matter what" client (described in Chapter Two) when the therapist gave her the sentence, "The truth is, up to now my unhappiness over feeling unloved by my father is bigger than any happiness I've been able to have." The immediate upwelling of deep, poignant grief and sorrow that this woman experienced upon saying this sentence unlocked her chronic depression and restored her connection to a deep region in her own being that she had sealed off.

Once the client has emotionally dropped fully into the position verbalized in the statement, additional elements of emotional truth may very likely come into awareness spontaneously—the process of serial accessing. Then either further radical inquiry or further position work is pursued, as needed.

The following transcript illustrates position work carried out using overt statements. This is a continuation of a session (see pp. 168–170) with a woman whose symptom was a repeating pattern of compulsively becoming obsessive and emotionally dependent upon a certain type of man (a problem of symbiotic attachment). Radical inquiry had revealed how she knows to whom to attach (someone charismatic with an emotional wound or hole needing healing) and what her attachment does for that person (relieves his wound) and for herself ("They'll need me, and if they need me, they'll stay around" and be the one remaining "kidney" that keeps her alive).

From the therapist's point of view, each of the overt sentences offered to the client is merely a handing back of an element of emotional truth that the client had already made known to the therapist. The therapist chooses a wording, though, that is so blunt and vivid that in reencountering her own truth in this form, the client enjoys a small shock of new awareness of her own position. The transcript begins as the therapist is about to have her openly declare her pro-symptom position directly to her image of three men from her past with whom she enacted this unconscious position:

Therapist: So would you picture Alex—and Jeff—and your father—standing there in front of you?

Client: OK. [Pause] There they are.

Therapist: And try out saying to them some sentences I'll give you, to see if they're true for you. Change the words to make them more accurate, or let me know if they're just not true. First, try out saying to the three of them, "I know how to fill your hole—"

Client: I know how to fill your hole—

Therapist: "—and make you feel like *you're* really special."

Client: —and make you feel like *you're* really special—and really *whole.*

Therapist: "And I can spot you a mile away."

Client: [Laughs] And I can spot you a mile away.

Therapist: "And I move in faster than the speed of light."

Client: [Laughs harder] And I move in faster than the speed of light. It's *true.* [Pause] But then, I lose *myself.* It totally wipes out my own power.

Therapist: Yes, so say that, too. Tell them the whole thing: "Getting a strong connection with you is so important to me that it's worth wiping out my own power."

Client: Connecting with you is worth wiping out my own power. [Pause] Yes, that *is* true for some part of me.

Therapist: *That's* the part that matters here. I know you have other parts that feel differently, but stay with this one for now.

Client: OK.

Therapist: So try saying it again.

Client: Connecting with you is worth wiping out my own power. [With zeal] 'Cause it's like I *have* to have it—it's the only thing.

Therapist: What's "it"? More important than having your own power is having—

Client: This *connection.* I've *got* to have this connection more than anything.

Therapist: And tell them what this connection is going to do for you, why it's so important to you.

Client: This connection with you allows me to feel alive— *that's* the thing. And without it I feel dead, and that's

why I need it. It's like life or death. One way I feel
alive and the other way I feel dead.

Therapist: Like having no kidneys?

Client: Right.

Therapist: And what good is having your own power if you're
dead?

Client: Right, *exactly.* That's right.

Therapist: So why wouldn't you go for that connection *instantly,*
whenever you see that right kind of person?

Client: Right. It's like a drowning person seeing the surface of
the water from underneath. There's only *one* thing
you're gonna try for.

[The client is now lucidly inhabiting her pro-symptom position, in
which spotting a willing attachee and symbiotically attaching is
nothing short of lifesaving.]

Therapist: Stay with that, and let it show you more about what
happened for you with your mother.

Client: [Pause] There's a way I couldn't get air from my
mother, so these other people are like air sockets.

Therapist: So you feel that your mother stopped giving you
something vital, and without it you feel dead.

Client: Yes.

Therapist: And what is that vital something that she didn't give
you?

Client: Love. Something like love.

Therapist: And this dead feeling—what's the common word for
that state of feeling dead, lifeless?

Client: [Pause] Depressed.

Therapist: Yes.

Client: Right, right. Without it I feel depressed . . . I think
that's true, that there's this underlying depression
that's there all the time. Sometimes it *seems* not to be.

[The idea of depression arose for the first time in a previous session but was too threatening and frightening for her to feel and
know as true about herself, so this is something of a breakthrough.]

Therapist: One way to look at that is to ask yourself, do you ever
not make that speed-of-light reach for the right kind of

Therapist: person with a hole in the middle, when he or she appears on the radar?

Client: I probably always go for it.

Therapist: So the depressed, dead side of you is—

Client: —actually always happening. Right, right.

Therapist: So I'd like you to try on this sentence: "I'm always depressed over not getting love from my mother, whether or not I'm actually feeling it."

Client: [Big exhale] I'm always depressed over not getting love from my mother. It's true. It feels really—it's that quality of deadness. Grey. It just makes me want to go to sleep. *That's* the depression—I just want to go to sleep, or *die.*

Therapist: [Referring to a spontaneous memory in a previous session] Just like you sometimes wanted never again to wake up from sleep, as a little girl.

The position work recorded above enabled the client to voice the pro/anti synthesis, "Getting [someone like] dad to attach to me and give me life by needing me and loving me is urgently important and is worth the obsessing and the emotional dependency, because without that I'm dead." Her depression became the next focus of therapy, but after this session she never again lost herself in a compulsion to attach symbiotically and soon became involved with the "balanced" sort of person she had never found exciting.

Cycling In and Out of a Symptom-Free Position

This is a repetitive use of the technique of viewing from a symptom-free position described in Chapter Five. In this technique the therapist evokes the client into an imaginal experience of being in a situation in which the symptom normally happens strongly, and then further guides the client to construct an experience of herself as being without the symptom in this situation. For the purpose of position work, the technique can simply be applied in a repetitive manner, evoking the client alternately into and out of a symptom-free position, guiding the client to attend to what is lost when symptom-free and what is gained when the symptom is allowed to return, and asking the client to notice and verbalize the value of having the symptom. The alternation is done as many times as is necessary for the client to achieve her own experiential clarity as to the value of having the symptom. The exercise is then ended, but the therapist must then deliberately, repeatedly, and explicitly make the identified value of the symptom a focus of attention in one way and another, continually requiring the client to accommodate his conscious position to this new knowledge.

Following the Client a Little Bit Ahead

Our name for this technique of position work is an apt phrase coined by psychotherapist Kenneth Rhea. What this phrase means in DOBT is that the therapist verbally sums up the client's pro-symptom position in a concise, unified, emphatic way, bringing together what the client has already revealed of it in bits and pieces without realizing their pro-symptom significance. This is done again as additional pro-symptom material emerges until finally the therapist repeats back key elements of pro-symptom *and* anti-symptom meaning in a way that calls attention to and makes plain the linkages between them, forming a pro/anti synthesis, and does so with a condensed, sharply etched phrasing that makes a strong impression and is easily remembered. The final step, of course, is to have the client voice the synthesis to the therapist as his own emotional truth.

A short example: Having done enough radical inquiry to grasp the pro-symptom significance of a thirty-three-year-old male client's pervasive pattern of underachievement, the therapist took a first step of position work by empathically reviewing this man's dual positions in a way that drew him into a pro/anti synthesis. The therapist said, "I want to make sure I'm accurately understanding what I've learned from you. Please tell me if I've got this right. You want very much to 'amount to something,' and you're genuinely troubled over how little you're achieving or building in your life so far, and you want this pattern to change. At the same time, in another area of your feelings, you have another concern, also a passionate concern—a concern that your father shouldn't get away with how he treated you. You have an intense feeling of outrage and injustice that after treating you 'like absolute shit for sixteen years,' he thinks he did *fine* as a dad and is respected as a family man by his well-to-do friends. And you figure that if he sees your life coming together just fine, with solid achievements and success, it will prove to him irreversibly that he *did* do fine as a dad. And you're determined not to let that happen. In this area of your inner feelings you feel you *have* to keep your life a shambles to show him how badly he 'damaged' you. And even though it really does cost you dearly to keep your life in shambles, and even though you would want for yourself to be achieving things, even more urgently important to you is this need to present your father with a shambles, as the proof of how bad a job he actually did. Is that right? Is that the emotional truth for you?"

It is well known that for the therapist to repeat back the key constructs or elements of meaning already identified by the client has an awareness-enhancing effect for the client, particularly if no interpretive meaning is added by the therapist. Hearing the therapist state the client's own important meanings places the client momentarily outside of them and separate from them, allowing the client to attend reflectively to those meanings as objects within a larger field of consideration, rather than remain subjectively absorbed in those meanings with little or no awareness of them, as was previously always the form of contact with them. Achieving a reflective awareness of these meanings brings them into material contact with other meanings, knowings, and purposes in the client's conscious world, an interaction likely to be transformative.

Confronting with Emotional Truth

This is a technique also used for radical inquiry as described in Chapter Five, where we saw how a first-time assertion to visualized figures of previously unspeakable emotional truths can begin a serial accessing of a chain of deeply unconscious meanings and memories, illuminating the core of the pro-symptom construction. In confronting with emotional truth for position work, the client explicitly and very bluntly voices to the relevant person (either imaginally or in vivo) his previously hidden pro-symptom position or the pro/anti synthesis, whichever is appropriate. While for radical inquiry the client is only initially trying out an expression of emotional truth to see if it feels true, in position work the client is now squarely asserting his emotional truth as an actuality and as a basis of future decisions, actions, and relations. For the client to access and strongly express his pro-symptom position in this way tends to be a conclusive step toward integrating this material. Confronting with emotional truth means saying all that needs to be said, all the words of emotional truth that the client never dared say or couldn't conceive of saying. To this end, a useful task is that of the client writing a never-to-be-sent letter fully expressing the uncensored emotional truth to the appropriate person(s), even if deceased. Other examples follow later in this chapter in a transcript from couples therapy.

This is a deceptively simple technique. To confront with emotional truth is a deep affirmation of self because it expresses a fundamental ontological (fourth-order) position: I am a being capable of sound knowing; I am a being who is worthy of being taken seriously and treated with respect; my own knowledge is separate from your knowledge; and so on. If taking this ontological position is a significant change for the client, it will, because of its high level of superordinacy, immediately challenge and displace various old constructs of (third-order) purpose, (second-order) meaning and (first-order) behavior. If this shift involves more disorientation or loss than the client is ready to experience, he or she will either revert to the old constructions and/or manifest resistance (go blank, dissociate, intellectualize, get distracted, and so on). In that case the therapist accepts and acknowledges to the client that the therapist had invited the client to take too big a step; the therapist then pursues radical inquiry into the emotional truth of specifically which consequences of that new self-affirming position would be intolerable and why. Position work and other experiential shift work can then be carried out as necessary to dispel each such obstacle until the client succeeds at holding the new position from which to confront with emotional truth.

Traumatic Incident Reduction (TIR)

Traumatic incident reduction (TIR) is a technique developed by psychotherapists Frank Gerbode and Gerald French for fundamentally resolving (rather than merely managing or controlling) post-traumatic stress symptomatology. It is a process for rapidly accessing and dispelling the unconscious traumatic memory and the associated unconscious constructions of reality set up by the client during a traumatic event.

In DOBT terms, the TIR technique efficiently carries out radical inquiry and position work in relation to a particular type of pro-symptom position, one in which the (ongoing) emotional reality was formed by a traumatic incident. The technique involves a very specific protocol for ushering the client repetitively through the memory of the traumatic event. This repetitive, detailed, subjective review instigates a thorough emotional processing of this memory, progressively filling in lost details and unfolding the crucial moments of meaning-formation that occurred during the incident. This brings about a spontaneous emergence into awareness of the symptom-generating meanings, construals, intentions, and protective actions that were unconsciously formed. Thus, the TIR process fits very well within the DOBT framework of psychotherapy.

The note at the end of the chapter will guide interested readers to further details.

So far we have been considering in-session techniques of position work. Now we turn to between-session techniques, which are fully as important for achieving time-effective results.

No matter how well position work is carried out in the therapy hour, integration of the pro-symptom position's altered, unfamiliar reality is neither complete nor stable until the client consistently accesses the pro-symptom position and pro/anti synthesis during ordinary life between sessions. The following three techniques are designed to extend position work beyond the therapist's office door at the end of the session. Without such between-session tasks, the integration achieved by the in-session work may quickly *dis*integrate as the client walks onto the street, where the cues of the therapist's office-world recede and the cues of everyday life densely arise.

In position work, Alice steps through the looking glass into the unfamiliar reality in her pro-symptom position, and then she must bring back what she has found, *all the way home,* and live with it. Without special measures this is unlikely to occur, and the client may arrive at the next session not even aware of having lost what she had found. Her pro-symptom position has submerged again into unconsciousness and autonomy, allowing for continued production of the symptom and for a separate, conscious anti-symptom position in which the symptom again seems involuntary, completely undesirable, and devoid of sense or meaning.

When unconsciousness of the pro-symptom position recurs, the therapist simply repeats position work as necessary to retrieve it. Actually, the process of integration often involves a transitional period of alternating between the pro/anti synthesis and the pro/anti split for a few days to a few weeks. During this period, whenever the client drops the reality of the synthesis and speaks from the anti-symptom position, the therapist immediately requests the client to retake the synthesis position, for example by asking, "How would you say that from the point of view of your emotional truth about this?"

As a rule we prescribe a between-session task of position work at the end of every session.

Index Card Tasks

Simplest is to assign daily reading of an index card on which the therapist has written a succinct formulation of a key, fresh-caught emotional truth. The pro/anti synthesis is of course the emotional truth most important to catch and hold in a verbal net. The therapist and client collaborate on finding the wording that most adequately and accurately captures the client's felt sense of meaning, but it should be the therapist who writes the words on the card. Within the client's view, the therapist also writes down his or her own copy of exactly what is on the card. The therapist recommends the client read the card each morning and evening, or tape it to their mirror or dashboard, so as to encounter it frequently but unexpectedly. At or near the beginning of the next session, the therapist asks what the client experienced in relating to the emotional truth on the card. This follow-up is essential.

Daily Review Tasks

Another simple between-session task is a nightly, five-minute review of the day in which the client identifies and jots down any situation in which a newly discovered pro-symptom position was in fact operating, noting specifically what made the symptom important to have in that situation. The client brings this record to the next session to review with the therapist.

Using the Symptom as a Signal to Take the Pro-Symptom Position

In the ultimate technique of between-session position work, the therapist explains to the client that as a result of experiencing and recognizing the symptom's emotional truth, the meaning of the occurrence of the symptom has changed. Whenever the symptom now begins to occur, it can now be experienced as a *signal* to the client to knowingly take the (pro-symptom) position of his emotional truth and to let himself feel the emotional truth of in fact currently needing or wanting the symptom, despite its very real costs. The therapist gives the client the between-session task of watching for the symptom to occur so that he can use it in this way.

As part of this task the therapist assigns the client to have the symptom happen at predictable times when it would happen anyway, but to do so knowingly and purposefully for its now-conscious value, accepting the pain or trouble that it brings. The therapist explains that this means there will be a change not in behavior but in the client's awareness and appreciation of the emotional truth of what the symptom is doing for him at such times, and of actually implementing it for that purpose.

This task, coming after position work has been done in session, is not the same as the paradoxical intervention of prescribing the symptom in strategic therapy, because it is carrying out a different therapeutic strategy and has different effects on the client. Doing this task in DOBT more fully integrates the previously unconscious pro-symptom position. This dissolves the client's anti-symptom construal of the symptom as involuntary and of the self as helplessly afflicted with a pathology. The task also causes the client to become more aware of the symptom-positive context and of when and how it arises. All of this further sharpens the client's direct knowledge of how the symptom is important to have and of the loss that will have to be accepted in living without it.

In formulating this task, the client and the therapist should very explicitly identify specifically what constitutes having the symptom happen. It is also most important that an imaginal rehearsal of the symptom happening and of recognizing it as a signal be done in session. The therapist also gives the client an index card on which is written the emotional truth and purpose of the symptom, to be read immediately upon noticing the signal—the symptom—occurring.

Systemic Position Work with Couples and Families

Locating and making conscious a pro-symptom position is as therapeutically potent in couple and family therapy as it is for individual therapy. We find that carrying out position work with one or more participants during a couple or family session is one of the most effective ways to unlock a symptom-generating pattern of interaction.

The key notion, already introduced in Chapter Three, is that of the couple or family's ecology of meanings (our extension of Gregory Bateson's "ecology of ideas"). The relationship system is viewed rather concretely as an interaction between the current constructions of meaning of the individual family members. What depth-oriented brief therapy emphasizes is that the "understanding" that each family member has of the others' behavior is often unconscious. This unconscious construal of meaning lives within an unconscious position that then expresses itself with a behavior that is the presenting symptom, or part of it. This problem behavior indecipherably expresses some hidden emotional truth but is construed by others as showing bad intentions or bad character, and they react accordingly, which only further wounds the first one and proves to him how bad the others are, and so on. The others, of course, had responded in terms of *their* private and largely unconscious worlds of meaning, making their own contribution to the circulation of reactivity and misconstrued signals, all comprising the family's unrecognized ecology of meanings. This circular self-consistency of behaviors and of construed meanings of behaviors locks the ecology into its current, symptom-generating, mutually adversarial, reactive, or alienated configuration, because each member views her or his own interpretations and behaviors as perfectly justified.

In DOBT, systemic position work interrupts and permanently dissolves whole segments of this symptom-producing ecology of unconscious meanings, ending it. This position work consists of having family members access and reveal their emotional truth or pro-symptom position in the presence of each other.

In the following example from family therapy, the therapist spots an opening for position work and then focuses the session on this process, which produces a breakthrough that resolves the problem. The presenting symptom is the ten-year-old son's behavior of hitting other children at school, which had recently been happening several times each week. The parents, Beth and Jack, described their son, Bobby, as having been diagnosed with attention deficit disorder and as always having been difficult, temperamental, and aggressive, "losing control" and hitting, biting, and scratching ever since he was a toddler. Their daughter Molly, twelve, was in contrast the good child who felt neglected because of how focused on Bobby both parents continually were. All four of them were in the sessions.

Both parents regarded the boy's hitting as the problem, but it was the father, the stricter, more controlling parent, who was emotionally battling with the boy over this behavior, taking it personally as a defiance of both his express wishes and his paternal authority. He was at this point emotionally rubbed raw by the stress of frequent parent-teacher conferences and by the continual tension at home due to an endless series of new incidents. Shortly before therapy began, a psychologist at the family's HMO recommended putting Bobby on Ritalin.

What follows is a transcript of fourteen minutes from this family's eighth session. Previous sessions had focused largely on the father's obsession with controlling his son, which, it emerged, was actually father's imagined solution to *another* problem—the problem of avoiding incurring his octogenarian mother's shaming criticism for being unable to control his children. The therapist, in other words, had been viewing father's continual attempt to control the son as "the symptom," perceiving the father as having a pro-symptom position consisting of an emotional wound of inadequacy in relation to his mother and a protective action of shielding this wound by suppressing his son in order to avoid his mother's attacks. The therapist had done much position work of having the father acknowledge his emotional vulnerability to his mother's criticism and had worked with the family to support father in solving that problem in a new way: by wrestling with his mother instead of with his son. This work had seemed important and fruitful, but in the eighth session father was again full of blame and anger at Bobby for a record-setting week of hitting.

In this session an entirely new and unsuspected pro-symptom position of the father emerges, and the therapist immediately and persistently does position work that transforms the ecology of meanings and resolves the problem.

> *Father:* [With a weary and castigating tone] Bobby, when
> mom comes home from work at the end of the day,

there isn't a note from her supervisor telling me that she's been in a fight. When your sister comes home from school at the end of the day, there isn't a note from her teacher telling me that she's been in a fight. When I come home from work at night, I don't bring a note from my boss telling mom or you or Molly that I've been in a fight. Who in this family brings home the notes?

[The son appears to take his father's last few words as an emotional blow: he visibly crumples in his chair, slumping sideways to hide his face.]

Therapist: Jack, what's your intention right now? What is it you want Bobby to—

Son: To make me feel bad.

Therapist: To make you feel bad?

Father: [Angrily] I want him to hear the *truth!*

Therapist: You think he doesn't already *know* that he's the one who gets in trouble?

Father: I think he's in *incredible* denial.

Therapist: Well, maybe that's so, but look at the effect that's actually being created by your words.

Father: It's not an effect I'm unfamiliar with. I'm at an absolute loss how to try and convey this message to him.

Therapist: What's the message?

Father: [Silence; looks down; appears to be reflecting]

Therapist: So far the message is, "You're different than all the rest of us; you do bad things and you're different. You're bad." And he's definitely feeling very bad.

Son: [Sits upright suddenly and asks father] So what would you—what do you want me to do about it? Leave the family? Go somewhere else?

Therapist: [To father] That's the feeling he winds up getting from that form of the message.

Father: [To son] I'm glad that you can say that to me. I want you to keep saying things to me. OK?

Son: OK.

Father: I love you, Bobby. I don't want you to go away. You're a very important part of my life and you're a very important part of this family. What I want is very plain and simple. I want the notes to stop coming home. I want to be able to go to your classroom at the end of the day and not have your teacher call me and say Bobby has been in another fight. That's very stressful for me, Bobby. It *hurts.* I want to come home at night and not have your sister come to me, the first thing I come home, and complain to me, "Bobby did this and Bobby did that." I want to go and find your mother in the kitchen smiling and happy, and not stressed and yelling because there's been another conflict. [Long pause] I know, Bobby, that this is not such a simple thing that I can just say to you, "Stop doing this," and it stops and it ends and it changes. I mean, I know it's not that simple. Because if it *was* that simple it would have happened already, wouldn't it?

Son: Well, there wouldn't be any notes.

Father: Bobby, you're a terrific kid. [Reaches arm to daughter and says to her] *You're* a terrific kid. We have terrific kids.

Son: Not so terrific.

Father: You *are* terrific; we're *all* of us terrific. That's the truth.

[The father, three years a recovered alcoholic, seems to the therapist at this point to be careening from one kind of emotional theme and mood to another.]

Father: None of this stuff that has happened is the end of the world. In a way, I'm actually rather pleased—that you're standing up for yourself with your friends. 'Cause I knew a little boy one time who didn't stand up. Who couldn't strike back. Who didn't know how to stop the taunting and the teasing. And I'm glad that isn't happening to you. Nobody—

Therapist: Who was that little boy?

Father: —messes with you.

[This is a previously undisclosed theme that strikes the therapist as revealing a pro-symptom position held by the father.]

Son: [Answering the therapist's question by pointing at father] Him.

Father: That little boy was me, yes.

Son: Dad used to tell me that whenever there was a conflict he'd find a way to get out of it and hide.

Therapist: So, would it be true, Jack, for you to tell Bobby, that there's a *part* of you, just a *part* of you, that's glad that he hits the other kids when they mess with him? Is that—is that true?

Father: Yes. I did say that. Part of me is very pleased, in a way, that you don't get pushed around.

Son: But part of you wants me to stop. Practically all of you.

Father: [Now with an annoyed tone again] It's very hard for me, Bobby. *Every day* last week I got called into your classroom by your teacher.

Therapist: Jack, would you be willing to say to him, "I wish I could have made as much trouble as you're doing."

Father: [Nodding his head in assent and speaking with obvious, open earnestness] I wish I could have made as much trouble as you. *Darn* right—wish I could have.

Son: But I never hear you say that.

Mother: But each is a different way of not taking responsibility either.

Therapist: Beth, can I ask you to hold on to that? Something important is happening right there that I want to allow to flow. Try to remember what you're saying. Thanks.

[As soon as the therapist blocks the mother's interruption of the father-son interaction, the son, who had comfortingly taken father's hand when father spoke of his childhood woes, with his other hand now reaches to take his mother's hand; smiles lovingly at her; says, "Group hug," with a sweet voice; and leans his head down onto mother's forearm. The son is now emotionally comforting both parents at once.]

Therapist: Jack, would you say that to him again?

[The son now rises from his chair, lets go of his parents' hands, and steps over to be in front of his father, facing him, as if to receive very directly the words that the therapist has asked father to say to him.]

> *Father:* Bobby, I wish I could have made as much trouble. I wish I could have *gotten* into as much trouble.

[The son now leans down into a full hug with his father, who responds warmly, rubbing the son's back. The daughter fidgets unhappily. After ten seconds, the son again stands and speaks to father.]

> *Son:* Sometimes I wish I could have not gotten into as much trouble as you. Everybody wants to be like somebody else—
> *Daughter:* Maybe we should just have them trade bodies.
> *Therapist:* It sounds like that, doesn't it?
> *Son:* —and that somebody else usually wants to be that everybody. [Pause] So everybody wants to be somebody; somebody wants to be everybody.
> *Therapist:* It's true, Bobby.
> *Father:* Sometimes you know [at this moment the son looks at the video camera and starts clowning for it] you amaze me with how wise you are—and silly.
> *Son:* Helloo, helloo.
> *Mother:* They're both at such a wonderful age.
> *Therapist:* So Bobby, you seemed surprised to hear—it seemed like a new thing for you to hear from dad that part of him is glad you have the strength to hit other kids [daughter now stands, puts hands on father's shoulders, gently massaging them] and not let them mess with you, and—
> *Son:* —First time ever.
> *Therapist:* Yeah, first time you've ever heard that he wishes, he wishes he could have been like that himself. . . .
> *Mother:* Bobby takes no responsibility for his actions; he just acts. He doesn't consider—
> *Son:* —I used to.
> *Mother:* You used to what? Consider?
> *Son:* Consider what the heck would happen. But now I just do it.

Mother: Anyway.

Son: Even though I didn't want to.

Father: I would really like to ask Bobby a question which at least to me is important that I try and get an answer about. I think we both agree this was a difficult week. Can you tell me why this was a difficult week for you? Not just, I mean, in the context of the troubles in the yard but the troubles in the classroom as well.

Son: Well, you see, I think it was Tuesday that my teacher told me I made a mistake and she didn't like what I did, and then from there on it kept happening. She kept saying that, and I kept on getting angry, and then the next day I'd do it again. I think it was like a challenge to see how mad I could get her. How mad I could get her?

Therapist: And Bobby, I'm wondering if you could say those same words—if that would be true—to say the same words to dad: "Sometimes I want to see how mad I can get you." Try saying it to him.

Son: Sure. How mad can I get you, dad? Soooo mad.

Father: Did you think I was mad at you this week?

Son: Yeah.

Therapist: So is it like this: sometimes dad says or does things and *you* feel really mad at *him,* and you want to get *him* mad back at you? Is it like that?

Son: Yup.

Therapist: Yup. And you know how to do it. What do you have to do to get dad mad?

Son: I don't really mean to make dad mad. I don't ever want to make my parents mad, *except* when they make *me* mad.

[Bobby, in describing his views and patterns of managing anger in relation to his teacher and parents, has now revealed a key pro-symptom position he holds, a very purposeful and self-affirming position of not being anyone's powerless victim, which he carries out by returning perceived provocation in equal measure.]

Therapist: So Jack, I think you're doing very successfully—and I'm not being facetious—at teaching your boy not to be the defenseless little kid that you were. The side effect is that *you* have to deal with that same spirit. It's, you know, it's not just out there in the school yard. It comes home and then is a parent problem.

Father: I did not want him to be a defenseless little kid.

Therapist: Well, you've succeeded!

Father: [Smiling broadly] In spades.

Son: But isn't there still a part of you, dad, that still wants me to be, kind of, not a defenseless little kid but not a bully?

Father: I would worry just as much about you being a bully, Bobby, as I would about you being a defenseless little kid.

Mother: But you're not a bully.

Father: You're not a bully. I've seen you, and you're not a bully, and I'm very pleased about that, too. [Father reaches over, ruffles his son's hair affectionately, and then takes the son's hand in his.]

Therapist: Jack, would it be going too far for me to ask you to say to Bobby—by "too far" I mean not true—you know, to say to Bobby something like this: "Bobby, even though it's a lot of trouble for me, I'm *glad* you can hit those other kids when you need to."

Son: Well—

Therapist: Wait Bobby, let's see if that's true for dad.

Father: Bobby, even though it's a lot of trouble for me—and it is a *lot* of trouble for me—I'm glad that you can take care of yourself, and when you feel it's necessary, I'm glad that you can hit back.

Therapist: Bobby, how does it feel to *hear* that from him?

Son: [Joyfully flings an arm wide] Wonderful! I feel I've gotta hit *everybody* in the world at least once!

Father: [Looks down into his lap somberly]

Mother: [Hand goes to forehead.] Oh, swell.

Therapist: I think mom's having a hard time with this.

Son: I once saw this Ren and Stimpy show [father lets go of son's hand; appears to be suffering son's enthusiasm for aggression]; it was a cartoon about this kid who was a bully and his father who was a bully also. And his father, um—they stop by this—Ren and Stimpy were at this little kid's house when Victor, the bully, came, and they were in the car and his dad was driving it, and he—the dad waited in the car while the son got out, and the son beat up Ren and Stimpy, and the kid then got back in the car, and you heard the dad say, "Nice job, son!"

Therapist: And you're hearing that from dad right now! It's just like in that cartoon! And it feels *wonderful.*

Son: I never knew cartoons could be so educating.

Therapist: How you doing, Jack? It's like you've given an airing to another side of yourself that's been quite hidden in all this. And it's emerged that maybe your struggle isn't so much really with Bobby as with your own two sides. You're of two minds—

Father: Oh, absolutely.

After this session there was an immediate falling away of Bobby's prior lifelong disposition to be easily provoked to aggression. The hitting disappeared. There was one more family session in which Molly was made part of the breakthrough, and then four couple sessions in which the focus was on marital issues rather than parenting problems. In a follow-up inquiry by telephone, Jack, the father, described with great pleasure that during the next four months of school there had been only one minor incident involving some pushing and that Bobby's grades had improved significantly. Ritalin was no longer being considered.

The symptom-maintaining ecology of meanings in this family was transformed when the father expressed sincere admiration and approval of his son's hitting, the symptom that he had until then so stridently attacked. Getting the father to openly take his pro-symptom position was the position work that brought about the breakthrough. The father's expression of his emotional truth of the symptom, combined with the boy's new awareness of dad's approval, completely changed the meanings operating between the two of them. Dad's continual, castigating disapproval had been for Bobby a trigger of continual anger at dad, which, as Bobby so openly explained, made him want to make dad angry, too, and hitting other children was clearly the best way to do that.

We find in general that if the symptom bearer in a family is a child, then in most cases at least one of the parents, in addition to the child, has an unconscious, pro-symptom position, just as this father did. We consider the pro-symptom positions of elders in the family to be the most superordinate or governing feature of the system and the most important focus of attention (which is why, once the father's pro-symptom position emerged in the session above, the therapist did not deviate from position work to respond to other systemic phenomena occurring in the room, such as children emotionally caretaking parents, and so on).

Note that the therapist's manner with the father was devoid of blame. Blame would have been implied, for example, if the therapist had offered an interpretation that the father had needed and induced his son to be aggressive as a vicarious undoing of father's own childhood behavior of fearful flight. No such interpretation was used or needed in order to carry out the position work that dismantled the old ecology of meanings operating here. Only in cases of overt exploitation or violation does it become appropriate for the therapist to negatively connote a client's behavior, and when possible this is done even then in the context of the emotional truth of those behaviors.

Position Work and the Loss of a Familiar Reality

The client's emotional truth regarding the presenting symptom is unconscious because awareness of that emotional truth would entail some degree of disorientation, emotional disturbance, or pain that the client wants forever to avoid. The therapist must not collude with this avoidant stance of the client. The therapist needs the conviction that integrating the emotional truth of the symptom will be liberating and healing even if initially and temporarily disturbing, and he or she must be ready to assist the client with any disorientation or emotional pain that the client may temporarily experience.

Position work entails disorientation because the client suddenly inhabits the pro-symptom position's unfamiliar reality. In our clinical experience, preserving the familiarity of one's experiential reality is one of the most powerful and highly superordinate purposes operating in the human psyche. "Familiarity is far more desirable than comfort" said Virginia Satir at a 1983 San Francisco workshop. However, the familiarity of some part of the client's habitual reality is squarely challenged when the client owns the reality in the emotional truth of the symptom. Aspects of the nature of the world, of significant others such as parents, or of the self may suddenly appear substantially altered. This shift may be sudden not because of hurriedness or clumsiness on the part of the therapist, but because reality in the emotional truth of the symptom may be so qualitatively different than the familiar, conscious reality that even if parceled down to a small-as-possible first encounter, the shift will still feel sudden.

Here is an example of position work generating a modest degree of disorientation and emotional distress. A woman lawyer explained in her first session that sculpting is what matters most to her and has always been her first love, but that her legal work keeps crowding it out, sometimes to the point of nonexistence for extended periods of time. She was now forty-five, and because this pattern was out of control, she was concerned that her life would pass by with her neglecting what she wanted most to be doing.

The therapist, assuming coherence, tentatively inferred that this woman's behavior pattern was produced by a pro-symptom position in which pursuing her legal work *was* more important than her art, despite her conscious belief that sculpting was more important. After about twenty minutes of radical inquiry the therapist wrote down what she understood this woman's pro-symptom position to be and gave this to her to read aloud as a way of "trying on" this position for emotional truth, and as a task of position work.

The client read, "The truth is, my legal practice is actually *more* important to me than my sculpting because it more fully carries out my values. I'm actually willing to endure the painful loss I feel when expanding my legal work eliminates my sculpting. My values come first; the joy of art comes second. I'm a lawyer first, then a sculptor." This was not an interpretation offered by the therapist but a summing-up or synthesis of what she had learned from the client.

After reading this out loud the woman said, "I have to say this feels absolutely true," but she now seemed shaken and added that this was "very disorienting" and that she felt "a kind of stab of fear in realizing this."

In her conscious position, her identity during all of her adult life had been very strongly based on the image of herself as an artist, and she viewed her legal work as something she did to earn a living and support herself as a sculptor. To experience suddenly that in her emotional truth she was "a lawyer first, then a sculptor" involved both a sizable change in identity and an emotional loss of some fond expectations of how her work life would unfold, bringing a stab of fear. (She could, of course, now reassess and revise her priorities in order to pursue those fond hopes as a sculptor. In fact, only by the client's having faced her emotionally true position were those hopes salvageable.)

Multiglobal Constructions and the Length of Therapy

Significant as these changes in the client's experiential reality were, they affected a limited region of it. She could therefore tolerate the full, rapid encounter with the changes of reality needed for resolution. Difficulties in keeping the therapy time-effective develop when the position work required to dispel the presenting symptom challenges and would change a far greater expanse of the person's *entire* experiential reality. This occurs most commonly with clients who in childhood suffered severe, sustained abuse (emotional, physical, or sexual) and whose presenting symptoms are features of abuse-related constructions.

With such clients, the emotional truth of the symptom is a construction of reality that not only makes the particular presenting symptoms necessary but also defines in a global way virtually all of the person's experiential reality and does so through numerous, highly superordinate constructions and pro-symptom positions.

Let's take as an example low self-esteem, which is perhaps the abuse-related symptom most frequently encountered by therapists. The following lists spell out some of the unconscious purposes (third-order constructs) served by maintaining the (second-order) strategic construal of low self-worth, that is, the construal of self as inadequate, defective and unlovable, and therefore deserving of the rejection, criticism, or abuse received. (A *strategic* construal is one whose value is in serving an unconscious, third-order purpose—a hidden agenda—rather than in the truth of its content.)

Initial Purposes Served in Childhood by Inventing and Adhering to Self-Blame

- Avoid an emotional disconnection from the parents, which would be a massive threat to survival and create unbearable anxiety. Self-blame avoids disconnection because it (1) avoids the alienation and disloyalty of perceiving the parents as the bad ones and (2) keeps oneself in a shared reality with the parents, a reality in which all agree that *I'm* the bad one.
- Preserve the illusion of possible control over stopping the abuse and avoid the terror of powerlessness and helplessness: If it's my fault, then I can stop it by becoming good enough to deserve love.
- Preserve safety by disentitling oneself to any aspect of self-expression that triggers the abuse (including rage, which would be especially dangerous, and any other predictable triggers).

Purposes Served by Maintaining Low Self-Worth in Adulthood

- Preserve the emotional connection with one's family of origin by (1) avoiding the alienation and disloyalty of perceiving the parents as having been abusive and (2) maintaining the original sense of being in a shared reality with the family.
- Avoid immensely painful grief over a wasted life and sense of betrayal by parents that would arise if one realized, "I am, and was all along, a perfectly lovable, adequate being."
- Avoid further blows: If I don't stand up in any way, I can't be knocked down again in any way.
- Retribution: My failure to amount to anything is my proof of how badly you treated me.
- Restoration: Only my unwellness will attract the nurturing attention I never got but should have gotten and still hope to get from someone.
- Restoration: As a child I didn't get to be carefree, as I should have been, and now that I'm big it's my turn to feel uncontrolled and free. I don't want anyone to see me as capable, and I don't want to *feel* capable, so I'll be free of demands and pressures.

Someone who was severely abused may habitually harbor most or all of the third-order purposes listed. Note the extremely large region of experiential reality encompassed by a collection of purposes and meanings such as this. If any one of these purposes remains intact, so does the experiential state of low self-esteem. For the client to relinquish the low self-esteem construction requires the dissolution of all such unconscious, third-order purposes that are operating. This entails an essentially global transformation of identity, motivation, and relationship to others that few people can allow to occur within a few sessions (but which *can* occur in far less time than is assumed in traditional long-term therapies).

A child who experiences recurring abuse or negativity from his parent(s) consciously dislikes it intensely but nevertheless unconsciously construes the parent as being right to treat the child so hurtfully, in effect going into agreement with the parent's apparent view of the child as unlovable. This construal or assumption about the parent's rightness is a second-order construct, a meaning attributed to a particular perception. (The child makes this second-order construal, rather than the opposite one that the parent is wrong to behave thus, as a protective action in consequence of his third- and fourth-order constructs, "I am a helpless being totally dependent for survival on these large others" [fourth-order ontology] and "I must preserve my connection with them at all cost" [third-order purpose], respectively. If the child did *not* go into agreement with the parent's apparent attitude, the child would feel emotionally disconnected from the parent and intolerably vulnerable to annihilation.) This second-order construal that the parent is correct to be treating the child harmfully inevitably doubles as a superordinate fourth-order ontological construction, "I am a bad, unlovable, repellant being"—the basis of the emotion of shame that figures so strongly in the lives of such clients.

Thus low self-worth stemming from abuse has a unique construction in which fourth, third, and second orders circularly reinforce each other, making the state of low self-esteem especially tenacious and locked, as therapists well know it to be.

As we saw in Chapter Two, it is by rendering a third-order purpose conscious and exposed that the second-order, strategic construction carrying it out can most effectively be dispelled. The purposes presented in the list above maintain such second-order construals as the following:

If I show any imperfection I'll be rejected or attacked.

If I express any feelings I'll be severely burdening others.

I'm not worthy of attention.

I'm bad and dirty, and it was my fault he would have sex with me again and again.

If I was any good they wouldn't have beat me so much.

If anyone saw the real me they'd leave me.

A raised voice means I'm about to be beaten.

I hate myself for being so unlovable.

As always in depth-oriented brief therapy, it is the client's capacities that set the rate of the work. When there are multiple, global pro-symptom constructions structuring virtually all of the client's reality, the client may require a slower pace of change.

We term such clients *multiglobal.* These are the clients with whom effective work in every session may not be brief, because of both the slower pace that may be required by the client in order to tolerate the necessary, sweeping changes in reality, and because each of the many global, pro-symptom constructions requires therapeutic attention. Even a self-avowed "brief therapy evangelist" such as therapist and trainer William O'Hanlon acknowledges the need for longer work with some clients and that ultimately, "the real question is not how long therapy takes, but how effective it is and whether it serves those who seek it. I believe effective therapy is usually brief, but not in every case." Still the therapist should never think statistically or stereotype any one person as a "long-term client," which would dull the therapist's active intentionality, inevitably making therapy longer than it need be. No matter how many sessions are required, every session is always regarded as one of depth-oriented brief therapy and as one in which a major breakthrough could occur. Then the work will prove to be brief (less than twenty sessions) in many multiglobal cases, and in others it will be as brief as possible (seldom exceeding forty to fifty sessions).

In addition to adults heavily abused as children, multiglobal clients include those who would be described psychodynamically as having distinct character disorders. All of the methodology of DOBT still applies, namely, discovering and working directly with the client's pro-symptom constructs through carrying out DOBT's two top priorities for effectiveness, radical inquiry or experiential shift in every session.

Transformation of the Pro-Symptom Position

Coaching the transformation of constructs is the further process of experiential shift used when the problem is not resolved solely by position work. Essentially the therapist prompts the client to use his or her control of the *existence* of constructs (the native ability to create, preserve, or dissolve constructions of reality) in order to transform the pro-symptom position so that there is no longer a view of reality in which the symptom is necessary to have.

To bring about a transformation of the client's pro-symptom reality, the therapist utilizes this fundamental principle: *Within any one of the versions of reality it harbors, the mind does not tolerate inconsistent representations of reality.*

From this principle follows this methodology: (1) Have the client access the pro-symptom emotional reality by vivifying and experiencing it, and then, *in the same field of awareness,* (2) Evocatively coach the client to create and experience a new, devictimized reality, inconsistent with the victimization, powerlessness, or woundedness in the old one, motivating the client to dissolve the old one.

In this state, with both the old, pro-symptom construction and the newly created, incompatible constructs vivified, the client actually experiences the inconsistency or disconfirmation and resolves the conflict by dissolving the old construction in favor of the new (*accommodation* in Piagetian terms). Note that as a rule people dissolve old constructions of reality only if an acceptable replacement already is at hand, in order to avoid the anxiety that would arise from a void of meaning. If the new constructs are created while the old position is not activated, the client does not actually experience an inconsistency or disconfirmation. *The simultaneous vivifying of the old and the new constructs in the same field of awareness is the essential condition for the transformation of position to occur.* This process is fundamentally different from a mere cognitive refuting or "correcting" of the client's beliefs, as was practiced in the early history of cognitive therapy.

Techniques for Transformation of the Pro-Symptom Position

To carry out this process of transforming the pro-symptom position, we principally use three well-known techniques:

1. Reenactment
2. Creating connection between positions
3. Construct substitution

Reenactment

The technique of reenactment is used widely by experiential therapists for fostering recovery from the sequelae of traumatic events that occurred at any point in life, such as symptoms experienced by adults abused as children and by victims of assault. The therapist orchestrates a revision of reality in the client's pro-symptom position by first evoking the client into accessing the original, subjective experiences during which he or she installed that reality and then having the client vividly replay these pivotal experiences in a new way (hence the other name for this type of work, revising personal history). As described earlier, the reality that was being experienced at the time of the original formation of an emotional wound or trauma is the reality in the pro-symptom position containing that wound or trauma. This means that in doing position work—in drawing the client into experientially inhabiting her pro-symptom position (such as, "I'm seven, and I wish I would die in my sleep")—the stage is automatically set for the vivid replay and revision.

For successful reenactment it is essential for the therapist to understand that an unresolved emotional trauma is an unconscious knowing that is largely kinesthetic and somesthetic—that is, more neuromuscular in construction than verbal-cognitive. Major emotional wounds and traumas are held as a specific pattern of unconscious emotional-somatic tensions that continue for decades to restimulate a state of fear and helplessness.

For reenactment, then, the client first does the position work of attending in detail to the unfolding of the original emotionally wounding or traumatic situation. This involves as much kine/ somesthetic experience and expression of the body's knowings of the event as possible, using breathing, vocalization, expressions of terror or rage, and so on. When the emotional truth of the experience is well accessed, the client again visualizes this situation developing in the original manner almost up to the point at which the trauma occurs. This time, however, the client is guided, encouraged, and supported by the therapist in imaginally responding to the situation in some strongly assertive, effective new way that prevents the harm and the trauma from ever occurring. This creates a new construction of reality that substantially dissolves and revises the old one, dispelling ongoing feelings of victimization and disempowerment and releasing the neuromuscular tensions that were set up and locked in during the original event.

In a subsequent session, the therapist has the client again view the original scene and notice what his or her emotional response is now. If the client is sufficiently devoid of original reactions, the process is complete; otherwise, another round or two of reenactment is indicated, based on the client's current model of the scene.

An example of reenactment within couples therapy follows later in this chapter.

Creating Connection Between Positions

This is a class of techniques in which the client's wounded or deprived state in the pro-symptom position receives a transforming contact from another position in which the client has emotional and cognitive assets needed in the pro-symptom position.

Perhaps the best-known example of this is what is widely termed *inner child work,* applicable whenever the client's experiential identity in the pro-symptom position is that of being a child needing a safe, caring adult to provide love, attention, understanding, help, or rescue. The child position is brought into the needed kind of relationship with an adult position of the client, which for both positions is an emotionally real and transformative experience. Jungian active imagination, described in Chapter Five, also creates transformative interaction and relationship between conscious and unconscious positions of all sorts, personified in visual imagery. The imaginal-interactive techniques of Gestalt therapy do likewise, as does the more recently developed voice dialogue approach.

All such methods are useful within DOBT if applied in the completely phenomenological manner of DOBT—that is, the therapist always elicits and follows the *client's* emotional truth and never imposes the existence of, say, a presumed "inner child" position on the client. If a child position figures importantly in the client's construction of the problem, then as a rule the visualized image of that child-self and the state of being that child will be easily accessible and quite real to the client and will have a distinct voice and character of its own, autonomous from the client's familiar ego-identity. If not, then the therapist should drop the "inner child" or any other motif and work in some other way that feels emotionally real for the client.

Construct Substitution

A client can substitute a new construct for an old one—revising a piece of reality—if the therapist sets up the conditions for this to occur. The new construct or view of reality must be clearly and compellingly inconsistent with the view of reality in the client's pro-symptom position. It can come in the form of a perception, a new experience, a communication of information from someone, an image, or an idea. The task of the therapist is to arrange for the client to take in this new construct *while inhabiting and vividly experiencing the pro-symptom position,* so that both the new and the old constructs are vivified and experientially real to the client at the same time. A previous example of this arose in Chapter Two, in which the client, while accessing her cutting shard of believing herself repulsively ugly, was guided by the therapist into simultaneously experiencing the totally incompatible construct of her third-order protective purpose for viewing herself as ugly. This interaction of incompatible constructs dissolved the capacity of the "I'm ugly" construct to define reality. Later in this chapter we consider construct substitution in which the new, incompatible construct comes from the client's partner as a result of position work during couples therapy.

Case Example: Couple Abused as Children

Since Chapter Two provided detailed examples of the transformation of pro-symptom positions in individual therapy, we will illustrate the transformation of pro-symptom positions here with the first three sessions of a six-session couples therapy. This example will show the entire methodology of DOBT, including radical inquiry, position work, and transformation of an ecology of meanings, as well as transformation of pro-symptom positions. Techniques of radical inquiry illustrated are viewing from a symptom-free position, sentence completion, experiential questioning, and mind-body communication. Illustrated also are techniques of position work, including following a little bit ahead, overt statements of position, confronting with emotional truth, cycling between symptom and symptom-free positions, and using the symptom as signal. Transformation of pro-symptom positions is carried out in these sessions both by construct substitution and through reenactment.

Kate and Alan, in their mid-thirties and married for five years, came for therapy on Kate's initiative because of her anguish over the relationship. She described the problem as "lack of communication," as so many couple therapy clients do. She said she felt painfully alone in the relationship because Alan is so regularly "closed down" emotionally and doesn't interact with her about personally meaningful things. The therapist asked Alan if Kate's description of him as "closed down" made any sense to him. He said it did because he does go into a state in which he knows he is closed down and "uncomfortably tight," but that was how he had always felt in a relationship, and so it hadn't occurred to him that he could be any different. Asked if he wanted to be any different, he said, "Yes, sure. But I have no idea how."

At this point the therapist, viewing through the conceptual lens of depth-oriented brief therapy, was beginning to see the two pro-symptom positions in an ecology of meanings: Alan evidently had a position that made it important to be closed down emotionally, and Kate had a position that made it important to be with a man who wouldn't be a close, intimate participant in the relationship. It is these unconscious, pro-symptom positions that fit together ecologically, hand in glove. The therapist could begin to infer these positions simply on the basis of how the two partners had structured their pattern of relating. As always, in DOBT the therapist views the presenting symptom as being exactly what some position of the client wants or needs to be doing. The gist of a pro-symptom position often becomes apparent simply by noting what people actually do, as distinct from how they think and feel about what they actually do. Kate was genuinely suffering the costs of being with a closed-down man, and so had an anti-symptom position that she presented in therapy, but evidently these costs were less important than whatever made it important to be with such a partner. Of course, the therapist's early inferences about these pro-symptom positions merely serve as an initial guide for beginning the process of radical inquiry, to be followed by position work and transformation.

Therapist: [To Kate] You've described this important experience that's missing for you in the relationship. You want to experience Alan as being emotionally open and coming *toward* you emotionally, really tuning *in* to you instead of tuning *out*. Is that right?

Kate: Mm-hm.

[To test his inference about her pro-symptom position, the therapist is beginning to do radical inquiry by evoking in Kate a symptom-free position of receiving close attention from her husband.]

Therapist: How does it actually feel to you when you *do* have that experience of him?

Kate: Well, it hasn't happened in so long that I'm not sure. On and off he was sometimes more open in the first year after we were married.

Therapist: So would you be willing to turn your chair a bit more toward Alan right now, and just look at him—yes— and just *imagine* for a few moments having him actually coming *toward* you emotionally, actually *wanting to know what's going on in your feelings*? [Pause] And as you imagine him *all focused on you* like that, also imagine yourself being *about to reveal to him* some very personal feelings and thoughts that are important to you. [Pause] And how does this feel to you?

Kate: Not good.

Therapist: How do you know it's not good?

Kate: Well, the moment you said those words, "what's going on in your feelings," I just felt my stomach lurch and clench up.

[Kate is now accessing a pro-symptom position of needing Alan to be emotionally distant. This confirms experientially the therapist's initial inference.]

Therapist: Uh-huh. Anything else?

Kate: Well, then when you said he's "all focused" on me, I felt, "No, get *away.*" And because of *that* feeling, I couldn't do the last part—I couldn't imagine really feeling ready to reveal something real personal.

Therapist: I see. OK. You did that exercise very well, actually, just by letting yourself feel whatever actually happened, so thank you. Would you be willing to do one more step of this?

Kate: OK, if it will help.

Therapist: I think it will. What I'd like you to do is to say this sentence to Alan: "If I do let you come close and see who I really am . . ." and then when you reach the blank at the end, just let it complete itself, without pre-thinking the ending. Willing to do that?

[The therapist is using sentence completion to carry radical inquiry further and elicit the emotional truth of why it is important to her to maintain emotional distance.]

Kate: Well, I'll try. [Looking at Alan] If I do let you see who I really am—[Pause; looks down in her lap, face flushing, eyes getting teary; seems unable to speak]

Therapist: What are you feeling right now?

Kate: Well, the sentence didn't finish with words, I just kept getting a picture.

Therapist: What's the picture?

Kate: [Through sniffles and tears] It's a picture of me. I'm like covered with tar. And he'd see *that.*

Therapist: Did something happen to you that covered you with tar?

Kate: [Begins crying] Yes.

Therapist: Do you know what it was?

Kate: Yes. [She now gives a general account of the "nightmare" of living with an uncle for several summers in her early teenage years: This uncle, "Henry," continually predated after her sexually, always pointedly blaming her for making him talk sexually to her, peep at her in the bathroom, and commit other violations. This resulted in a deep sense that it *was* all her fault and that the "dark, dirty feeling" she experienced—as represented by the image of herself covered with tar— was a quality of her self. Henry finally physically molested her when she was fifteen. She awoke in the middle of the night to find him fondling her, but she pretended not to be awake and endured this violation for what felt like a very long time.]

Therapist: What an ordeal you went through—really a nightmare. And the way he made it seem led you to feel that it was your fault, and that the real you is this dark, dirty thing.

Kate: Mm-hm.

[Important parts of Kate's pro-symptom position are now clear to the therapist.]

Therapist: So let's do one more small step for now. Could you look for the *connection*— What's the *connection* between this secret feeling or view of yourself as a dark, dirty being and having this lack of close emotional attention in your couple relationship? What's the connection?

Kate: [Pause] Oh—he won't find out.

Therapist: Yes. You said Alan knows a little about what happened with that uncle, but he doesn't know about "dark and dirty," does he?

Kate: No.

Therapist: [Pause] So, even though it *hurts* to feel so alone in the relationship, you expect it would feel even *worse* to be really seen and found out?

[This is an initial step of position work: following the client a little bit ahead, the therapist empathically voices his understanding of her pro/anti synthesis.]

Kate: [Looking into her lap] Yes.

Therapist: And is *that* what makes it important to be with a man who's safe because he won't pay close attention and see who you really are?

Kate: Yes. [Pause] I had no idea that that's behind all this, but yes—I mean, right now I can feel how true that is.

Therapist: Mm-hm. [Pause] There may be things we can do to change how this is for you, if you want. Not necessarily in this session, but "dark and dirty" could change for you.

Kate: Yeah, I'd really like that.

Therapist: OK, so we'll see how to fit that into our work. So, Alan, are you feeling left out?

Alan: No. That was really something. But now you're coming after *me*! [All laugh]

Therapist: Well, we've learned something really important, I think. We've learned that even though Kate is very dissatisfied with your pattern of interacting with her, and feels very unconnected-with by you, that same pattern is keeping her feeling *safe* in a way she really values. I'm wondering if knowing that is something new, for you.

Alan: Yeah. I'm amazed to see that. I thought it was all bad.

[The therapist is making sure that the changed meaning of the problem has entered into Alan's side of the couple's ecology of meanings.]

Therapist: So did she. I think she may be at least as surprised as you are. But what about *you*? Didn't you say earlier that *you* don't like feeling all closed down and tight so much of the time?

Alan: Yeah, it feels lousy, but it's like something comes over me.

Therapist: I'd like to know what that experience is like, for you. How would you teach me to have it?

Alan: [Laughs] How would I teach *you* to have it?

Therapist: Yeah. Tell me exactly what I'd have to feel in my body and think in my head and feel emotionally, to experience it exactly as you do.

Alan: Well, OK. I'll try. I've never thought about it this way. Umm—it feels like I'm in a dense fog—like my head and shoulders are in a dense fog. Or all stuffed with cotton.

Therapist: OK, got it. What else?

Alan: And my throat feels pressure, or kind of choked off. And my neck feels sort of rigid. Yeah, a kind of tight, pressured, stiff feeling in my throat and neck.

Therapist: OK, good. Very clear instructions. Anything else?

Alan: Well, let's see. Kind of a knot in my stomach, a tense feeling.

Therapist: A knot with a tense feeling—a feeling of—?

Alan: The knot is a kind of anxious feeling, yeah.

Therapist: OK: Thick fog or cotton in your head and shoulders; throat feeling tight, and pressure, and rigid; and a knot of anxiety in your stomach.

Alan: Yeah.

[The therapist recognizes this as a description of a dissociative state, a protective action by which a person does indeed close down emotionally when there is a perceived danger of reopening an extremely vulnerable, unhealed emotional wound. The therapist, always looking for signs of the pro-symptom position and how to evoke it, now knows that Alan's pro-symptom position is a reality based in an old wound that feels regularly threatened.]

Therapist: So how do you know when to go into this state?

Alan: You ask the weirdest questions.

Therapist: And you give such good answers to them! How *do* you know when to go in to this state?

Kate: It's whenever I *want* anything from him!

Alan: Oh, come on.

Kate: It's true! All I have to do is want anything, like just to have him tell me what he's feeling about something *important* in our lives, and he shuts down. Why am I *in* this relationship?

Therapist: [To Alan, who was about to respond to Kate] Let me

> change my question: With *whom* do you go into this
> state?

Kate: With me and with his mother.

Therapist: Kate, I need to hear from Alan about this.

Alan: She's right about that.

Therapist: What happened with your mother that you'd have a
knot of anxiety in your stomach?

[The therapist intends to usher Alan into directly experiencing
the wound that he normally avoids experiencing by dissociating.
The themes and meanings within this wound will be the emotional truth of the symptom of his closing down emotionally so
often. To be experiencing that emotional wound directly would
be to have direct access to it as a construction of reality, and to
have that access would make a transformation of the wound-con-
struction immediately possible.]

> *Alan:* I don't know. I mean, when I was little she drank a lot,
> but I don't know exactly what I'd have a knot of anxi-
> ety over.

Therapist: Well, *something* would happen that was pretty scary for
you, to knot up like that. Could you let yourself feel
that knot right now?

Alan: Actually I sort of already am, because of how angry
Kate just got at me.

Therapist: Good, good. Just give that knot your whole attention.
[Alan lowers his eyes as he attends to the knot.] Yes.
Let yourself kind of get into the emotional atmosphere of it, that familiar climate of tension and fog
that you feel. [Pause] Good. And I wonder if that knot
will tell you something about what in the situation is
so scary. Because the knot knows everything this is
about. Maybe the knot can send you an image of a
scene, a scene that shows what it's about.

Alan: [His eyes and attention jumping up and away from
the knot] Well, yeah, when you said that a picture did
come up, and it—

Therapist: Could you stay down there with the knot as you tell
me what the picture is?

Alan: Oh, OK. Well, my mom would get drunk and like tell me her problems.

Therapist: So stay in that picture—and tell me, how old are you?

[The client may be regarding his picture as "the past," but the therapist understands it to be a visual representation of a current construction of meaning that is *currently* involved in generating symptoms.]

Alan: Starting at about seven and until I was about twelve. So she'd get drunk at night and come into my room, and sometimes it was really late, so she'd wake me up and start talking to me about all kinds of stuff that she was miserable about—really personal stuff.

Therapist: So there you are at seven or eight, waked up by her late at night, and she's drunk and talking to you like that, and I'll bet you get whiffs of her breath—

Alan: Yeah, it's horrible.

Therapist: —and see if you can feel what's *scary* to you in what's happening.

Alan: The whole thing.

Therapist: Yes, the whole thing is scary. I imagine it's scary in a bunch of different ways all at once. See if you can put your finger on some of the ways it's scary.

Alan: [Puts hand on his stomach] Well—umm—it's like I'm supposed to *fix* it for her. I'm supposed to know how to do whatever will make her feel better [bursts into tears], but I *don't* know how. [Cries] And that's what's scary, because if I can't fix it she'll stay miserable and it'll be my fault and she'll blame me. [Cries harder]

[Alan is now accessing the emotional wound in his normally unconscious pro-symptom position; he is in the experiential reality of that wound.]

Therapist: Keep seeing that image of mom in the scene, and try out saying these words to her: "I don't know how to make you feel good."

Alan: [Crying] I don't know how to make you feel good— and I'm really scared you'll stop loving me.

Therapist: Yes. There it is.

Alan: Yeah. God.

Therapist: Alan, would you look at Kate and say those same words to her? Not about mom, but to Kate herself— how you feel the same things with Kate herself.

Alan: Yeah, I do. When you want to talk to me it's like, "Oh shit! I'm not gonna be able to fix it, and you're gonna think I'm not worth being with."

Therapist: So try out saying the same thing to Kate: "I don't know how to make you feel good, and I'm really scared you'll stop loving me."

Alan: [Through tears] I don't know how to make you feel good, and I'm really scared you'll stop loving me.

[The therapist is having Alan do position work by overtly stating to Kate the emotional truth of his symptom of dissociating.]

Kate: But I'm not trying to get you to make me feel good or *fix* me.

Therapist: He can't let that in yet. We'll get to that in a minute. The thing is, Kate, knowing that's what *he's* assuming, does it make new sense why he goes into fear and tightens up and closes down?

[The therapist is now reinforcing the change wrought in *her* part of the ecology of meanings by what has been revealed of the emotional truth of *his* behavior.]

Kate: Yes, it does, because all along I thought it means he doesn't really love me and doesn't share my goals and doesn't want to be with me.

Therapist: When actually it means you're *so* important to him that the thought of losing your love actually *panics* him. [To Alan] Am I right?

Alan: Yeah, that's about it.

Therapist: Alan, there's one more part we should do. Can you stay with that feeling of, "I'm really scared you'll stop loving me if I can't fix it and make you feel better"?

Alan: Yeah, OK.

Therapist: Good. Let yourself feel that in relation to Kate, and look at her. And where in your body do you feel it?

Alan: Right here. [Indicates the knot in his stomach]

Therapist: OK. When Kate says what she's going to say in a moment, see if you can let what she's saying flow right into that place. It's OK if it flows into your ears, too, as long as it also flows right there, too. Willing to do that?

Alan: Yeah.

Therapist: OK. Kate, if these words are true for you, would you just say to Alan, "I love you even if you don't know how to help me with my problem"?

Kate: I do love you even if you don't know how to help me with my problem.

[The therapist is attempting to orchestrate a transformation of Alan's emotional wound through the technique of construct substitution. It has become clear that an integral component of his wound is the unconscious presupposition he holds in the emotional (not cognitive) representation, "My value to a female is in my ability to relieve her emotional distress." It is this presupposition that constitutes his knowing to expect rejection and abandonment when he does not see how to fix or relieve Kate's problems. The sentence Kate is now saying disconfirms Alan's old presupposition; she had already stated that she does not share it. However, in order for Kate's sentence to be effectual in dissolving his presupposition, it is necessary for Alan to be positioned in the emotional reality of his presupposition *as he hears her words*. With the old presupposition already accessed experientially, the new construction of meaning he is receiving creates an experiential disconfirmation that both motivates him to dissolve the old view and provides the alternative construction he needs in order to do so.]

Therapist: [To Alan] Can you let it in there?

Alan: I think so, yeah.

Therapist: [To Kate] Give him another dose of that.

Kate: Alan, I love you even if you don't know how to help me with my problem.

Therapist: [To Alan] How's it feel to let that in *there*?

Alan: It's like a picture of a soapsuds commercial I used to

see on TV when I was a kid, like a clean white cloud
coming in and washing away the grime.

Therapist: Can you actually feel it?

Alan: Well, kind of a fresh, lighter feeling down there.

Therapist: Do you believe it when she says, "I love you even if
you don't know how to help me with my problem"?

Alan: [Looks closely at her face] Yeah. I think I do.

Therapist: OK, good. Our time's up for today, and I want to give
you something that will help you keep these new
things we've done.

The therapist gave each of them an index card and recommended
they look at their card twice a day, morning and night. On Alan's
card was written, "I truly believe that if I don't solve your problem,
you'll think I'm worthless." For Alan this was position work; it
would keep this position consciously accessed and diminish or
eliminate its capacity to come over him autonomously. On Kate's
card was written, "I love you even if you don't know how to help
me with my problem." This sentence would keep her positioned
in the new way of making sense of Alan's emotional withdrawals
rather than in the old way of construing them to mean he doesn't
love her. These cards would maintain the new ecology of meanings
developed in the session.

The therapist suggested that the second session could focus, if
Kate wished, on her "tar" and the lingering effects of being
molested. That session, one week later, included the following work:

Kate: I do affirmations and meditations, but I can't get rid
of this yucky feeling about myself. People who know
me will say really nice things about me, and secretly I
feel like I've got them totally fooled . . . I remember
Henry [the uncle who molested her] would always say
to me, "How do you *expect* me to behave, lookin' like
you do?" He was always making comments about how
I dressed, how I was trying to get him excited, and I'd
get so mixed up. He found any excuse to talk about
sex. I'd never know when he'd be spying on me when
I'd come out of the shower, or if I'd wake up in the
middle of the night because he'd be touching me.

And it all felt like it must be my fault. And actually, when *anything* feels bad between people I feel like it must be my fault.

Therapist: So that whole experience with him was nightmarish in itself, and in addition you feel it was your fault. And this feeling that it's you who makes bad things happen has stayed with you.

Kate: Yeah. Right. That's the tar, like the real me is this really dark, bad influence. If things start to feel bad with anybody for any reason, it's like, "Uh-oh, it's coming out again." I mean, it's always in there, but now it's coming *out.*

[This imagery constitutes an important pro-symptom construct, a fourth-order presupposition of the nature of her self as dark, bad, contaminating. Since this presupposition is already in awareness, it is available for transformation by introducing incompatible constructs for her to hold simultaneously. The therapist will now attempt to guide her to create new, incompatible constructs.]

Therapist: Sounds like you got tarred.

Kate: I sure did.

Therapist: Now, there's something that's very important to know about the ordeal of getting tarred. Should I tell you what it is?

Kate: You better!

Therapist: It's this: Getting tarred means you get tar on you because *somebody else puts it on you.* It's somebody else's tar.

Kate: [Pause] I never thought of that.

Therapist: I know, because I can hear that you've been assuming that it's your *own* darkness or dirtiness.

Kate: Right.

Therapist: But when you get tarred, it means somebody else puts that tar on you. It still feels very yucky to have it *on* you, but you can know that it's *not coming out of you.*

Kate: Yeah.

Therapist: It's not your own badness. That's the important thing about it. [Pause] How does it feel to see it this way?

Kate: Umm—it's kind of a *relief,* you know? I mean, I still don't see how to get it off me, but it's a relief to think of it like—like foreign matter.

[Her sense of "relief" indicates that she has taken in the therapist's offer of a new construal and is dissolving her previous presupposition that the tar is of her own being. This is a step in the right direction. However, the fact that "I still don't see how to get it off me" indicates that she has an unconscious position of needing the tar to stay. In other words, the therapist assumes coherence: whatever is, is because some position of the client requires it to be. The therapist will now do radical inquiry and position work to find and bring her into experiential knowledge of that position.]

Therapist: Want to find out how to get it all off?

Kate: Is that possible?

Therapist: I think so. Want to find out?

Kate: Yes.

Therapist: OK. Do you ever picture Henry and his house?

Kate: More than I'd like to.

Therapist: Mm-hm. I know it was really horrible for you there, so if it's too uncomfortable to imagine being there, and being fifteen, that's really OK and we'll find another way to do this.

Kate: No, it's OK. For years I couldn't *stop* picturing exactly that, so one more time won't hurt.

Therapist: OK. Let the scene form, and it's in any one of the rooms in Henry's house, and he's there, with all his creepy energy, and you're fifteen. [Pause] And let me know when you're in that scene.

Kate: OK, I've got it.

Therapist: Good. And I wonder if you can be in this scene in a certain way that I'll describe, a certain version of yourself. See if you can be the version of yourself where there is no tar on you at all. See what it's like to be there, fifteen, with Henry, *knowing* that you're a clean person, with no tar on you. And you notice that Henry has with him a large bucket—yes, a big bucket, and you can see that the bucket is full of tar. All the tar is over there with Henry, and it's clear that the tar is *all his.*

[The therapist is pursuing radical inquiry through the technique of viewing from a symptom-free position.]

Kate: [Eyes closed; face now looking strained] This is feeling really uncomfortable. Really uncomfortable.

Therapist: OK, stay with it. See if you can put words on what's uncomfortable for you, in knowing that *you're clean,* and all the tar is Henry's?

Kate: I, ah, feel scared, like I'm in danger, worse than before somehow.

Therapist: In a new way. What is it about *this* situation that you know to understand as a danger?

Kate: Ah, I feel really vulnerable, or helpless. God, I just flashed on being locked in with Blue Beard. Yeah, I feel totally like I'm with a really evil monster in his castle, and I'm helpless.

[She is now to some degree directly contacting the core emotional wound created by the sexual abuse, a state of utter horror and helplessness to prevent a predatory monster from violating her at his whim. It is now clear that her second-order construal of *herself* as the cause of this badness spared her a conscious experience of this state of utter helplessness. The therapist next will follow her a little bit ahead, in order to foster position work.]

Therapist: So let me see if I'm understanding. By having all the tar over there with Henry, and none on you, which makes it clear that none of this is *your* doing, then you feel helpless and trapped with him, and you see him as a dangerous monster who has all the power. And that's *really* scary.

Kate: Yes. Oooh, it's creepy.

Therapist: OK. Now let the version of you change back to the familiar one of feeling *you're* the tarry one who brings the tar. Can you do that?

Kate: [Pause] Yes.

Therapist: And let that be the reality of the scene now. Now you feel *you're* dark and dirty, and it's *you* that makes bad things happen. [Pause] And see how the situation feels now.

Kate: Well, it's interesting, because—I mean, I'm yucky, but it's familiar and it's not *near* as scary and dangerous-feeling as the other.

[To further the position work, the therapist has done some cycling between symptom-free and symptom-bearing positions, and as a result, Kate is consciously realizing that viewing herself as the dark, dirty cause of the molestation is a strategic protective action that keeps her from experiencing the much worse horror of knowing that she isn't the cause at all, and that the abuse occurs because she is with a monster over whom she has no control whatsoever. Having now found the position in which having the tar on her is needed, and since she understands the meaning of what was found, the therapist will immediately continue position work by inviting her to make an overt statement that will integrate the pro/anti synthesis.]

Therapist: So would you try out saying this sentence and seeing if it feels true to you? Try out saying, "I'd rather believe the tar is from *me*, because then Henry's *not* a monster, I'm *not* helpless, and being here is much less scary."

Kate: I'd rather believe the tar is from *me*, because then Henry's not a monster, and, um—

Therapist: "And I'm not helpless, and being here is a lot less scary."

Kate: —and I'm not helpless, and being here is a lot less scary. [Pause] Yeah, that's right. Wow. [Cries]

Therapist: Could you say the whole thing now?

Kate: OK. I'd rather believe the tar is from *me*, because then *Henry's* not a monster, and *I'm* not helpless, and being here is a *lot* less scary.

Therapist: [Pause] Would you tell us what you're feeling, Kate?

Kate: [Speaking through tears] I didn't realize I was so terrified in all that. I didn't realize I was trapped with a monster.

Therapist: You're realizing it was even more of a nightmare than you let yourself know?

Kate: Yes. [Cries]

Therapist: And are you realizing this because now you're letting yourself know that the tar was really his, all along, and not yours?

Kate: Yes. [Cries] And it's so sad, and it really *hurts,* to
see that I've felt so bad about myself for so many
years, [Cries] when really it was all *him.* That really
hurts. [Cries]

[The painful grief she is now experiencing confirms that she has
allowed the old strategic construal of herself to dissolve, revealing to her the decades of tragic cost in self-regard accompanying
how she protected herself from the horror of the situation.]

Therapist: Yes, it hurts to see that. Really hurts. [She nods] I
need to ask Alan something. How are you doing with
Kate hurting like this? Feeling a knot or fogging up?
Alan: No. It's pretty obvious nobody's expecting me to fix
anything. But I *would* like to hold you. [They hug]
Kate: I can see us out with friends sometime, and I'll ask
you, "How's your knot?" and you'll say, "Fine. How's
your tar?" [Both laugh]

The session ended a few minutes later. The therapist gave her a
card with the words of her pro/anti synthesis, "I needed to pretend being molested was my fault, even though this really cost me,
because otherwise it would have been too horrifying to know I was
with a monster." She was to read this daily and at any time when
feelings of "tar" occurred (the position work technique of using
the symptom as a signal to take the pro-symptom position).

At the start of the third session, Kate reported, "Some people
at work pulled some really sneaky moves that felt really bad, and I
felt myself getting really anxious and *guilty* and feeling like it was
all because of *me,* but then I read the card and realized, no, it's not
me, it's what *they're* doing that's rubbing off on me. It's not me. It's
not me!"

Most of the session was used to bring about a further transformation of the core wound from the molestation through the technique of reenactment: The therapist had Kate again imaginally
focus on the incident of the abuse and coached her through making new, powerful, self-protective responses to her uncle based on
knowing that *he* was the bad one. In this replay she awoke from
sleep just before he was about to begin touching her and screamed
at him, "You're a monster! You're trying to molest me!" She then

got up, threw a chair at him, and ran out of the house screaming for the police. At that point she saw Alan (also visualizing the scene and imaginally participating in it) who now helped her in her moment of need by bringing her to a neighbor's house to phone the police, who came and locked Henry up in a "jail car" and took him away. All of this was emotionally vivid for her. When it was over and their eyes were again open, the therapist said to her, "So this time you knew Henry was being very, very bad to you, and you stopped him, and Alan helped you. How does it feel?" She said, "It feels like I'm finally waking up from a very long, very bad dream."

Therapy ended with three more couple sessions at three-week intervals, sessions that were used mainly to help them adjust to the new internal and interpersonal realities. This included writing and sending a letter to her father and mother revealing what father's now deceased brother, Henry, had done to her. In the last session, Kate said, "Everything has changed. I came in wanting *Alan* to open up to *me,* but then *I* wound up opening up to *him* about *my* dark secret. It feels like we're a lot closer now, like we're really friends and I can trust him to really know me." Alan said the fog and the knot were gone and that "it's so clear now that she loves me whether or not she's upset about something. It's becoming hard to remember what my problem with that was."

Summary

Change in depth-oriented brief therapy means creating an experiential shift in the client's construction of reality, resolving the presenting problem. The therapy client has two fundamental abilities to change emotional-cognitive reality: the ability to control the *illumination* of constructs and the ability to control the *existence* of constructs. We have described techniques by which the therapist guides, coaches, and induces the client to use these native abilities to bring about experiential shifts in his or her initially unconscious, pro-symptom position.

In *position work* the client illuminates the pro-symptom position, experientially inhabits it, apprehends the coherent emotional meaning or value of having the symptom, and creates a *pro/anti synthesis* by asserting the emotional truth that the meaning or value of having the symptom warrants the costs. The client discovers that he or she is the ingenious architect and purposeful implementor of the symptom.

For many clients, resolution occurs at this point, either because the client spontaneously dissolves the position that has been made conscious, or because the symptom, reframed to its emotional truth, is no longer seen as a problem. For others, the therapist guides the client through an additional stage of carrying out the *transformation of the pro-symptom position* by creating new constructs that dissolve the emotional wounds and presuppositions comprising the pro-symptom reality.

Notes

P. 203, *People wish to be settled . . .:* R. W. Emerson (1990), "Circles," in R. D. Richardson, Jr. (Ed.), *Ralph Waldo Emerson: Selected Essays, Lectures, and Poems* (p. 199), New York: Bantam.

P. 204, *We define psychotherapy . . . presenting problem:* This definition of psychotherapy is similar to others previously formulated. For example, Montalvo has defined psychotherapy as an "interpersonal agreement to abrogate the usual rules that structure reality, in order to reshape reality" [B. Montalvo (1976), "Observations of Two Natural Amnesias," *Family Process, 15,* 333]. For us this approaches a suitable definition, provided the "reality" twice mentioned is understood to be specifically the "reality" inhabited by the client as an individual, and the "rules" are understood to be the client's conscious and unconscious ways of making sense of experience (of self, others, events, and so on). Our definition emphasizes our view that in psychotherapy it is always the client who transforms his or her own experiential world so as to become symptom-free, using native constructivist abilities to do so, including the ability to arrange to interact with a therapist who prompts the effective use of those abilities.

PP. 206–207, *"As long as I attend . . . keep change from occurring":* N. Shuler (1985). "Trying to Change as Denial," *California Association for Counseling and Development Journal, 6,* 49–51.

P. 215, *an apt phrase coined by psychotherapist Kenneth Rhea:* K. Rhea (1993), "Essential Considerations in the Practice of Psychotherapy," *The California Therapist, 5*(5), 60–61.

P. 217, *Traumatic Incident Reduction . . . developed by psychotherapists Frank Gerbode and Gerald French:* F. Gerbode (1988), *Beyond Psychology: An Introduction to Metapsychology,* Palo Alto, CA: IRM Press. Information on TIR is available from the Institute for Research in Metapsychology, 431 Burgess Drive, Menlo Park, CA 94025. The Psychosocial

Stress Research of Florida State University has conducted comparative research on the effectiveness of TIR and several other techniques for rapid resolution of post-traumatic stress syndrome, but as of this writing these results have not yet been finalized or published. For information contact Psychosocial Stress Research Program, 103 Sandels Building, Tallahassee, FL 32306–4097.

P. 235, *"the real question . . . but not in every case."*: W. H. O'Hanlon (1990), "Debriefing Myself," *Family Therapy Networker, 14*(2), 48.

P. 236, *dissolving the old construction in favor of the new* (accommodation *in Piagetian terms):* J. Piaget (1971), *The Construction of Reality in the Child,* New York: Ballantine (original work published in 1937); and J. Piaget (1985), *The Equilibration of Cognitive Structures: the Central Problem of Intellectual Development,* Chicago: University of Chicago Press.

P. 237, *The technique of reenactment:* See, for example, J. Moreno (1962), *Psychodrama* (vol. 3), New York: Beacon House; N. Drew (1993), "Reenactment Interviewing: A Methodology for Phenomenological Research," *IMAGE: Journal of Nursing Scholarship, 25*(4), 345–351; L. D. Crump (1984), "Gestalt Therapy in the Treatment of Vietnam Veterans Experiencing PTSD Symptomatology," *Journal of Contemporary Psychology, 14*(1), 90–98.

P. 237, *revising personal history:* R. Bandler and J. Grinder (1982), *Reframing: Neuro-Linguistic Programming and the Transformation of Meaning,* Moab, UT: Real People Press.

P. 238, *inner child work:* See, for example, J. Abrams (Ed.) (1990), *Reclaiming the Inner Child,* Los Angeles: Tarcher.

P. 239, *voice dialogue:* H. Stone and S. Winkleman (1989), *Embracing Our Selves: The Voice Dialogue Manual,* San Rafael, CA: New World Library.

Conclusion

He looked at his own Soul with a Telescope.
What seemed all irregular, he saw and shewed
to be beautiful Constellations; and he added
to the Consciousness hidden worlds within worlds.
SAMUEL COLERIDGE, *Notebooks*

In this book we have presented a comprehensive, nonpathologizing approach that reconciles the perennial opposites of "deep" and "brief" in psychotherapy. It is an approach organized around the understanding that unconscious emotional realities are immediately accessible and changeable.

This way of working challenges conventional, limiting assumptions about what is possible in psychotherapy. To do depth-oriented brief therapy is to know that clients can be guided to rapidly experience and express their unconscious, symptom-generating constructions of meaning; that these constructions are transformed by the individual not over time, but in moments when they enter awareness and when alternative acceptable positions are created; that significant change is an immediate possibility in every session, from the first session; that brief therapy can produce change beyond symptom relief by generating the experience of intrinsic wellness and worth; and that the authenticity and poignance of the work—for the therapist as well as for the client—need not be sacrificed because the work is brief.

The conceptual framework and the therapeutic logic of depth-oriented brief therapy is actually extremely simple: the client has a pro-symptom emotional truth; do nothing but empathically find it; usher the client into experiencing it; and then, if necessary, assist the client to change it.

For some therapists, however, learning this approach means learning a new way of thinking and a new style of interacting with clients. This can at first feel very difficult, especially if an old, familiar construction of therapy is being shed at the same time. But once familiarity with depth-oriented brief therapy develops, its great simplicity becomes apparent, and the advanced trainee wonders what made it seem difficult at first.

The therapeutic benefits of working with the emotional truth of the symptom are numerous, as we have shown in these pages. Some of the most salient are listed below.

Leverage: Recognizing and accepting the client's pro-symptom position gives the therapist an alliance with the functional region of the client's psyche that has the most power over the symptom, maximizing therapeutic leverage for change and minimizing or eliminating resistance.

Trust: The client's experience of the therapist as interested in and unafraid of the client's most important emotional truths, and able to understand and accept them sensitively, rapidly engenders trust and accelerates the psychotherapeutic process.

Permanence: Living as though the symptom's emotional truth weren't the case is what generates the symptom in the first place. Resolving the problem at the level of the emotional truth of the symptom has the greatest potential for eliminating the symptom permanently and preventing emergence of alternate symptoms.

Potent reframe: Repositioning the client within the emotional truth of the problem is inherently a compelling reframe—a contextual shift that constitutes a second- or higher-order transformation of meaning. This reframe is highly effective at dispelling the problem because (1) it registers strongly as true (a high degree of "fit" to the client's psychology is achieved) and (2) it automatically transforms the client's construal of being the *victim* of the symptom into a position of being the *creator* or *implementor* of the symptom.

Easy hypnosis: Themes from the client's emotional truth are the most evocative for hypnotic induction. These themes make induction easy, because they are the very themes with which the client's unconscious mind is already strongly preoccupied, and the full force of that unconscious involvement immediately absorbs the client's attention.

Gain of meaning: Symptoms arise precisely because of *un*awareness of the meaningful personal themes generating them. Conscious retrieval of these themes puts clients back into the experientially true stories of their lives, which brings new energy, aliveness, and wholeness along with new engagement in personally meaningful issues and choices.

Realization of self-worth: Working at the level of the emotional truth of the symptom achieves resolution and healing of a deeper kind than is the current norm or aim in the brief therapy field—a realization of core well-being and self-worth that comes from finding that symptoms regarded as evidence of defectiveness or craziness turn out to be full of sense and coherent personal meaning.

Of course, in keeping with the constructivist paradigm on which depth-oriented brief therapy is based, we cannot claim that its description of symptoms, therapy, and change is *objectively* true. We know only that for a therapist to view the client's problem in this way will in the end always *seem* and *feel* true to both client and therapist and will make therapy remarkably time- and depth-effective. And we know that what seemed all irregular will come to be known as marvelously coherent and saturated with deeply felt meaning and intelligence.

P. 259, *He looked at his own Soul . . .:* K. Coburn (Ed.) (1957), *The Notebooks of Samuel Taylor Coleridge,* Princeton, NJ: Princeton University Press.

References

Bandler, R., & Grinder, J. (1982). *Reframing: Neuro-linguistic programming and the transformation of meaning.* Moab, UT: Real People Press.

Bateson, G. (1972). *Steps to an ecology of mind.* New York: Ballantine.

Bateson, G. (1979). *Mind and nature: A necessary unity.* New York: Dutton.

Berger, P., & Luckman, T. (1966). *The social construction of reality.* New York: Doubleday.

Bogdan, J. (1984). Family organization as an ecology of ideas: An alternative to the reification of family systems. *Family Process, 23,* 375–388.

Boszormenyi-Nagy, I., & Spark, G. (1973). *Invisible loyalties.* New York: HarperCollins.

Bouchard, M.-A., & Guérette, L. (1991). Psychotherapy as a hermeneutical experience. *Psychotherapy, 28*(3), 385–394.

Bower, G. H., and Hilgard, E. R. (1981). *Theories of learning* (5th ed.). Englewood Cliffs, NJ: Prentice-Hall.

Bruner, J. (1990). *Acts of meaning.* Cambridge, MA: Harvard University Press.

Bugental, J.F.T. (1978). *Psychotherapy and process: The fundamentals of an existential-humanistic approach.* Reading, MA: Addison-Wesley.

Bugental, J.F.T., & Bugental, E. K. (1984). A fate worse than death: The fear of changing. *Psychotherapy, 21,* 543–549.

Chomsky, N. (1969). *Deep structure, surface structure, and semantic interpretation.* Bloomington, IN: Indiana University Linguistics Club.

Coale, H. W. (1992). The constructivist emphasis on language: A critical conversation. *Journal of Strategic and Systemic Therapies, 11*(1), 12–26.

Coyne, J. C. (1985). Toward a theory of frames and reframing: The social nature of frames. *Journal of Marital and Family Therapy, 11,* 337–344.

Dell, P. (1982). Beyond homeostasis: Toward a concept of coherence. *Family Process, 21,* 21–41.

Dell, P. (1985). Understanding Bateson and Maturana: Toward a biological foundation for the social sciences. *Journal of Marital and Family Therapy, 11*(1), 1–20.

Derrida, J. (1981). *Positions.* Chicago: University of Chicago Press.

Derrida, J. (1992). Mochlos: Or, the conflict of the faculties. In R. Rand

(Ed.), *Logomachia* (pp. 3–34). Lincoln, NE: University of Nebraska Press.

de Shazer, S. (1985). *Keys to solutions in brief therapy*. New York: W. W. Norton.

Erickson, M. H. (1980). *Innovative hypnotherapy: Collected papers of Milton H. Erickson on hypnosis* (Vol. 4, E. L. Rossi, Ed.). New York: Irvington.

Erickson, M. H., & Rossi, E. L. (1979). *Hypnotherapy: An exploratory casebook*. New York: Irvington.

Feixas, G. (1990). Approaching the individual, approaching the system: A constructivist model for integrative psychotherapy. *Journal of Family Psychology, 4*(1), 4–35.

Feixas, G., Cunillera, C., & Mateu, C. (1990). A constructivist approach to systemic family therapy: A case study using dream analysis. *Journal of Strategic and Systemic Therapies, 9*, 55–65.

Festinger, L. (1957). *A theory of cognitive dissonance*. Evanston, IL: Row, Peterson.

Fisch, R., Weakland, J., & Segal, L. (1983). *The tactics of change: Doing therapy briefly*. San Francisco: Jossey-Bass.

Fish, V. (1993). Poststructuralism in family therapy: Interrogating the narrative/conversational mode. *Journal of Marital and Family Therapy, 19*(3), 221–232.

Fodor, J. A. (1983). *The modularity of mind*. Cambridge, MA: MIT/Bradford Books.

Foerster, H. von. (1981). *Observing systems*. Salinas, CA: Intersystems.

Foerster, H. von. (1984). On constructing a reality. In P. Watzlawick (Ed.), *The invented reality* (pp. 41–62). New York: W. W. Norton.

Foucault, M. (1980). *Power/knowledge: Selected interviews and other writings*. New York: Pantheon.

Foucault, M. (1982). The subject and power [Afterword]. In H. L. Dreufu & P. Rabinow, *Michel Foucault: Beyond structuralism and hermeneutics. With an afterword by Michel Foucault* (pp.208–226). Chicago: University of Chicago Press.

Frank, J. D. (1973). *Persuasion and healing* (2nd ed.). Baltimore, MD: Johns Hopkins University Press.

Frankl, V. E. (1959). *Man's search for meaning: An introduction to logotherapy*. New York: Washington Square Press.

Geertz, C. (1973). *The interpretation of cultures*. New York: Basic Books.

Gendlin, E. T. (1978). *Focusing*. New York: Bantam Books.

Gergen, K. (1985). The social constructionist movement in modern psychology. *American Psychologist, 40*, 266–275.

Glasersfeld, E. von. (1979). Radical constructivism and Piaget's concept of knowledge. In F. B. Murray (Ed.), *The impact of Piagetian theory on education, philosophy, psychiatry, and psychology* (pp. 109–122). Baltimore, MD: University Park Press.

Glasersfeld, E. von. (1984). An introduction to radical constructivism. In P. Watzlawick (Ed.), *The invented reality* (pp. 17–40). New York: W. W. Norton.

Glasersfeld, E. von. (1987). *The construction of knowledge.* Salinas, CA: Intersystems.

Glasersfeld, E. von. (1988). The reluctance to change a way of thinking. *Irish Journal of Psychology, 9*(1), 83–90.

Greenberg, L. S., Rice, L., & Elliott, R. (1993). *Facilitating emotional change: The moment-by-moment process.* New York: Guilford.

Greenberg, L. S., & Safran, J. D. (1984). Hot cognition—emotion coming in from the cold: A reply to Rachman and Mahoney. *Cognitive Therapy and Research, 8*(6), 591–598.

Greenberg, L. S., & Safran, J. D. (1984). Integrating affect and cognition: A perspective on the process of therapeutic change. *Cognitive Therapy and Research, 8*(6), 559–578.

Greenberg, L. S., & Safran, J. D. (1987). *Emotion in psychotherapy: Affect and cognition in the process of change.* New York: Guilford.

Guidano, V. F., & Liotti, G. A. (1983). *Cognitive processes and emotional disorders.* New York: Guilford.

Guidano, V. F., & Liotti, G. A. (1985). A constructivist foundation for cognitive therapy. In M. J. Mahoney & A. Freeman (Eds.), *Cognition and psychotherapy* (pp. 101–142). New York: Plenum.

Haley, J. (1973). *Uncommon therapy: The psychiatric techniques of Milton H. Erickson, M.D.* New York: W. W. Norton.

Haley, J. (1976). *Problem-solving therapy.* New York: HarperCollins.

Haley, J. (1978). Ideas which handicap therapists. In M. M. Berger (Ed.), *Beyond the double bind.* New York: Brunner/Mazel.

Held, B. (1990). What's in a name? Some confusions and concerns about constructivism. *Journal of Marital and Family Therapy, 16,* 179–186.

Held, B., & Pols, E. (1985). The confusion about epistemology and "epistemology"—and what to do about it. *Family Process, 24,* 521–524.

Hermans, H.J.M., Kempen, H.J.G., & van Loon, R.J.P. (1992). The dialogical self. *American Psychologist, 47*(1), 23–33.

Hoffman, L. (1988). A constructivist position for family therapy. *Irish Journal of Psychology, 9,* 110–129.

Hoffman, L. (1990). Constructing realities: An art of lenses. *Family Process, 29,* 1–12.

Horner, A. J. (1994). *Treating the neurotic patient in brief psychotherapy.* Northvale, NJ: Aronson. (Originally published in 1985)

Huxley, A. (1954). *The doors of perception.* New York: HarperCollins.

Johnson, S. M. (1994). *Character styles.* New York: W. W. Norton.

Joyce-Moniz, L. (1985). Epistemological therapy and constructivism. In M. J. Mahoney & A. Freeman (Eds.), *Cognition and psychotherapy* (pp. 143–179). New York: Plenum.

Jung, C. G. (1952). *Symbols of transformation.* New York: Bollingen Foundation.

Jung, C. G. (1961). *Memories, dreams, reflections.* New York: Vintage.

Keeney, B. (1983). *The aesthetics of change.* New York: Guilford.

Kelly, G. (1955). *The psychology of personal constructs.* New York: W. W. Norton.

Kelly, G. (1969). *Clinical psychology and personality: The selected papers of George Kelly* (B. Maher, Ed.). New York: Wiley.

Kohut, H. (1971). *The analysis of the self.* New York: International Universities Press.

Kohut, H. (1977). *The restoration of the self.* New York: International Universities Press.

Krause, I.-B. (1993). Family therapy and anthropology: A case for emotions. *Journal of Family Therapy, 15,* 35–56.

Kristeva, J. (1980). *Desire in language: A semiotic approach to literature and art.* New York: Columbia University Press.

Lacan, J. (1977). *Ecrits: A selection* (A. Sheridan, Trans.). New York: W. W. Norton.

Laing, R. D. (1967). *The politics of experience.* New York: Pantheon.

Laing, R. D. (1969). *Self and others.* New York: Pantheon.

Laing, R. D. (1972). *The politics of the family and other essays.* London: Vintage.

Laing, R. D., Phillipson, H., & Lee, A. (1966). *Interpersonal perception.* New York: Perennial Library.

Levi-Strauss, C. (1963). *Structural anthropology.* New York: Basic Books.

Lipchik, E. (1994). The rush to be brief. *Family Therapy Networker, 18*(2), 35–39.

Luepnitz, D. A. (1988). *The family interpreted: Feminist theory in clinical practice.* New York: Basic Books.

Lyddon, W. (1990). First- and second-order change: Implications for rationalist and constructivist cognitive therapies. *Journal of Counseling and Development, 69*(6), 122–127.

Lyddon, W., and McLaughlin, J. (1992). Constructivist psychology: a heuristic framework. *Journal of Mind and Behavior, 13,* 89–107.

Madanes, C. (1981). *Strategic family therapy.* San Francisco: Jossey-Bass.

Mahoney, M. J. (1988). Constructivist metatheory: I. Basic features and historical foundations. *International Journal of Personal Construct Psychology, 1,* 1–35.

Mahoney, M. J. (1988). Constructivist metatheory: II. Implications for psychotherapy. *International Journal of Personal Construct Psychology, 1,* 299–315.

Mahoney, M. J. (1991). *Human change processes: The scientific foundations of psychotherapy.* New York: Basic Books.

Maturana, H. R., & Varela, F. J. (1980). *Autopoiesis and cognition: The realization of living.* Boston: D. Reidel.

Montalvo, B. (1976). Observations of two natural amnesias. *Family Process, 15,* 333–342.

Napier, A., & Whitaker, C. (1978). *The family crucible.* New York: Harper-Collins.

Neimeyer, R. A. (1984). Toward a personal construct conceptualization of depression and suicide. In F. R. Epting & R. A. Neimeyer (Eds.), *Personal meanings of death: Applications of personal construct theory to clinical practice* (pp. 127–173). New York: Hemisphere.

Neimeyer, R. A. (1993). An appraisal of constructivist psychotherapies. *Journal of Consulting and Clinical Psychology, 61*(2), 221–234.

Neisser, U. (1976). *Cognition and reality.* San Francisco: W. H. Freeman.

Nylund, D., & Corsiglia, V. (1994). Becoming solution-focused forced in brief therapy. *Journal of Systemic Therapies, 13*(1), 5–12.

Ogden, T. H. (1994). *Subjects of analysis.* Northvale, NJ: Aronson.

O'Hanlon, W. H. (1990). Debriefing myself. *Family Therapy Networker, 14*(2), 48–49, 68–69.

Papp, P. (1983). *The process of change.* New York: Guilford.

Pascual-Leone, J. (1991). Emotions, development, and psychotherapy. In J. D. Safran & L. S. Greenberg (Eds.), *Emotion, psychotherapy and change* (pp. 302–335). New York: Guilford.

Pearce, W. B., & Cronin, V. E. (1980). *Communication, action, and meaning: The creation of social realities.* New York: Praeger.

Perls, F. S. (1969). *Gestalt therapy verbatim.* Lafayette, CA: Real People Press.

Perls, F. S. (1973). *The Gestalt approach: Eyewitness to therapy.* Palo Alto, CA: Science and Behavior Books.

Piaget, J. (1970). *Psychology and epistemology: Toward a theory of knowledge.* New York: Viking Penguin.

Piaget, J. (1970). *Structuralism.* New York: Basic Books.

Piaget, J. (1971). *The construction of reality in the child.* New York: Ballantine. (Original work published 1937)

Piaget, J. (1985). *The equilibration of cognitive structures: The central problem of intellectual development.* Chicago: University of Chicago Press.

Rachman, S. (1984). A reassessment of the "primacy of affect." *Cognitive Therapy and Research, 8*(6), 579–584.

Rice, L. N. (1974). The evocative function of the therapist. In L. N. Rice & D. A. Wexler (Eds.), *Innovations in client-centered therapy* (pp. 289–311). New York: Wiley.

Satir, V. (1964). *Conjoint family therapy.* Palo Alto, CA: Science and Behavior Books.

Satir, V. (1972). *Peoplemaking*. Palo Alto, CA: Science and Behavior Books.

Schwartz, R. (1992). Rescuing the exiles. *Family Therapy Networker, 16*(3), 33–37, 75.

Selvini-Pallazoli, M., Boscolo, L., Cecchin, G., & Prata, G. (1980). Hypothesizing-circularity-neutrality. *Family Process, 19,* 3–12.

Sherman, R., & Fredman, N. (1986). *Handbook of structured techniques in marriage and family therapy*. New York: Brunner/Mazel.

Shuler, N. (1985). Trying to change as denial. *California Association for Counseling and Development Journal, 6,* 49–51.

Siegelman, E. (1990). *Metaphor and meaning in psychology*. New York: Guilford.

Sluzki, C. (1992). Transformations: A blueprint for narrative changes in therapy. *Family Process, 31*(3), 217–230.

Sontag, S. (1966). *Against interpretation, and other essays*. New York: Farrar, Straus & Giroux.

Spence, D. P. (1982). *Narrative truth and historical truth*. New York: W. W. Norton.

Szasz, T. (1961). *The myth of mental illness*. New York: Hoeber-Harper.

Waters, D. (1994). Prisoners of our metaphors. *Family Therapy Networker, 18*(6), 73–75.

Waters, D., & Lawrence, E. (1993). *Competence, courage, and change*. New York: W. W. Norton.

Watzlawick, P. (Ed.). (1984). *The invented reality*. New York: W. W. Norton.

Watzlawick, P., Beavin, J., & Jackson, D. (1967). *Pragmatics of human communication*. New York: W. W. Norton.

Watzlawick, P., Weakland, J., and Fisch, R. (1974). *Change: Principles of problem formation and problem resolution*. New York: W. W. Norton.

White, M., & Epston, D. (1990). *Narrative means to therapeutic ends*. New York: W. W. Norton.

Wylie, M. S. (1990). Brief therapy on the couch. *Family Therapy Networker, 14*(2), 26–35, 66.

Zajonc, R. (1980). Feeling and thinking: Preferences need no inferences. *American Psychologist, 35,* 151–175.

Zajonc, R. (1984). On the primacy of affect. *American Psychologist, 39,* 117–123.

The Authors

BRUCE ECKER is a psychotherapist in private practice in Oakland, California, and teaches brief therapy at John F. Kennedy University. He is active as a clinical staff trainer and consultant at numerous therapy centers, provides training intensives for professionals nationally, and is coauthor and coeditor of *Spiritual Choices: The Problem of Recognizing Authentic Paths to Inner Transformation* (1987). His work in psychotherapy follows a career of well over a decade in physics research with numerous professional publications.

LAUREL HULLEY is in private practice in Oakland, California, and, as director of clinical training for Pacific Seminars, develops and designs professional trainings in depth-oriented brief therapy. She has been engaged for over ten years in the issues and theory of training therapists for effectiveness. Her clinical interests include the treatment of schizoid constructions in brief therapy, which is the topic of a book in progress.

The authors are the originators of depth-oriented brief therapy.

.

Index

LaVergne, TN USA
04 September 2009
156883LV00002B/71/P